Benjamin Britten

NEW PERSPECTIVES ON
HIS LIFE AND WORK

ALDEBURGH STUDIES IN MUSIC

General Editor: Christopher Grogan

Volume 8

ISSN 0969-3548

Other volumes in this series:

Benjamin Britten

NEW PERSPECTIVES ON HIS LIFE AND WORK

Edited by

Lucy Walker

THE BOYDELL PRESS

THE BRITTEN–PEARS FOUNDATION

First published 2009
The Boydell Press, Woodbridge

ISBN 978-1-84383-516-5

The Boydell Press is an imprint of Boydell & Brewer Ltd
PO Box 9, Woodbridge, Suffolk IP12 3DF, UK
and of Boydell & Brewer Inc.
668 Mt Hope Avenue, Rochester, NY 14620, USA
website: www.boydellandbrewer.com

A catalogue record for this book is available
from the British Library

This publication is printed on acid-free paper

Designed and typeset in Adobe Warnock Pro
by David Roberts, Pershore, Worcestershire

Printed in Great Britain by
CPI Antony Rowe, Chippenham and Eastbourne

Contents

Illustrations

Acknowledgements

On behalf of the contributors I would like to thank my colleagues at the Britten–Pears Foundation for their help in providing information for the chapters here, particularly: Jude Brimmer, Nick Clark, Chris Grogan and Jonathan Manton. For their help with several chapters thanks are also due to Mervyn Cooke and Colin Matthews. I would also like to thank Britten's publishers (Boosey & Hawkes, Chester Music and Faber Music) for their permission to reproduce musical examples from those of Britten's works in which they hold copyright. The following music examples are reproduced by kind permission of Boosey & Hawkes Music Publishers Ltd: chapter 3, exx. 1, 2, 6b © Copyright 1962 by Boosey & Hawkes Music Publishers Ltd; chapter 5, exx. 4a, 4b, 5, 6, 7, 8a, 8b, 8c, 9 © Copyright 1955 by Hawkes & Son (London) Ltd; chapter 3, exx. 3, 4, 5b, 6a © Copyright 1970 by Boosey & Hawkes Music Publishers Ltd; Chapter 9, ex. 1 © Copyright 1905 by Adolph Furstner. U. S. Copyright Renewed. Copyright assigned 1943 to Hawkes & Son (London) Ltd for the World excluding Germany, Italy, Portugal and the former territories of the U.S.S.R. (excluding Estonia, Latvia and Lithuania). The following music examples are reproduced by kind permission of Chester Music Limited: Chapter 5, exx. 1, 2, 3 music © Copyright 2002 by The Britten Estate Limited. All publishing rights exercised worldwide by Chester Music Limited, London. All Rights Reserved. International Copyright Secured. The following music examples are reproduced by kind permission of Faber Music: chapter 8, exx. 1-6 © Copyright 1973 by Faber Music Ltd, London; chapter 9, exx. 6, 7a, 7b, 9 © Copyright 1979 by Faber Music Ltd, London. The diagram in chapter 9 (ex. 2b) is based on Tethys Carpenter's 'Tonal and Dramatic Structure' in Deryck Cooke, ed., *Richard Strauss: Salome* (Cambridge: CUP, 1989) and appears by permission of Cambridge University Press. The poem on p. 60 ('O lurcher-loving collier') is number 11 of *Twelve Songs* by W. H. Auden, © Copyright Faber and Faber Ltd.

Illustrations of Britten's unpublished manuscripts (plates 1, 2, 3, 5, 6 and 7) appear courtesy of the Britten–Pears Foundation, and special thanks are due to Nick Clark and Jonathan Manton. The photographer of the Britten and Shostakovich image (plate 4) is currently unidentified. Plate 8 is © David Myerscough-Jones. Every reasonable effort has been made to trace the copyright owners and we would be pleased to hear from those whom we have been unable to locate.

Quotations from Britten's unpublished material, including correspondence and diaries, are reproduced courtesy of the Britten–Pears Foundation. I would like to acknowledge the following for their kind permission in allowing us to reproduce unpublished material: Irina Shostakovich for permission to reproduce extracts from Shostakovich's correspondence; Elizabeth Wilson for permission to reproduce extracts from Sir Duncan Wilson's correspondence with Britten and Elizabeth Wilson's private correspondence with the author (chapter 3); Clarissa Lewis for permission to quote from Myfanwy Piper's letters and other writings; Roderic Dunnett for permission to quote from his private correspondence and tape recordings (chapter 7); Barbara Mobbs for permission to quote from Patrick White's libretto for *A Fringe of Leaves*; the estate of Sidney Nolan for permission to quote from his correspondence with Britten (chapter 10); and Pierre Barrat for permission to cite his correspondence (chapter 11).

Special thanks are due to: Levon Hakobian, Alexander Ivashkin, Liudmila Kovnatskaya, Hugh Lunghi, Eric Roseberry, Kathryn Bailey and Kristian Hibberd (chapter 3); Michael Fend, Christopher Wintle and Philip Rupprecht (chapter 6); and Philip Reed, Sarah Francis, Jeremy Polmear and Stephen Powell (chapter 4). My own personal thanks are to: Chris Grogan for much advice and editorial help; Jude Brimmer, Nick Clark, Caroline Harding, Jonathan Manton, James B. Spence and Nick Walker for proof-reading and many helpful comments; the staff at the John Innes Centre, Norwich, for their help at the original Britten Study Day in 2008; the contributors for making this process a pleasant and interesting one; Richard Northedge for providing the index; Michael Middeke at Boydell & Brewer for overseeing the project and answering my thousands of queries; and to James for endless patience and everything else.

Notes on Contributors

Jane Brandon studied for her MMus at King's College London, completing a dissertation focusing on the influence of Italian vocal writing on Britten's *The Seven Sonnets of Michelangelo*. Her PhD, centring on Britten's and Verdi's operas, was completed at King's College London with AHRC funding in 2008. The thesis, entitled ' "The Secret of Perfection": Britten and Verdi', investigates Britten's appropriation and re-invention of Verdi's operatic style. In addition to her enthusiasm for 20th-century opera, 19th-century Italian opera and British music, her wider research interests include source studies, intertextuality and genre studies. She is currently revising her thesis for forthcoming publication by Cambridge University Press.

George Caird studied at the Royal Academy of Music and Cambridge University before pursuing a freelance career as an oboist which included orchestral playing, chamber music and solo engagements. He worked with many of London's major orchestras, particularly as a member of the Academy of St Martin in the Fields from 1984 to 1991. He has also been a member of a number of leading ensembles, notably as a founder-member of The Albion Ensemble. He is on the board of numerous trusts and has chaired several committees associated with music education. He was appointed as a professor of oboe at the Royal Academy of Music in 1984 and since September 1993, has been Principal of Birmingham Conservatoire. He has written articles on music education, the oboe and other woodwind instruments and on British music for a variety of journals.

Sharon Choa is Lecturer in Music, Director of Performance Studies and conductor of the UEA Symphony Orchestra at the University of East Anglia, School of Music. She studied as a violinist at the Royal Academy of Music and at King's College London, where she graduated with a first-class BMus degree and was awarded a PhD on the subject of 'sonata-fugue' processes in Haydn's string quartets. Her research interests have since extended to Beethoven, Martinů, Britten, and have increasingly employed research approaches that are 'practice-based'. She is an editor for the Martinů critical edition to be brought out by Bärenreiter, and was Director of the AHRC-funded Britten Thematic Catalogue from 2006–9 in collaboration with the Britten–Pears Foundation.

David Crilly studied at Leeds College of Music and the University of Southampton, before undertaking doctoral research on positivism in twentieth-century musicology at Magdalen College, Oxford, with Bojan Bujic. He then took up an appointment as Senior Lecturer and Director of Research at Anglia Ruskin University. For 18 years he was Director-in-Residence for Anglia Opera and also founded the internationally renowned annual Cambridge Shakespeare Festival, of which he remains Artistic Director. He is a performer, conductor and composer, and author of a range of musicological publications, including work on music analysis, aesthetics, Charlie Parker, Astor Piazzolla and Debussy, although his main research explores issues of influence and intertextuality in the music of Benjamin Britten. His focus on interdisciplinary study led to him taking up the post of Head of Creative and Performing Arts at Liverpool Hope University in 2008.

J. P. E. Harper-Scott is a Lecturer in Music at Royal Holloway, University of London. He is the author of *Edward Elgar, Modernist* (Cambridge University Press, 2006) and *Elgar: an Extraordinary Life* (ABRSM, 2007), the co-editor with Julian Rushton of *Elgar Studies* (CUP, 2007) and with Jim Samson of *An Introduction to Music Studies* (CUP, 2009). Current research includes an analytical study of Wagner's *Ring* and a monograph, *William Walton and National Modernism*, which is under contract with Cambridge University Press.

Brian McMahon is from Dublin. He retired early from business and enrolled in University College Dublin, taking a degree in History and Politics. As a postgraduate History student he chose to research Benjamin Britten's pacifism culminating in his *War Requiem,* for his Master's degree. He is currently a PhD candidate under Professor Richard Aldous, researching the lifelong relationship between the BBC and Benjamin Britten. Brian, who is married with three adult sons, has been involved with music all his life. He is currently a member of one of Ireland's foremost choral groups, Tallaght Choral Society.

Colin Matthews studied at the Universities of Nottingham and Sussex, where he also taught, and subsequently worked with Britten in Aldeburgh 1972–6, and with Imogen Holst. He collaborated with Deryck Cooke for many years on the performing version of Mahler's Tenth Symphony. Since the early 1970s his music has been performed worldwide, ranging from solo piano music through three string quartets and many ensemble, orchestral and choral works, with recordings on major labels. He was Associate Composer with the London Symphony Orchestra, 1992–9, and since 2001 has been Composer-in-Association with the Hallé, for whom he has recently completed his orchestration of Debussy's 24 *Préludes*. He is a founder trustee and Music Director of the Britten–Pears Foundation.

Arne Muus studied Musicology, German Literature and Modern History at the Universities of Freiburg-in-Breisgau (Germany) and Bristol. He has worked as an opera dramaturg and assistant stage director and is currently reading for a DPhil in Musicology at the University of Oxford (Christ Church) under the supervision of Prof. Jonathan Cross. He has presented papers at the 2008 RMA Research Student Conference and at the Third Biennial Conference of the North American British Music Studies Association (NABMSA).

Maéna Py is a doctoral student at the Université François Rabelais de Tours. After studies in comparative literature at the Sorbonne, she obtained l'agrégation de Lettres Modernes and is now working towards a thesis of comparative literature/performing arts on Benjamin Britten's operas, supervised by Isabelle Moindrot. At the same time, she has pursued her musical studies, in the cello and in musical analysis. She has participated in many university colloquia and conferences devoted to opera and the performing arts, including: 'L'Opéra dans le monde Anglophone' in Caen (October 2006); 'Koltès et les Amériques' in Metz (December 2006); 'Les Livrets d'opéra 1930–1945' in Nantes (November 2007); 'Le Monologue contre le drame' in Arras (March 2008); 'La Traduction des livrets d'opéra au XXe siècle' in Tours (May 2008) (these papers are all due to be published). Since 2007 she has been teaching in the Performing Arts department at the Université François Rabelais de Tours.

Cameron Pyke read History at Sidney Sussex College, Cambridge from 1989 to 1992. He taught History and Classics at Lancing College from 1993 to 1998 and is currently Head of Upper School at Dulwich College. He is researching Britten's creative response to Russia as a PhD under the supervision of Professor Alexander Ivashkin at Goldsmiths College, University of London. In August 2008 he delivered a paper on the theme of attitudes to death in Britten and Shostakovich at Salzburg University.

Claire Seymour is Head of the Senior College at Queen's College London, where she teaches English Literature. In addition, she is an Open University Associate Lecturer in both English Literature and Music, and a Tutor in Opera Studies for Rose Bruford College. She is the author of *The Operas of Benjamin Britten: Expression and Evasion* (Boydell and Brewer, 2004). From 2004 to 2008 she was the editor of the *Thomas Hardy Journal*, and has introduced several Wordsworth Classics editions of Hardy (*Under the Greenwood Tree*, *The Return of the Native* and *Life's Little Ironies*) and other writers. She researches and lectures on the interdisciplinary relationship between words and music, and has contributed a chapter on 'Hardy and Music' to Blackwell's *Companion to Thomas Hardy* (Spring 2009). She is a regular critic for *Opera Today*.

Frances Spalding is an art historian, critic and biographer. She has published extensively on twentieth-century British art and is the author of a centenary history of the Tate. She has written lives of Roger Fry, Vanessa Bell, John Minton and Gwen Raverat, and her joint biography of John and Myfanwy Piper will be published by Oxford University Press in September 2009. She is a Fellow of the Royal Society of Literature, Honorary Fellow of the Royal College of Art and currently Professor of Art History at Newcastle University.

Lucy Walker has been Project Manager of the Britten Thematic Catalogue since 2006. Several publications have arisen from this project, including articles for *Notes* and *Fontes Artis Musicae*. Her PhD was on the operas of Francis Poulenc and was completed at King's College, London in 2005, where she was also an occasional lecturer for several years. She now teaches on a regular basis at the School of Music at the University of East Anglia and is responsible for fostering collaboration between the Britten–Pears Foundation and other academic institutions in the UK.

Abbreviations

BBAA   Benjamin Britten, *On Receiving the First Aspen Award* (London: Faber, 1964)

BBD   Britten's unpublished diaries. The diaries are, at the time of writing, being prepared for publication and many diary entries will, in due course, be available in print.

BPF   Britten–Pears Foundation

CPBC   Christopher Palmer, *The Britten Companion* (London: Faber, 1984)

CSOB   Claire Seymour, *The Operas of Benjamin Britten: Expression and Evasion* (Woodbridge: Boydell Press, 2004)

DHOB   David Herbert, ed., *The Operas of Benjamin Britten* (London: Hamish Hamilton, 1979) [revised edition (Herbert Press: 1989) noted where appropriate]

HCBB   Humphrey Carpenter, *Benjamin Britten* (London: Faber, 1992)

MCCC   Mervyn Cooke, ed., *The Cambridge Companion to Benjamin Britten* (Cambridge: Cambridge University Press, 1999)

MCWR   Mervyn Cooke, *War Requiem* (Cambridge: Cambridge University Press, 1996)

MRLL   Donald Mitchell and Philip Reed, eds., *Letters from a Life: Selected Letters and Diaries of Benjamin Britten* (London: Faber, 1998), vol. 1: *1923–1939*; vol. 2: *1939–1976*

PKBM   Paul Kildea, ed., *Britten on Music* (Oxford: Oxford University Press, 2003)

Britten's unpublished correspondence (to and from the composer) and diaries are held at the BPF unless otherwise stated. Catalogue numbers have not been noted here as they are currently in the process of being altered.

Introduction

Lucy Walker

In his introduction to *The Cambridge Companion to Benjamin Britten* (1999), Mervyn Cooke remarks in some astonishment that, 'as the century draws to a close' there persists a noticeable strain of 'bigoted views' towards Britten, particularly with regard to his sexuality.[1] This trend, as his introduction then goes on to explore, serves mainly to distract from the remarkable breadth and scope of Britten's repertoire and also to imbue studies of his works, particularly the operas, with a very specific slant. The *Companion*, until now the most recent book of essays on Britten to be published, successfully counteracts such narrowness of perspective. Yet Cooke also recounts the history of 'Britten criticism', and we find that, although 'posterity, on the whole, continues to serve Britten well',[2] some writers have tended to throw a protective arm around the composer, shielding him from potential disapprobation; and even as recently as 1999 it appeared that certain elements of Britten studies required particular pleading. The result of this has been that, at times, negative critical readings of the composer's works or, more particularly, his life may have been blue-pencilled.

This collection was not specifically devised in opposition to previous Britten literature, or to draw direct comparisons with Cooke's collection. However, *Benjamin Britten: New Perspectives on his Life and Work* arrives exactly ten years after the *Companion*, and the intervening years have quite definitely witnessed a noticeable shift in perspective. For example, it is a feature of this new volume that while some of the 'controversial' elements of Britten's history are engaged with head-on – most notably his pacifism – they are not necessarily explained away or excused. Furthermore, a palpable objectivity towards the composer is in evidence here, and this is most likely due to the 'newness' of the contributors, most of whom are entering the world of Britten criticism for the first time.

These essays had their origin in papers presented at a Britten Study Day held at the University of East Anglia (UEA) in April 2008, and, although they have undergone considerable revisions since then, the spirit of the original study day is preserved in the order of the collection and in the freshness of the approach. The 'New' of the title draws attention to several elements. First, some of the writers are not only new to Britten studies in terms of their publishing history but are publishing for the first time, having recently completed or reached a significant stage in Britten-related doctoral theses. Others are established scholars who are writing on Britten for the first time. Only a couple can be said to be 'Britten scholars', and thus the collection represents something of a break with the past in incorporating a mix of postgraduate writers and more experienced scholars in the same volume. Additionally, the collection reveals the extent to which Britten scholarship is reaching outside the confines of Anglo-American criticism.[3]

Secondly, *New Perspectives* represents a new type of structure. Previous volumes of Britten essays have been in the form of 'Companions',[4] with the aim of achieving comprehensiveness where such a prolific composer was concerned – chapters on the early years, vocal music, orchestral music, operas, and pieces for children, etc. This group, on the other hand, was serendipitously formed from its origins in a conference that had no specific theme, other than to discuss Britten. As a result, the collection can be seen to represent the Britten 'Zeitgeist': a 'snapshot' of what researchers happened to be working on at the time of the call for papers.

One final element of 'newness' is that the original study day – and thus the book – was initiated by a new venture: the online Britten Thematic Catalogue, a collaborative research project between the Britten–Pears Foundation and the UEA.[5] In itself, this is a hugely important and pioneering project that will make accessible for the first time the entire range of information regarding Britten's *œuvre* online, providing a model for other catalogues and extending the debate on the use of the internet as a tool for the capturing and dissemination of these resources. As some of the essays demonstrate, the project has also given rise to the exploration of a wide diversity of other ethical, cultural and psychological issues concerning the development of an artist and the responsibilities towards their legacy of those who come after them. I very much hope that the project will inspire further 'new perspectives' on Britten during its genesis over the next few years, and after the catalogue has been unveiled in completeness for the composer's centenary in 2013.

The collection follows, more or less, the pattern of the original study day. It begins with Colin Matthews' 'Going behind Britten's back' which outlines the ethical concerns that he – as Music Director of the BPF – must address when considering the publications of works that Britten may well have wished to suppress. In the context of the Britten Thematic Catalogue, which has to date catalogued over 700 works of the composer's unpublished juvenilia, this chapter will gain increasing relevance as Britten's 'bottom-drawer manuscripts'[6] become fully documented, available to research, and attractive to publishers.

Some of the works may also be available to perform, which is the subject of Sharon Choa's 'Performing Early Britten'. Choa, who directed premières of several pieces of juvenilia during the Study Day, discusses these and other orchestral works by Britten from 1926–7, which could be described as 'turning points' in his early compositional career, and in particular which raise a variety of problems concerning the performance, and performance expectations, of Britten's early 'masterpieces.'

What follows is a group of essays concerning Britten's absorption of and expression in his works of various musical and non-musical influences, including the works of Shostakovich and Verdi, the poetry of Ovid, and the audio-visual phenomena of the cinema. Cameron Pyke's 'Shostakovich's Fourteenth Symphony: A Response to *War Requiem*?' outlines two significant, ostensibly very different works in the context of Britten's and Shostakovich's friendship and creative relationship. Pyke argues the case for a strong interconnectivity between symphony and requiem especially in relation to the chosen texts, the exegesis of the theme of death and the characteristic deployment of orchestral forces. Despite what amounts to almost a coyness in directly commenting on each others' work, Pyke reveals that Britten and Shostakovich demonstrated a long-distance and long-term mutual assimilation of musical and extra-musical *topoi*.

Assimilation is also the subject of George Caird's '*Six Metamorphoses after Ovid* and the Influence of Classical Mythology on Benjamin Britten'. In terms of mainstream critical literature on the subject the 1951 work for solo oboe has been somewhat neglected, as has, Caird suggests, the importance to Britten's *œuvre* of classical mythology. Britten had written for the oboe at different times in his life and for different individual players, but in this work – composed for Joy Boughton – Britten made use of the instrument to represent certain tropes in classical mythology, a subject which, as Caird proposes, is of as much significance to Britten's repertoire as liturgical or biblical texts.

David Crilly's 'Britten and the Cinematic Frame' discusses the influence of cinema on Britten, specifically the significant effect that working for the GPO Film Unit in the 1930s had on his compositional style. During this period of somewhat hectic activity, the composer was required not only to provide soundtracks but to 'integrate sound into the fabric of the visual dramatic narrative'.[7] This practice, in such early collaborative films as *Coal Face* and *Night Mail*, argues Crilly, established in Britten's compositional technique a sophisticated manipulation of the visual and oral perspectives expressed by the multivalence of the 'cinematic frame'; and this he later made use of in his stage works, notably *The Turn of the Screw* and *Peter Grimes*.

Jane Brandon's chapter, 'Storms, Laughter and Madness: Verdian "Numbers" and Generic Allusions in Benjamin Britten's *Peter Grimes*', concludes this eclectic gathering of influences and allusions and also introduces the next group of chapters on Britten's operas. While Britten's admiration of Verdi has often been noted, Brandon's is the first study in any detail to examine how Verdi's operas, and Italian 'number operas' in general, influenced the genesis of Britten's operas as well as their structure, stagecraft and characterization. However, as Brandon points out, a study of Verdian manifestations in, for example, *Peter Grimes* 'often reveals more about Britten's innovations than his reliance on tradition.'[8] Brandon's chapter reminds us that Britten filtered the past through his own lens and for his own purposes; and *Grimes* can be seen as both tribute to and subverter of Italianate tradition.

The 'neglected' opera *Owen Wingrave* surprisingly found itself the subject of two independently formed papers at the study day, reflecting perhaps its recent smattering of productions in the UK. *Wingrave* is an opera often considered 'difficult': it received a mixed reception after its television broadcast in 1971 and reviews of modern revivals tend to be prefaced with a description of the opera's 'problems'.[9] Frances Spalding (in 'Dramatic Invention in Myfanwy Piper's Libretto for *Owen Wingrave*') argues for a reconsideration of the dramatic qualities of the opera through a close study of the genesis of Piper's libretto. Spalding describes Piper's collaborative relationship with Britten and the particular problems encountered in devising an opera that would suit the needs of both a television broadcast and future performances on a stage. Piper was not, interestingly, entirely satisfied with certain elements of the libretto – notably the characterization of Kate, over which she strongly disagreed with Britten – but Spalding, and Piper, convincingly present the case for a re-examination and re-hearing of this work.

Arne Muus also examines the libretto in ' "The Minstrel Boy to the War is Gone" – Utterance and Dramaturgy in Britten's *Owen Wingrave*' and challenges the critical reception of the work's supposedly weak structure and dénouement. Taking as a critical standpoint various seminal works of Sigmund Freud, Muus investigates Owen's often contradictory behaviour, and suggests that – far from being a weakness in the libretto – the paradoxes in Owen's character are informed by his problematic relationship with his late father. Owen is thus a 'Winslow Boy' first and foremost, and it is his Oedipal struggles which contribute most strongly to the opera's dramatic impact.

J. P. E. Harper-Scott's 'Made You Look! Children in *Salome* and *Death in Venice*' scrutinizes the cultural themes of another recently much-performed opera, *Death in Venice*. Richard Strauss and Britten both produced, for their respective times, scandalous and morally risky depictions of children on the operatic stage partly, it seems, for the scopic gratification of the audience.

While *Death in Venice* and Strauss's *Salome* are – superficially – two operas with very little in common, Harper-Scott places them side by side as unlikely comrades in order to highlight structural and ethical elements both operas address, whether purposefully or not. In Britten's case, suggests Harper-Scott, the composer's intentional classical Greek aesthetic in *Death in Venice*, expressed through the character of Aschenbach and his love for Tadzio, is largely overturned as a result of its intertextual similarities with the 'decadent' *Salome*, and we are 'invited to entertain the thought that the child might be the monster.'[10]

Drawing the section on opera to a close, Claire Seymour's 'From the Borough to Fraser Island' takes Britten to Australia and back by way of an imaginative, indeed imaginary, account of an opera-that-might-have-been – an opera whose subject matter was very much the outsider in society. Seymour describes the genesis of a libretto written by the novelist Patrick White and submitted to Britten with the hope of a future collaboration. White's *A Fringe of Leaves* is a fictionalized true story of a Scottish woman who was ship-wrecked on an Australian island in the 19th century and who remained there, an outsider inhabiting a world of submerged menace, for ten weeks. Many characteristic elements of Britten's operas can be found in this story: the challenging of innocence, the 'odd one out', the physical power of the sea. While Britten did not in fact set the libretto, largely, it appears, because he took an instant dislike to White, through White's draft text Seymour offers an entirely new angle on Britten's dramatic preoccupations.

The final two chapters consider, in their various ways, a vision of Britten somewhat removed from most narratives of his life and works. Maéna Py's 'Britten and France, or the Late Emergence of a Remarkable Lyric Universe' uncovers the generally hostile critical reception Britten's operas received in France, principally in Paris, from the 1940s until around the 1990s, thus providing a perspective that is largely new to British readership. Only in the provinces, reveals Py, where French musical life was not in the grip of such figures as Pierre Boulez – who actively resisted the performance of non-serialist music in the 1950s and 1960s – did Britten's operas find sympathetic performances and hearings. We find that a staging of a Britten opera in Paris was often considered daring to the point of foolhardiness by the critics; performances were apparently deliberately sabotaged by the management; and while Britten's craftsmanship was often admired, his exactitude amidst the French preference for improvisation was not.

Finally, Brian McMahon, in 'Why did Benjamin Britten Return to Wartime England?', discusses Britten's status as 'outsider' in both the USA – for nearly three years during the early stages of World War II – and in his own country when he returned in 1942, and how this alienation may be interpreted today. It has long been the assumption that Britten returned to the UK following an acute attack of homesickness on reading E. M. Forster's article on the Aldeburgh writer George Crabbe while residing in Escondido, San Diego. McMahon suggests another, less romantic, and considerably less flattering possibility: that Britten was becoming nervous of the gathering US involvement in the war and the real chance he may be called up to serve in the US forces. Britten's attitude and behaviour during this period highlight some of the many contradictions in his character; McMahon's chapter describes in particular how the composer's fear of conflict collided with his strongly embedded principles – with some interesting results.

* * *

It may be that *New Perspectives* will be the first of many such collections born out of the Thematic Catalogue project, although we have a trap to avoid in perpetually and self-consciously striving for newness ('New Perspectives II'; 'More New Perspectives'; Newer Perspectives; 'Newest Perspectives', etc). I also take heed of Colin Matthews' warning against any tendency to announce 'discoveries' of 'new' Britten works, which, although attractive to the media, are not likely to take place now. Ideally, what the project and this most recent crop of Britten scholarship will encourage is a freshening of attitude towards the composer; a healthy detachment from the subject in order to generate further insight; and, possibly, a further serendipitous batch of responses to a call for papers in the future. It certainly seems as if Britten scholarship is wide open: more so now than at any time in the past.

Notes

1 *MCCC*, p. 1.

2 *MCCC*, p. 7.

3 Other works on Britten not in the English language include: Liudmila Kovnatskaya, *Benjamin Britten* (Moscow: All-Union Publishing House, 1974); Andrzej Tuchowski, *Benjamin Britten: twórca dzieło epoka* (Kraków: Musica Iagellonica, 1994); Xavier de Gaulle, *Benjamin Britten, ou l'impossible quiétude* (Arles: Actes Sud, 1996); Mildred Clary, *Benjamin Britten, ou le mythe de l'enfance* (Paris: Buchet/Chastel, 2006); and Norbert Abels, *Benjamin Britten* (Hamburg: Rowohlt Tb, 2008).

4 See *CPBC* and *MCCC*. Other collections have included Philip Reed, ed., *On Mahler and Britten: Essays in Honour of Donald Mitchell on his Seventieth Birthday* (Woodbridge; Aldeburgh: Boydell Press; Britten–Pears Library, 1995) and the earlier volume, Donald Mitchell and Hans Keller, eds., *Benjamin Britten: A Commentary on his Works from a Group of Specialists* (London: Rockliff, 1952).

5 This project will include details of Britten's manuscripts and other related documentary information. As the project is a work-in-progress any detailed information given here will rapidly go out of date; for current information and regular updates see www.brittenpears.org.

6 This term is from Michael Berkeley's 'Life after death', *The Guardian* (13 March 2004), http://www.guardian.co.uk/music/2004/mar/13/classicalmusicandopera1 accessed 7 February 2007.

7 David Crilly, 'Britten and the Cinematic Frame', p. 56 below.

8 Jane Brandon, 'Storms, Laughter and Madness: Verdian "Numbers" and Generic Allusions in Benjamin Britten's *Peter Grimes*', p. 74 below.

9 Anna Picard, in a review of a 2007 production, begins '*Owen Wingrave* is a sorely compromised work … Musically weak, structurally clumsy, morally simplistic, cavalier in its interpretation of the source material, and uneven in its embrace of televisual techniques' (*The Independent*, 29 April 2007); while Andrew Clements, reviewing a 2008 recording, writes 'what makes *Wingrave* problematic is its failure to be innovative, and how the score is too obviously content to revisit musical ideas and moral themes that Britten had explored more memorably in earlier works.' (*The Guardian*, 6 June 2008).

10 J. P. E. Harper-Scott, 'Made You Look! Children in *Salome* and *Death in Venice*', p. 130 below.

1 Going Behind Britten's Back

Colin Matthews

The extraordinary scope of the archive held by the Britten–Pears Foundation, with its cache of something like 750 pieces of juvenilia, along with what amounts to at least 95 per cent of the manuscripts of mature works, including many which were withdrawn or unfinished or have been published posthumously, must be unique for any composer. It is a special privilege to have access to so much material, but it brings with it responsibilities, as well as a number of moral questions. Just as biographers are often taken to task for burrowing too deeply into the minutiae of an artist's life, and thereby perhaps missing the bigger picture, or misinterpreting the life, so musicologists may be tempted by this extraordinary abundance of new information – especially about the composer's early development – to place undue weight on it, or exaggerate its importance. In addition, because music is not directly accessible in the way that words (or pictures) are, there is the vexed question of whether or not works that the composer might have suppressed should see the light of day in terms of performance, or publication. Since we have many hundreds of unperformed works in the archive (most, but by no means all, consisting of juvenilia) this is an important question for us. It is an issue which we need to consider in several different ways.

When a lost manuscript of a composer of several centuries ago resurfaces, no one is likely to dispute whether or not the music should be performed, even if it adds little or nothing to our understanding of the composer. But we start to feel uneasy when missing or incomplete works are reconstructed – Bach's St Mark or St Luke Passions, for instance, or Mozart's *Zaide*, or Schubert's five unfinished piano sonatas, or his and Beethoven's more tenuous Tenth Symphonies.

The most significant unfinished piece to have fully entered the repertoire is, of course, Mozart's Requiem. There can be very few, if any, who would maintain that it should not be performed at all, as not representative of Mozart's final wishes, but of course there has been controversy for over 200 years about Süssmayr's contribution as regards both its extent and its competence; and as scholarship has become more focused, different versions have emerged, although none has completely won the day and supplanted the standard editions.

Schubert's Unfinished Symphony is a different case, since it seems just as likely that Schubert was content with it in its incomplete state as that he tried but failed to complete it. Like the Mozart Requiem, it has been a repertoire piece from the outset, as has the torso of Bruckner's Ninth Symphony; but here we have a different and tragic state of affairs. It is almost certain that Bruckner not only finished the Finale in sketch form, but completed a much larger proportion than survives in orchestral score. The chaotic dispersal of the manuscript after his death, with his friends appropriating pages of the Finale as souvenirs, means that – unless those missing pages turn up (which is not impossible even now) – the Finale cannot be reconstructed other than hypothetically.

As we move nearer to our own time – with the unlikelihood of discovering, say, a previously unknown Strauss symphonic poem – attention turns to juvenilia or to earlier versions of well-known works. Here the record industry, in its insatiable quest for novelty (as long as this does not mean recording genuinely new music) has been responsible for unearthing works that might be better forgotten. In many cases the presentation of obscure or immature works unbalances our view of the composer, and gives a false perspective on the work: for instance the recording of all of Dvořák's early quartets, which has particular relevance, as we shall see, to Britten.

In some cases recent revivals of early versions of works that the composer subsequently revised have brought new insights. In the cases of Sibelius' Violin Concerto and Vaughan Williams' *London Symphony* for instance, the original versions are, unusually, more complex than the final ones, and have proved to be valid works in their own right, and certainly worth hearing – although no one would suggest that they should supplant the composers' second thoughts. But this is not always the case, and there is no real need to hear Sibelius' clumsy first attempts at his Fifth Symphony more than once, since the final version is so superior.

Before returning to Britten, I would like to refer to two major works with whose reconstruction I have been closely involved: Mahler's Tenth Symphony and Elgar's Third. My views on Mahler's Tenth are on record elsewhere,[1] and if I still have any unease about the perception of this work, it is because it cannot be emphasized enough that, although it is a symphony that is complete in sketch, without a missing bar, it is very much a work in progress. No amount of reconstruction can reflect what Mahler would have done with it had he lived. For all its beauty and significance, it is a very imperfect work, and its audience needs to be fully aware of this state of incompleteness. It is, in Deryck Cooke's words, *not* Mahler's 'Tenth Symphony', but a performing version of the sketches in the state in which Mahler left them when he died.[2] The waters have in recent years been muddied by alternative versions, most of them simply reworkings of Cooke's pioneering edition, and to my mind lacking all validity.

Because Mahler's working method was always to through-compose, we have a complete but imperfect musical argument. With Elgar's Third Symphony we have a patchwork of musical ideas, some ordered, some not, which only the composer could have put together as he intended. This was Elgar's way of working throughout his life. Anthony Payne's great achievement is to have created a framework for these sketches which, to my ears, is totally convincing: *not* Elgar's Third Symphony, but a hybrid work which stands in for it, full of a vitality which belies the received opinion of a composer with nothing left to say.

The Thematic Catalogue of Britten's music will comprise a completely open and unexpurgated account of everything he wrote. There will in future be no excuse for the kind of misinformation where, for instance, works are regularly described as having been 'discovered' at the Britten–Pears Foundation, as though they had been previously unknown or unrecognized. In fact the basic listing of works, including juvenilia and unfinished pieces, was made while Britten was still alive, and at his instigation. Myth and misinformation tends to become attached to 'unknown' works, and especially to the music that I have been discussing – Mozart's Requiem most notably, of course, but at the first performance of the three completed movements of Bruckner's Ninth, seven years after his death, the existence of even the sketches for the Finale was deliberately denied. Those musicologists who examined Mahler's Tenth largely failed to grasp the scope of the work, or its scale; there are still some today who wish it had remained in manuscript and unplayed. No one, before Anthony Payne, thought to look properly through Elgar's sketches; and the announcement of the reconstructed Third Symphony's first performance in 1997 brought forth howls of protest from devoted Elgarians who would have preferred that Elgar's wish that the manuscript should be burned – expressed once only and immediately contradicted – had been carried out.

What is it that can so concern musicologists about unfinished works? I quote the words of a noted authority on the subject of Mahler's Tenth:

> the author inclines to the view that precisely someone who senses the extraordinary scope of the conception of the Tenth ought to do without adaptations and performances. The case is similar with sketches of unfinished pictures by masters: anyone who understands them and

can visualise how they might have been completed would prefer to file them away and contemplate them privately.[3]

This is none other than Theodor Adorno. Elsewhere in his writing on the Tenth he shows that he simply has not understood the stage that Mahler had reached with the music; but here he is making a statement that I find abhorrent. It is to my mind unthinkable that musicologists should be able to gloat in private over music that they consider unsafe for ears other than their own. That Adorno goes on to apply the same standards to unfinished works of art only compounds the infamy.

Clearly we have no intention of taking such a line where Britten's music is concerned. But, as custodians of his manuscripts, how should we fulfil our responsibility toward the public? In the first place, we intend, as I have already stated, to be completely open about what we hold, and to make it, in one form or another, as widely available as seems appropriate. But the Foundation is not a body that is concerned only with scholarship: the archive is largely maintained by the royalties that it earns from Britten's music, and the trustees have a consequent duty both to promote that music, and to protect it. We do our best to argue against cuts that opera houses want to make to the music; we are consulted about arrangements; and we do not allow commercial exploitation which we feel is inappropriate. Perhaps most important of all, we have had to take decisions on the publication of music that was not published in Britten's lifetime.

So, to return to the question that was implied at the outset: what is our responsibility towards music that the composer did not publish himself, or left incomplete, or withdrew, and which he might well have preferred to suppress? Of course there is a simple answer: if Britten had wanted to withhold any of his unpublished music then he was perfectly free to destroy it himself while he was alive. Yet this would have been alien to him, since he was an inveterate hoarder, keeping not just all of his early manuscripts – perhaps as much out of nostalgia as for any musical reason – but also everyday things such as cheque stubs, bills, and receipts. He was reluctant to throw anything away, useful or not; he was still using his old school exercise books at the end of his life. Alongside more or less every note of music he ever wrote, from scraps and exercises to full-blown works, we also have the everyday documentation of his life.

Alternatively he could have left an embargo on the performance or publication of this material after his death. Instead he left such decisions to his musical executors, one of whom was Peter Pears, who encouraged the publication of many early works. I suspect, though, that Britten would not have expected anyone to be sufficiently interested in this body of music to trouble with it: anyone who could describe writing such masterpieces as *The Young Person's Guide to the Orchestra* as a 'chore',[4] or the *Serenade* as 'not important stuff, but quite pleasant, I think'[5] is not likely to have given too much thought to what posterity might make of his legacy.

Yet even a work as well known as the *Serenade* has a hidden aspect: when Marion Thorpe discovered – and here for once the word 'discovered' is appropriate – the battered manuscript of Britten's setting of 'Now sleeps the crimson petal' for tenor, horn and strings in a suitcase (it had been given to her father, Erwin Stein), it proved not to only to be a strikingly beautiful omission from the *Serenade*, but the missing link between that work and the *Nocturne*, which Britten clearly remembered when he came to write the *Nocturne* 15 years later.

It is time to look in more detail at the archive itself, and what it contains. How have we dealt with it in the past, and how do we intend to deal with it in the future? In the case of juvenilia the scope of what we hold is so huge that it is here that we have to exercise the most discretion. While everything will eventually be made accessible in the online catalogue, the vast majority is never likely to be published. This applies just as much to the early piano pieces and songs as to the string quartets, a medium which Britten did not tackle for the first time until the relatively late age of twelve. Over the next six or seven years he wrote ten works for quartet in all, including six full-length quartets. Only one of these (the Quartet in D of 1931) was published in his lifetime (in fact towards the end of his life, in 1974); one (in G major from 1927) was given its first performance at a concert as part of the Britten Study Day in April 2008; another, in F major, from 1928, was published ten years ago. But the remaining unpublished works, while they might be given an airing, are unlikely to go any further. Although the proportion of ten early quartets to only three mature ones is fascinating, our considered opinion is that to publish or record 'the complete quartets' would give a false perspective. The vast array of works for solo piano contrasts even more strongly with the two works published in his lifetime. We have toyed with the idea of a 'piano marathon', presenting the entire corpus, but this essentially entertaining rather than scholarly project would be as far as it would go. Very few of these abundant but not very significant works will ever be seen in print.

The borderline between juvenilia and maturity is a fine one, but the *Sinfonietta*, as Britten's op. 1, obviously marks a boundary. But even that boundary is not a clear one, since it is already the 23rd work in chronological order in the *Catalogue of Published Works* compiled in 1999.[6] Ten of the 22 works that precede it were published in Britten's lifetime – either works that he did not feel at the time warranted an opus number (there are over 100 of these in this catalogue, as opposed to the 95 to which he gave opus numbers), or which he revised and published much later. From the time of the *Sinfonietta* – his final year at the Royal College in 1932/3 – there is a number of substantial works, any of which could have become opus 1, but which he abandoned. These include the Double Concerto for violin and viola, fully composed though never orchestrated, a work that is very similar in structure to the *Sinfonietta*, but nearly twice its length; the F minor *Phantasy* for String Quintet, which won the 1932 Cobbett Prize and was widely performed and broadcast, but not published until 1983; and the five-movement suite for string quartet which went under the title of 'Go play, boy, play', reworked many times between 1933 and 1936, most of it performed at the time, but never reaching a final form. From 1936 also come the posthumously published *Temporal Variations* for oboe and piano, but here we are well into Britten's early maturity, with *Our Hunting Fathers* and the *Frank Bridge Variations* either side of it, and the disappearance of such a major work after only one performance is inexplicable.

Moving on into a period that is well documented, we have four categories of what might be called 'unauthorized' works: 1. first versions of works subsequently revised; 2. works that were withdrawn by the composer (in several cases having already been given opus numbers); 3. works which were abandoned and left in an unfinished state; and 4. finished works which were performed but not given opus numbers nor published at the time.

The first category can be further subdivided: works that were later substantially revised, like the Piano Concerto, its original third movement replaced seven years later; *Billy Budd*, rearranged ten years after its first performance from four acts into two; or *The Rape of Lucretia*, whose libretto and music were both quite substantially reworked shortly after the first performance. All of these have been subsequently performed in their original versions. Alongside these there are works – like the *Serenade* – for which more music was written than was actually used. These are almost exclusively vocal works, like *Les Illuminations*, which was originally planned to have four additional movements, *Winter Words*, and *Who are these Children?* For all of these works Britten sketched additional songs, most of which have now been published; but with the injunction that they should be performed separately, not as if they were part of a supposedly 'original' song cycle. This music is, in most cases, no less inspired than the published work, but simply didn't 'fit' when it came to making the final choice.

The second category – of withdrawn works – includes both music that seems to have been withdrawn largely for personal reasons, such as *Young Apollo*, written as a portrait of Wulff Scherchen, the love of Britten's early life, or the *Occasional Overture*, written for the inauguration of the Third

Programme in 1946 but given a poor performance under one of Britten's least favourite conductors, Adrian Boult. The *American Overture*, composed in 1941 as an earlier *Occasional Overture*, was not so much withdrawn as forgotten, as Britten denied all knowledge of it until shown the manuscript in 1972, even though he had given it an opus number at the time. The opera *Paul Bunyan* was withdrawn because it needed revision, but also no doubt because Britten was hurt by the very adverse criticism at its first performance in 1941. When Britten revised it in 1974 he gave it the opus number 17, which had earlier been assigned to another withdrawn piece, the choral settings of Gerard Manley Hopkins under the title *A.M.D.G.* Although at least four songs from the seven intended for the latter work were performed in the early 1940s, the work as a whole was never completed, and one of the settings is even crossed out in the sketch. Since Britten declined to publish it when asked in the 1970s, its eventual publication in 1988 was somewhat questionable.

The third category – of abandoned works – is the smallest, since very few projects that Britten undertook (as opposed to works that were planned but never begun – these too will feature in the online catalogue) were left incomplete, particularly after Britten returned to the UK in the 1940s. Some were actual victims of the transatlantic crossing: he had to leave behind the manuscripts both of the Clarinet Concerto he was writing for Benny Goodman, and of the sketches for a 'Sonata for Orchestra'. Other abandoned works include a piece for four horns and strings intended as a memorial for Dennis Brain; and a set of piano variations from 1965 intended as a follow-up to the *Night Piece* written as a test piece for the 1963 Leeds Piano Competition.

This is where I have to hold up my hand, as in May 2008 I arranged the recording of not only the Clarinet Concerto, in a reconstruction which I have put together from various sources – including the *Sonata for Orchestra* – but also the Dennis Brain piece, the piano variations, and three of the songs composed for but not included in *Les Illuminations*.[7] Since I have had a hand in editing and preparing for publication not just these but a large proportion of the music that has appeared since Britten's death, I have to take no small measure of responsibility in answering the moral question that I posed at the beginning.

I am well aware of the accusation that has been made from time to time that the Britten–Pears Foundation, in turning out posthumous works, has not so much been mining the archive as scraping the barrel. While this criticism tends to come from those who have no idea of quite how big the barrel is, I am not so blinkered as to think that every note of Britten's is uniquely deserving of being presented to the public eye, and remain concerned that not all of the music that has been published posthumously has equal validity. But there is one aspect of Britten of which very few will be aware: even where the appearance of an unfinished or sketched work gives the impression of being scrappy and unformed, closer examination will reveal that it was thought through in nearly every detail. Consequently there is very little of what might be called reconstruction involved, and remarkably few editorial decisions that need to be made. This applies even to the early works that have been published – the *Quatre chansons françaises* from 1928, for instance, are printed almost exactly as Britten wrote them down. The orchestral detail, for someone who had barely heard an orchestra, is remarkable, and the only aspect that needed adjusting was Britten's rather poor knowledge of French inflection. But this was a work of which the composer made a careful fair copy, as a gift for his parents. On the other hand I can remember looking through the boxes of juvenilia many years ago with Rosamund Strode, and hardly giving a second glance to a folded piece of manuscript written in thick smudged pencil. When we finally examined it, it turned out to be a piece for solo viola – Britten's own instrument – of remarkable intensity, and complete in the sketch. It is dated 1 August 1930, so it was possible to check Britten's diary entry to find that this was the day after he left school at the age of 16, when he wrote 'I didn't think I should be so sorry to leave.'[8] The manuscript has no title, but it was published in 1985 as *Elegy*.

Would Britten have approved of works that he had put to one side being revealed for all to see? Probably not. But would anyone argue, given the archive that we have charge of, that we should not make it as accessible as we can? This does not mean publishing or recording everything – far from it – but so long as this 'unauthorized' music is given its proper perspective, it can only add to our overall understanding of the composer. I have to admit myself to a particular fascination with the hidden workings of composers, and have learned far more from pursuing this path than from analysis, whose insights by comparison can sometimes seem a little cold and clinical – something Britten himself is known to have felt. He would have been somewhat dismayed at the idea of a study day being devoted to him, especially one which brought so much attention to the juvenilia – 'here was no Mozart I fear', he wrote, in typically disparaging tone, in the introduction to a collection of his early piano pieces[9] – but I cannot help feeling that he would also have been secretly pleased.

The fourth category of 'unauthorized' works is – juvenilia aside – the largest of all, comprising the incidental music, ranging through the many film scores from the 1930s to the theatre and radio scores which he continued to write copiously until the late 1940s, when opera writing and festival running left him no spare time for such activities. I have omitted to describe this category in any detail, as much work has been done by others and it is proving to be an area of fruitful Britten scholarship.[10] When these works are included, along with the almost equally large body of arrangements of music by other composers, the Thematic Catalogue will run to more than 1,100 items. There is a lot of work to be done.

Notes

1 Colin Matthews, 'The Tenth Symphony', in *The Mahler Companion*, ed. Donald Mitchell and Andrew Nicholson (Oxford: Oxford University Press, 1999), pp. 491–507.

2 See Deryck Cooke, *Gustav Mahler: A Performing Version of the Draft for the Tenth Symphony*, second edition (New York and London: AMP/Faber, 1989), p. xvii.

3 Theodor Adorno, *Mahler: A Musical Physiognomy*, 2nd edition (Chicago: University of Chicago Press, 1992), p. x.

4 See *MRLL*, vol. 2, p. 1286.

5 See *HCBB*, p. 184.

6 Paul Banks, *Benjamin Britten: A Catalogue of the Published Works* (Aldeburgh: Britten-Pears Library, 1999).

7 Thomas Zehetmair conducting the Northern Sinfonia with soloists Michael Collins (clarinet), Sondrine Piao (soprano) and Rolf Hind (piano). The recording will be released under the NMC label in September 2009.

8 BBD, 1 August 1930.

9 Britten's introduction to *Five Walztes* (London: Faber Music, 1970).

10 See John Evans and Philip Reed, 'A Catalogue Raisonée', in *A Britten Source Book*, ed. John Evans, Philip Reed and Paul Wilson (Aldeburgh: Britten–Pears Library 1987), pp. 129–65; Philip Reed, 'Britten in the Cinema: *Coal Face*', in *MCCC*, pp. 54–77; Paul Kildea, *Selling Britten: Music and the Market Place* (Oxford: Oxford University Press, 2002), pp. 34–7, 49–52; David Crilly, 'Britten and the Cinematic Frame', chap. 5 below; and Mervyn Cooke, *A History of Film Music* (Cambridge: Cambridge University Press, 2008), pp 275–8.

2 Performing Early Britten: Signs of Promise and Achievement in *Poèmes* nos. 4 and 5 (1927)

Sharon Choa

One of the most exciting discoveries to have come out of work on the Benjamin Britten Thematic Catalogue has been the sheer scope and extent of the composer's juvenilia, now known to comprise over 700 distinct works, written between the ages of six and eighteen. These juvenile pieces and sketches, together with other documents such as diaries and letters from the period constitute, as Lucy Walker has noted, 'a substantial piece of his own childhood that he literally carried from place to place throughout his life'.[1] The 'value' that the composer invested in his early compositions, and his stated reason for keeping them throughout his adult life was, as he told Imogen Holst, 'the chance it gave of seeing how a child's mind worked' and this remains a valid reason for scholarly interest in the juvenilia today, now that the composer is firmly established as one of the most significant creative artists of the 20th century.

A particularly tantalizing thread running through the corpus of early work is the gradual development of Britten's orchestral technique in a sequence of scores written in a period when, prior to the start of his formal composition studies with Frank Bridge, the young composer was nevertheless able to impose upon himself a self-discipline that ensured, as Christopher Mark has noted 'a steady of improvement of skills and [an] expansion of creative vision', coupled with 'a determination to see a project to its conclusion'.[2] The Britten Study Day at the University of East Anglia in April 2008 provided an appropriate environment in which Britten's youthful 'determination' could at last be rewarded and his imagined sound world in some of these juvenile scores brought to life for the first time by real orchestral forces. The experience provided for the audience a powerful demonstration of the importance that performance can play in disseminating the research findings of the project as they relate to the development of Britten's early style. For me as the conductor it also presented a particular challenge to present the most convincing case both for the music itself and its orchestral presentation, balancing the problems created by the inevitable limitations in technique and weaknesses in form with a sensitivity to the young composer's individual voice and emerging creative vision.

The works chosen to be performed at the Study Day were the fourth and fifth of a sequence of '*Poèmes*' composed by Britten in late 1926 and early 1927, at a time when his early dependence on classical influences (most crucially Beethoven) had begun to be supplanted by an interest in more contemporary styles, reaching back to Wagner but embracing also most noticeably Debussy, Delius and Holst.[3] The idea of writing orchestral music was not new to him, however. As early as 1922, aged eight or nine, he had written a 'Symphony in C for Small Orchestra' scored for flute, piccolo, oboe, three percussion instruments (side drum, bass drum, kettle drum), harp, and strings. But 1926 was the first year to be dominated by orchestral composition. Two overtures had been completed earlier in the summer, one in C, and an 'Ouverture' in B♭ minor (composed between 1 and 29 June). Although both look back to classical models, the second in particular has a breadth suggestive, as Mark has observed, of Bruckner or (more likely) Sibelius, which points forward to the advances made in the *Poèmes*.[4] The 'Ouverture' was a particularly special achievement for the twelve-year old, as it was submitted to the BBC's 1926 Autumn Musical Festival Prize Competition by his father, with the identifying motto 'Never Unprepared'. Accompanying the score is a note from Mr Britten that reads:

> This composition was written by a lad of 12 years, in nine days: written in his very few spare moments snatched from the hourly routine of his 'Prep' school (in the early mornings for instance). He has only an elementary knowledge of harmony. Has had no instruction of any kind in Orchestration or counterpoint; a little in form. It is quite an original copy; no piano score written before. We thought it worth sending, if only for advice.[5]

The 'Ouverture' is an ambitious work scored for piccolo, two flutes, two oboes, two clarinets in B♭, two bassoons, four horns in B♭ alto, two trumpets in B♭, timpani and full strings. Beginning in the difficult key of B♭ minor, the piece charts a course to end in B♭ major via a middle section in A♭ major designated by a key signature change. And it is a self-consciously long score, filling out 90 pages of manuscript, although 12 pages in the middle are faintly crossed out as if either Britten himself or someone giving him advice had suggested that those pages could be cut.

Soon after the composition of the 'Ouverture', Britten reported to his mother on 28 August that he had taken 'a great like to modern Orchestral music', having heard Delius's 'lovely' *Life Dance* and three movements from *The Planets* at a Queen's Hall Promenade concert a few days' earlier, conducted by Henry Wood.[6] Soon afterwards, at the end of September, he began work on his *Poème pour Orchestra* no. 1. Two more such pieces followed around Christmas and the New Year before Britten embarked on his *Poème* no. 4, finishing the work in an astonishing three days, between 12 and 14 February 1927. A mere five days later, on 19 February, he completed the final touches to his fifth and final *Poème*.

The first two *Poèmes*, dated 26 September 1926 and 24 December 1926 respectively, employ the same orchestration as the 'Ouverture' with only minor adjustments.[7] No. 3, dated 29 December 1926 – 3 January 1927, sees the addition of two tubas and a harp – the latter perhaps one of the most difficult instruments for which to write. No. 4 settles for one flute, one oboe, one cor anglais, two clarinets in B♭, strings (specifying the exact numbers of players required), and harp; whereas no. 5 in F♯ minor, by far the longest of the set, expands the orchestral forces to include one flute, one oboe, two clarinets in A, two bassoons, two horns in F, three trombones and tuba, timpani and strings.[8]

On a first perusal of the orchestral score of *Poème* no. 4, a number of features are immediately impressive: how Britten manipulates orchestral texture; his sense of orchestral colour; and his understanding of how to exploit the technique of individual instruments. Less persuasive are his attempts at defining a coherent development of voice-leading within the structure, and his design of tonal-harmonic progressions. The aurally impressive beginning of the work has an identifiably Delian resonance but also seems to anticipate something of the 'dream world' that characterizes so many of Britten's mature works (see Plate 2). The use of arpeggiation in the harp, the *pianissimo tremolandi* in the strings, punctuated by occasional *pizzicato*, and splashes of trilling cymbals are unmistakeable Britten traits.

The process by which the composer develops his material through the rest of the piece is, however, a more clumsy affair. As both the length and the tonal journey of the 'Ouverture' were consciously designed to 'impress', so once again Britten shows himself keen to plunge into 'difficult' keys and exercise his understanding of 'clever' harmonic turns whenever the opportunity arises. Just seven bars into the score, the harmony shifts into G♭ major, then, using G♭ as an enharmonic pivot of F♯, passes through D major and back to G♭ immediately in the next bar. These harmonic transitions are abrupt, serve no particular expressive purpose and are not supported by equivalent motivic developments. This kind of rather awkward harmonic progression pervades much of the score, often endangering the coherence of its formal parts, both on the small and large scale. For these reasons, rehearsing and performing the score proved as difficult as it was pleasurable. It was exciting to explore and discover the boy Britten's sound world, a world full of colour and vivid imagination;

but it felt at times almost impossible to make the wealth of ideas that had been strung together somewhat haphazardly sound lucid in a performance. Inevitably, a great deal of adjustment in terms of dynamics and balance of parts was also necessary in order to create a dramatic narrative sufficient to sustain the interest of an audience.[9]

Many of the same comments can be applied to the experience of performing the *Poème* no. 5, although here the form employed is much larger and does not correspond to the sonata-form structure most often utilized by Britten at this stage of his development. At 368 bars, the piece is more than three times the length of its predecessor and formally much more complex and adventurous. It is divided essentially into three contrasting parts (which for this discussion are termed A, B and C) that are then repeated and varied. It begins with solemn brass chords reminiscent of the opening of the prelude to Wagner's *Lohengrin*, a score that the young Britten had acquired a few months earlier, in August 1926. This *Largo* section (A) leads into an *Allegro molto moderato* episode (B), concluding with a soft string passage that acts as a 'prelude' to the ensuing fugal section (C), marked *Presto*. This proves to be ultimately the most impressive span of the work, comprising nearly 100 bars.

In performance, the most problematic passages are undoubtedly the brass chorale sections that punctuate the work. The young Britten had identified some rather 'juicy' chords but had not yet learnt how to deal with their progression in terms of voice-leading. The individual lines make little melodic sense, so it is difficult for the players to find or define a direction. This then leads to the difficulty of phrasing the section in a musical way. So even though the brass sections occupy the least space in the piece, they actually need the most thought and careful rehearsal to bring out the underlying compositional intentions. Plate 3 shows the beginning of the section.

The (B) section, starting with an *ostinato* oscillating figure (see Example 1) in the second violin defining A major, is enveloped by string chords that are as 'juicy' as the brass chords heard earlier. This section, 24 bars in length, is structured as an arch, shaped by the organization of dynamics: beginning in *pp*, rising to *ff*, and then dying down to *pp* again with further *diminuendo* in the second violin *ostinato* line. Again, there is a distinct effect sought in these bars, but the effect is not supported by a logical voice-leading progression, resulting in rather jagged unfolding of parts. In purely technical terms, it is clear that the young Britten had not yet mastered first-species counterpoint – and indeed, from his father's note to the BBC less than a year before, we know that he had not yet been exposed to this kind of teaching. Nevertheless, in performance, articulating the chordal progressions in this section is less problematic as the *ostinato* figure keeps the exotic dissonances within a stable tonal framework, so that they can be rendered as pure colour surrounding a repeated motivic idea, and representing a single unvaried harmony. It is interesting to note that at this very early stage of Britten's composing career, he was already experimenting with a technique that he made use of so ingeniously in his later years: to 'harmonize' a single note with shifting chromatic harmonies to create an effect that makes the stationary note sound as if it is actually fluctuating. The resultant sound is both eerie and dreamy, as can be heard in the most well-known mature example of the application of this technique, the opening of the setting of Keats's 'Sonnet' in the *Serenade* (1943).

The fugal (C) section displays an altogether new level of skill. Whether it is because the fugue as a form is more formulaic, so that following its rules of development automatically places the parts in the 'right' order and controls the contrapuntal lines in a more restricted fashion, or whether the young

Example 1 Britten, *Poème* no. 5, bars 24–9

(The example reproduces the young Britten's sometimes idionsyncratic notation.)

Britten simply had a penchant for fugal writing, the technique underlying this section is far more sophisticated and the musical effect more fluent than in the earlier parts of the work. The unfolding of ideas is also far more organic, making both interpretation and performance easy and satisfying. The homophonic punctuation by the woodwinds adds to the dramatic movement, and the use of the timpani is particularly imaginative. Canon and *stretto* techniques are deployed, as well as transformations of the fugal subject in augmentation. The 14-year-old Britten had certainly learnt his basic fugal skills and might even have used a specific fugue as model. Whatever the process of composition, the outcome was a highly successful one.

Following the exposition of his three main sections, Britten begins again, revisiting the brass chorales of (A), this time with the chords punctuated by chordal responses from the woodwind. But here again Britten's imagination runs ahead of his technique. He writes *pppp* dynamics for two horns and the same for the oboe, and although it can be surmised that his underlying intention was to have all parts play as quietly as possible, in reality the balance does not work. Passing over for the time being the material of (B), Britten moves next to a reiteration of the fugue, now marked *Prestissimo* and in 2/4. The introduction of the subject in triplets is immediately accompanied by a countersubject that is made up essentially of *pizzicato* string chords. Lasting 60 bars, the section is quite a *tour de force* when played at *prestissimo* speed. At its end, the timpani is left on its own, pounding out the triplet figure in a passage which undoubtedly takes inspiration from the transition between the third and fourth movements of Beethoven's Fifth Symphony.

After a few brief interruptions by woodwind, string and brass chords, the timpani rhythm leads seamlessly into a varied repeat of the (B) section. This utilizes as a driving force the triplet figure established in the fugue while the upper strings and woodwind explode into exuberant high notes with capriciously fluctuating dynamics. The soundscape that Britten creates here is fantastic in every sense of the word, but again, the connection between parts is not sufficiently developed. The changes sound abrupt and some of the dynamic variations are almost unachievable; even then the thematic material does not easily lend itself to such extremes of dynamic treatment. Interestingly, the atmosphere of the passage suggests Schumann, but as part of the overall structure it fails to coalesce, appearing and then disappearing somewhat too unexpectedly. Britten had perhaps yet to learn the importance of a sense of organic development; even different dream episodes take time to come into being, as he discovered so well in his later life in works such as the *Nocturne*, op. 60.

Eventually the section fizzles out through the fragmentation of its themes and the dynamics are reduced to *pp*, then ultimately to silence over a pause. From this silence re-emerges the fugue, now in the minor mode and marked *poco più presto*. The voices enter in *stretto* and soon work themselves into a homophonic texture, with the woodwinds, brass and timpani as one group and the strings another, each playing in rhythmic unison. In many ways, the momentum generated by the fugue culminating in this mass of sound produced by the entire orchestra could have served as a convincing closing section for the work. However, Britten, in expansive mood, chooses instead to end this section after six *ff* chords in the strings and to reintroduce the (A) section brass chords yet again, creating a sudden halt in forward momentum. This, for one final time, is interrupted by a return to the (B) section material, gently introduced for two bars by the oboe and rumbling timpani, *ppp*. The exuberant Schumannesque passage immediately follows and it is with this material that Britten elects to close the entire work, not, however at the height of climax but in a moment of quiet, if misjudged, contemplation. From their height at *ff*, the dynamics in the final three bars are reduced rapidly to an implied *pp* in the strings, with the entire orchestra closing *pp* on an F♯ minor chord. Even if the ending here has not been calculated expertly enough to provide convincing closure, there can be little doubt of the creative individuality underlying the impulse that led the youthful Britten to provide a contemplative, rather than bombastic, end to the most extended and colourful essay thus far in his short career as a composer of orchestral music (see Example 2).

On 14 December 1926, while Britten was hard at work on the sequence of *Poèmes*, he received a letter from Charles Macpherson, the organist of St Paul's Cathedral, to whom a friend of his mother's had sent one of his manuscripts in search of encouragement and advice. Macpherson encouraged the young composer to

> go on writing whenever you have the chance. Hear all the music you can, and when you begin serious study you will find out a lot of things for yourself. Solving your own difficulties in music, without slavish imitation of others, or a too great insistence on some personal fancy or mannerism is one of the best things to have for composing.[10]

The evidence of the *Poèmes* nos. 4 and 5 is that Britten took this advice to heart, using the pieces as an opportunity to depart from the classical models he had until this point 'slavishly' imitated to develop a more personal style, influenced by the more modern music he had recently been exposed to and enjoyed, and experimenting with sounds, textures and structures that he had not previously felt confident to explore. In these pieces, with their deliberately chosen free programmatic titles, he could perhaps for the first time run with

Example 2 Britten, Poème no. 5, final bars

his creative imagination and pour out his ideas in as coherent a form as he was able to bestow within the limitations of his knowledge and technique. Less than a year later, the self-taught composer would come under the tutelage and guidance of Frank Bridge, and the fusion of the young Britten's artistic imagination with sound craftsmanship and robust technique would begin in earnest, and with it the beginning of the end of his long creative apprenticeship.

Notes

1 Lucy Walker, ' "How a Child's Mind Works": Assessing the "Value" of Britten's Juvenilia', *Notes* 64/4 (June 2008), pp. 641–58 at p. 644.

2 Christopher Mark, 'Juvenilia (1922–1932)', in *MCCC*, pp. 11–35 at p. 12. Mark's chapter includes brief discussions of the *Poèmes*.

3 As Mark has noted, 'the strongest influence up to the middle of 1926 ... was Beethoven.' See *ibid.*, p. 14. Britten turned distinctly against Beethoven's music later in his life.

4 *Ibid.*, p. 18.

5 See Plate 1.

6 *MRLL*, vol. 1, p. 88.

7 *Poème* no. 1 uses clarinets, horns and trumpets in different keys from those employed in the 'Ouverture' and *Poème* no. 2 omits the piccolo.

8 The five *Poèmes* are listed, and given numbers, in Britten's handwritten 'Catalogue of Works' which he compiled some time in late 1927. This catalogue is held at the BPF.

9 In both *Poèmes* 4 and 5 Britten has made a few obvious mistakes in terms of omissions of accidentals and the correct clefs. These were corrected for the performance, which, however, adhered to everything else that Britten wrote, even if it was felt that he might have misconstrued some of the notes in certain chordal writing. These instances, however, are not plentiful.

10 *MRLL*, vol. 1, p. 91.

3 Shostakovich's Fourteenth Symphony: A Response to *War Requiem*?

Cameron Pyke

The creative relationship between Britten and Shostakovich, spanning the period from their first meeting in 1960 until the latter's death in 1975, has been discussed by a number of musicologists, though not subjected to a full-length study in depth.[1] Britten himself described his compositions as 'so very different from [Shostakovich's] own, but conceived, many of them, in the same period, children of similar fathers, and with many of the same aims;'[2] and Shostakovich not only expressed admiration for Britten's 'deep musicality and lofty musical taste', 'the force and sincerity of his talent, his [music's] outer simplicity and [its] depth of emotional effect', he also consistently commended Britten's works to his own postgraduate students such as Boris Tishchenko.[3] Shostakovich's Fourteenth Symphony, first performed in 1969 and dedicated to Britten, who conducted its first performance outside the USSR a year later, is fundamental to a discussion of this relationship: both composers spoke of the work as 'our symphony' in their correspondence and musicologists have particularly emphasized the importance both of the work's dedication and the setting of Küchelbecker in the ninth movement, which we may assume to be addressed to Britten himself.[4]

Several of Britten's works can be regarded as influencing the symphony: *Spring Symphony* (1948–9), *Nocturne* (1958), *War Requiem* (1961–2), *Curlew River* (1964) and *The Prodigal Son* (1967–8), the latter containing Britten's own dedication to Shostakovich.[5] However, one should acknowledge that the composers do not seem to have discussed each other's music in depth on the relatively few occasions they met, nor are musical matters discussed at any length in their correspondence.[6] Nevertheless, Shostakovich's particular admiration for *War Requiem* is attested by a variety of sources. Shostakovich acquired a copy of the score in March 1963, and his correspondence with Britten indicates that he had listened to the recording 'many, many times' as early as December of the same year;[7] indeed, by August 1963 the composer was commending the work to his postgraduate students at the Leningrad Conservatory.[8] Shostakovich's admiration for *War Requiem* should also be viewed in the context of the considerable interest in Britten's music in the USSR following the

Khrushchev 'thaw'. In March 1964, for example, the Leningrad Conservatoire paid Britten 'the stunning compliment' of an 'improvised' performance of the first half of *War Requiem* and went on to organize a series of complete performances between 1964 and 1971.[9] This article will therefore examine the extent to which the Fourteenth Symphony can be viewed as a response to *War Requiem*, with particular reference to the conception and structure of each work, including choice of instrumentation, the setting of the poetic texts, and a comparison of their representation of death through satire.

Neither composer sheds extensive light on the two compositions in their private or public statements. Britten made few references to *War Requiem* in his correspondence, and his reticence was compounded by the widespread acclaim which greeted the work.[10] While *War Requiem* has usually been defined as a public statement of one of Britten's most cherished personal concerns, his pacifism, two further creative preoccupations are pertinent: first, there is Britten's personal response to the poetry of Owen, whom he regarded as 'by far our greatest war poet, and one of the most original and touching poets of this century', and as a genius unrecognized by the artistic and political establishment of his day.[11] The composer particularly admired the directness of Owen's poetry and its resonant association with the First World War, which enhanced its ability to highlight an 'ironic conflict of verbal and musical messages' when juxtaposed with the text of the Requiem Mass.[12] Secondly, Britten viewed *War Requiem* in terms of the responsibility of the creative artist to communicate directly to society, a theme he expounded in two speeches made in the year of its première and when receiving the first Aspen Award in 1964, and an aspiration comparable to the mature artistic credo of his Russian counterpart.[13]

Given the radically different political and social context of the Soviet Union in 1969, Shostakovich's choice of poetry for the symphony (by Lorca, Apollinaire, Küchelbecker and Rilke) was also unconventional, particularly its overall theme of death and the work's 'resolute denial of optimism, of "life-affirmation" ... the sine qua non of Soviet art'.[14] Moreover, Küchelbecker, the only Russian poet, was relatively unknown both in Russia and the West, while Rilke, Lorca and Apollinaire were, it has been argued, 'aeons removed from the psyche of the Soviet listener' and regarded with suspicion by the Union of Composers.[15] There is little evidence for Shostakovich's motivation in choosing the four poets, but it is clear that he also went to considerable trouble in selecting and, on at least three occasions, amending the texts.[16] If, in contrast to Britten's treatment of Owen, Shostakovich employed Russian translations and was also prepared to take extracts out of their original contexts, his identification with the poetry was as intense as Britten's; indeed, he saw the work as 'a turning point in my work in that everything that I have written for many years now has been in preparation for it'.[17] However, Shostakovich did not tend to comment on the significance of his music; moreover, when he did so one cannot be sure that his remarks represent his innermost feelings as opposed to wider ideological pressures.[18] In *Pravda*, for example, he expressed the hope that an audience would leave a performance of the symphony with the thought 'Life is beautiful', which was clearly not the reaction of those who attended its first performances. Indeed, Sir Duncan Wilson wrote to Britten from Moscow following the première: 'I think we all felt that here was a man who had looked all his eleven aspects of death in the face.'[19]

Three sources illuminate Shostakovich's selection of the poetry in the symphony and his conception of the work as a whole. The composer's letters to Isaak Glikman indicate that he viewed the symphony as an expansion of Musorgsky's *Pesni i pliaski smerti* [*Songs and Dances of Death*] which he had orchestrated in 1962; where Musorgsky had set four poems Shostakovich would set eleven. Secondly, in *Pravda* on 25 April 1969 the composer referred to his admiration for the 'profundity and beauty' of Küchelbecker's poetry, which he saw as unjustly neglected and to which he may also have been attracted by Küchelbecker's status as a Decembrist – that is, as a dissident of his day.[20] The other poets are not mentioned, but Lorca may also have been a figure towards whom Shostakovich felt an affinity: stigmatized and ultimately murdered for his non-conformity, he was also a pianist of considerable talent and a humanitarian who, through his open-air performances of plays, brought high culture to the rural masses during the Third Spanish Republic.[21] Thirdly, in Shostakovich's address at the closed dress rehearsal in the Small Hall of the Moscow Conservatoire on 21 June 1969 the composer explained his decision to treat the theme of death as a creative response to 'the great classics, who treated the theme of death in their work' but softened the depiction with 'a kind of brightening', 'beauteous serenity', and 'radiant music': Britten's *War Requiem*, Musorgsky's *Boris Godunov* and Verdi's *Aida* and *Otello* are cited as examples.[22]

In the light of this evidence, Levon Hakobian has developed the argument that the symphony 'seems to be a ... conscious, thoroughly premeditated polemical answer to the religious and humanistic conception of life' exemplified by *War Requiem*.[23] This may reflect Shostakovich's own attitudes towards religion, which seem to have coupled a rejection of religious belief with a knowledge of and respect for religious traditions such as – to judge from his orchestration of Musorgsky's *Khovanshchina* in 1958 – the Old Believers.[24] On the other hand, Shostakovich's public line in the 21 June 1969 speech on *War Requiem* may also have been a product of the ideological pressures under which he was compelled to work, as is illustrated by a contemporary description of the symphony's Moscow première:

> The programme ... included quite a long analysis of the new work. The introductory part of this clearly anticipates official criticism about its negative character, and takes the line roughly that such a series of protests against death is proof of a very 'positive' attitude to life, all in accordance with the humanism that informs D.S.' work throughout, and in contrast to the 'passive Christian acceptance' of death. I gather that this is the line taken on occasion by D.S. himself, and hope (without much faith) that it will succeed in getting the new symphony firmly into the Soviet repertoire.[25]

Fundamental to this debate is how one interprets the structure of the symphony, which is a setting of eleven poems:[26]

1   'De Profundis' (Lorca) Adagio

2   'Malagueña' (Lorca) Allegretto

3   'Loreley' (Apollinaire) Allegro molto

4   'The Suicide' (Apollinaire) Adagio

5   'On the Alert' (LES ATTENTIVES I) (Apollinaire) Allegretto

6   'Look, Madam' (LES ATTENTIVES II) (Apollinaire) Adagio

7   'At the Santé Jail' (Apollinaire) Adagio

8   'Zaporozhian Cossacks' Reply to the Sultan of Constantinople' (Apollinaire) Allegro

9   'O Delvig, Delvig!' (Küchelbecker) Andante

10   'Death of the Poet' (Rilke) Largo

11   'Conclusion' (Rilke) Moderato

Hakobian contends that Shostakovich's public division of the symphony into a conventional four-movement structure was primarily in order to allay criticism on account of its unpalatable theme; instead, 'consciously or unconsciously' the composer structured the symphony along the canonical lines of the *Missa pro defunctis*, that is, the liturgical structure of *War Requiem*.[27] Hakobian therefore divides the work into six 'movements of higher order', each with a canonical equivalent:

1   'De Profundis'; 'Malagueña' = Requiem/Kyrie

2   'Loreley'; 'The Suicide'; 'On the Alert'; 'Look, Madam' = Sequentia

3 'At the Santé Jail' = Offertorium

4 'Zaporozhian Cossacks' Reply to the Sultan of Constantinople';
  'O Delvig, Delvig!' = Sanctus/Benedictus

5 'Death of the Poet' = Agnus Dei

6 'Conclusion' = Libera me

Hakobian's thesis enhances one's understanding of a work which in many ways defies analysis as a conventional symphony, not least because – and in contrast to *War Requiem* – the work is tonally fluid and without key signatures. Moreover, it also accounts for the two settings which do not explicitly address the theme of death: 'Zaporozhian Cossacks' Reply to the Sultan of Constantinople' and 'O Delvig, Delvig!' The crudely explicit *(s)ff* curse and the musical language of the former can be viewed as a blasphemous counterpart to the paean to the Almighty in a Sanctus, while the D♭ major *andante* and expressive writing for voice, violas and divided cellos in 'O Delvig, Delvig' corresponds to a Benedictus, traditionally the most serene movement of the Requiem Mass and certainly so in Britten's *molto tranquillo* setting.

There are, however, several areas in which Hakobian's thesis requires qualification. First, on the central issue of the work's structure, Tishchenko recalls that

> Shostakovich played ... and sang for me the whole of the Fourteenth Symphony and then asked 'Is this a symphony? And if not what should I call it?' I answered that I did not think it was a symphony and that the first half should be called 'De Profundis'. Dmitri Dmitriyevich listened and then still chose to do it his way.[28]

Moreover, although Tishchenko's own *Rekviem* (1966) – a setting of Akhmatova headed by the phrases 'Requiem aeternam', 'Stabat Mater', and 'In memoriam' – was also admired by Shostakovich and may have influenced him in the symphony, Tishchenko does not detect a canonical structure in the Shostakovich work.[29] Secondly, beyond the 21 June 1969 speech there is no evidence that Shostakovich intended the symphony as a polemical response to *War Requiem* as opposed to a protest against death in the light of his own failing health, an interpretation supported both by Tishchenko and by Rudolf Barshai, who conducted the symphony's Moscow première.[30]

It is also worth noting that if Shostakovich regarded *War Requiem* as embodying a degree of religious consolation, this did not necessarily reflect Britten's fundamental conception of the work nor his own attitude towards religion. Although brought up as an Anglican and a regular churchgoer until the late 1930s, by the time of *War Requiem*'s composition it is unlikely that Britten possessed a belief in an afterlife beyond having a sense of the power of a work of art to live on beyond its creator.[31] The composer possessed considerable respect for the great traditions of religious music and regarded Christian imagery as a major means of musical communication; uniquely, however, in *War Requiem* he employed a variety of means to undermine the assurances of the Christian liturgy. For example, the placing of 'The End' within the 'Benedictus' accentuates its rejection of the prospect of Christian resurrection (Example 1), and the repetition of 'Quam olim Abrahae promisisti, et semini ejus' after Owen's depiction of the sacrifice of Isaac in the 'Offertorium' turns God's promise of holy light for the departed into a curse of everlasting violence for the living.

While it is therefore possible that Shostakovich structured the symphony along broadly canonical lines, in order, for example, to contrast the profanity of his 'Sanctus' with the brilliance of Britten's gamelan-inspired setting, one should not underestimate the extent to which Britten's own Sanctus and Benedictus are also radically subverted by the subsequent placing of the Owen poem and by its contrastingly subdued musical language. Hakobian, on the other hand, treats *War Requiem* as a work of Christian liturgy and does not highlight the function of the Owen texts as a means of undermining the liturgical text. Indeed, it seems that Shostakovich himself primarily viewed *War Requiem* as 'a great work of the human spirit' and therefore in the same light as the requiems of Mozart and Berlioz or Mahler's *Das Lied von der Erde*.[32]

It is possible that it was *War Requiem*'s final pages, not least the neutralization of the pervading C/F♯ 'mourning motif' into an F major chord in the final bar which Shostakovich, in common with some musicologists, interpreted as offering a degree of religious consolation (Example 2);[33] certainly the final two bars of the 'Conclusion' of the symphony are unambiguously bleak by comparison (Example 3). While Britten appears to have been sensitive on this point, and did in fact mark the bassoon, cello, viola and horn parts between R127 and R131 'sweetly', it is clear that he did not intend the conclusion of *War Requiem* to be a comforting experience.[34]

Example 1 War Requiem, from 'Benedictus'

The serenity of the two erstwhile combatants' final 'Let us sleep now' suggests that he envisaged sleep for the dead soldiers, but for the living there was to be no such consolation: indeed, if properly articulated – and performed in a suitably dry acoustic – the Owen settings 'should leave us wounded and bleeding.'[35] Britten was particularly concerned that the overwhelmingly positive reception of *War Requiem* would detract from the work's intended impact;

Example 2 *War Requiem*, final bars

Example 3 Shostakovich, Fourteenth Symphony, final bars

indeed, at a performance in 1968 the composer requested, without success, that the 'In Paradisum' should not be followed by applause, just as on 21 June 1969 Shostakovich requested silence in the intervals between the songs of the symphony, 'since they were concerned with the solemn theme of death'.[36]

Further expressive connections between these two works can be found in their shared, and particular, use of percussion. Britten was interested in the potential of using percussion as a means of representing violence in a pacifist context as early as 1936. The xylophone was utilized for this purpose in the 'Epilogue and Funeral March' of *Our Hunting Fathers*, engendering a creative trait which was to develop through the composer's association with James Blades and to find further expression in, for example, the use of percussion band in *Children's Crusade* (1969).[37] His treatment of percussion in *War Requiem* is partly symbolic, as in the prominent C/F♯ bell motif which disrupts the idea of rest in the opening 'Requiem aeternam' and at the work's conclusion; it is also employed to accentuate the most disturbing question the work poses, in the setting of 'The End' – 'Shall life renew these bodies? Of a truth / All death will He annul, all tears assuage?' – which is accompanied by a side drum with snares and marked 'agitated'. However, percussion is particularly used to represent slaughter, as in the vivid depiction of the binding of Isaac prior to his sacrifice, the use of bass and side drum sticks to accompany the word 'cattle' in the setting of *Anthem for Doomed Youth* (at six bars after R9), and in the cacophony of the 'Dies irae', graphically revisited in the 'Libera me' at R116.

The large percussion sections of Shostakovich's *Nos* (*The Nose*, 1927–8) and his Fourth Symphony (1935–6) – together with Tishchenko's more recent *Rekviem* – seem to have had more influence than Britten on Shostakovich's 'unexpected revival' of percussion in the symphony. Indeed, percussion is fundamental to the work: as Edison Denisov demonstrates, Shostakovich mostly uses wooden percussion instruments with a sharp, high and dry timbre; they are used in a very vivid way; and all timbres are hard and not linked to the timbre of the strings.[38] The overall effect is therefore devoid of texture, as in the *fff* use of woodblock in the 'Conclusion'. Whereas Britten's use of percussion in *War Requiem* is primarily a means of accentuating violence in a pacifist context, in the symphony Shostakovich seems to have employed it as a symbol of death. In 'At the Santé Jail', for example, the string fugato from R91 to R97 is accompanied by a dance-like rhythm on woodblock (Example 4), which bears a striking resemblance to the woodblock figure which accompanies the soloists' proclamation of Death's omnipotence in the 'Conclusion'.

Tishchenko links the use of percussion in the coda of the Second Cello Concerto (1966) and the Fourth and Fifteenth Symphonies, arguing that it

Example 4 Shostakovich, Fourteenth Symphony, from 'At the Santé Jail'

'evokes the sound of falling bones. When eternity comes, nothing remains but bones.'[39] It is significant that, of the three movements in the Fourteenth Symphony which do not employ percussion, 'Zaporozhian Cossacks' Reply to the Sultan of Constantinople' and 'O Delvig, Delvig!' do not address the theme of death and 'De Profundis' instead immediately highlights this motif by the quotation of the *Dies irae* chant in its first bar.

If the two works share both structure and symbolic utilization of instrumental forces, then *War Requiem* and the Fourteenth Symphony more fundamentally reflect a similar outlook, embodying a 'commitment to life in the context of a deeply tragic sense of our mortality.'[40] Indeed, although Britten only made very brief references to the symphony in his correspondence with Shostakovich, it is likely that he viewed the work in this light.[41] In their creative response to this attitude, both composers drew upon a variety of genres: in addition to the Owen settings which constitute, in effect, a song cycle for chamber orchestra within a liturgical frame, a significant amount of the vocal writing in *War Requiem* is operatic and the work as a whole can viewed as symphonic in scale, with whole sections corresponding to symphonic movements.[42] Similarly, if the symphony can be regarded as an orchestral song cycle, it also contains pronounced elements of chamber music, Russian art song and opera. One should further acknowledge that the symphony represents a wider response to Britten's music than *War Requiem*, an adoption of the model of Britten's own 'anthology' vocal works from *A Boy was Born* (1932–3) onwards, in which contrasting poetic extracts on a broad theme are set in a single work. Shostakovich himself had already employed an eleven-movement 'anthology' structure in *Iz evreiskoi narodnoi poèzii* [*From Jewish Folk Poetry*] in 1948 and was also to adopt this form in 1974 with his *Siuita na slova Mikelandzhelo Buonarroti* [*Suite on Words of Michelangelo*], which closely corresponds to the symphony not only in the tempo markings of individual movement but also in its themes of creativity and death.

Death has been regarded as a leading motif in both works and both composers were influenced by the 19th-century resurgence in Romantic music and literature of the motif of the Dance of Death. Donald Mitchell demonstrates the evolution of the Dance of Death motif across Britten's creative life, from *Our Hunting Fathers* (1936) through the 'Dies irae' of the *Sinfonia da Requiem* (1940), to its ultimate transformation in *War Requiem* into a fanfare-ridden

'Dies irae' graphically set on the battlefield.[43] Thus in *War Requiem*, death is depicted in this light within the 'Dies irae', in the tenor and baritone solos 'Out there, we've walked quite friendly up to Death': marked 'fast and gay', and 'bizarre in its music-hall evocation', Death the reaper is personified as a comrade of soldiers on both sides of the conflict.[44] Shostakovich's depiction of the Dance of Death is fundamentally similar: Musorgsky's settings of Golenishchev-Kutuzov in *Pesni i pliaski smerti* were a particular influence; and in choosing to set two lesser-known pieces from Lorca, it is also probable that Shostakovich was aware of Lorca's theory of the Duende highlighting the creative power of death as a driving force in the popular expression of Spanish musical culture and art, in contrast with the more ethereal Western notions of Muse and Angel as the source of artistic inspiration.[45] Thus, in 'Malagueña' the Dance of Death is given a Spanish flavour through the use of castanets and bolero-like dance rhythms; on the other hand, the glissandi for violin solo are reminiscent of a Russian folk style and, as with Britten's evocation, deliberately vulgar in effect.[46] Furthermore, the striking crescendos of accelerating notes from R13:10 and three bars before R20 – as well as in the final two bars of the symphony – suggest that Shostakovich also employed this musical device as a representation of Death.[47]

As has been observed, in *War Requiem* Britten refashioned the traditional liturgical context of the 'Dies irae' to depict the living hell of the battlefield; his closest musical model seems to have been Verdi's setting. During rehearsals for the 1963 Decca recording Britten stated that he wanted 'hysteria' in this movement, and that 'the words mean an awful lot ... make it sound creepy, make it alarmed.'[48] The composer did not employ the Western plainsong *Dies irae* chant (Example 5a), presumably because he wished to avoid the clichéd connotations it had assumed from the 19th century; Shostakovich, on the other hand, followed the use of the chant divorced from its liturgical text, not least by 20th-century Russian composers, as a recognizable symbol of death at the opening of 'De Profundis' (Example 5b).

Example 5 (a) *Dies Irae* chant;
(b) Shostakovich, Fourteenth Symphony, from 'De Profundis'

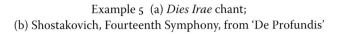

However, whereas the composer had earlier employed the chant satirically in 'Dance of Death' of the *Aforizmi [Aphorisms]* (1927) and the third of *Five Romances on Words from Krokodil Magazine* (1965), in this context its use is unambiguous and – to judge from the allusions to this passage in the Sonata for Viola and Piano (1975), the composer's final work – intensely personal. Further allusions to the chant reiterate the theme of death later in the symphony, most importantly, the reiteration of the opening twelve bars of the symphony in 'Death of the Poet', where it serves to accentuate the death of creativity, a preoccupation for the composer during the final eight years of his life in the context of increasing ill health and the renewed pressure on artistic life following the Soviet invasion of Czechoslovakia in August 1968.[49]

Shostakovich particularly, if not exclusively, chose poets whose work was influenced by the carnage of the First World War.[50] However, and despite Britten's choice of Owen, the commission from Coventry and the personal dedications of *War Requiem* indicate that the work was also intended to embrace the victims of the Second World War in addition to serving a polemical purpose as a warning to future generations. Thus, during the January 1963 recording rehearsals Britten remarked that 'The "Libera me Domine" happens *today* to mean something.'[51] Shostakovich himself was not unaware of the potential of a 'distant' event as means of contemporary reference, as in the case of his Eleventh Symphony (1956–7), which ostensibly commemorated the abortive Russian revolution of 1905 but also 'invited aesopian reading as a comment on the Soviet repression of the Hungarian uprising.'[52] However, while an ideal performance of *War Requiem* should achieve 'an unmediated confrontation with the horror, terror and pity of war',[53] this does not seem to have been Shostakovich's intention in this symphony, perhaps on account of his having already responded to the Great Patriotic War in earlier symphonies. In 'On the Alert' the tone is satirical rather than compassionate: the opening nine bars for xylophone imitate the fanfare of a reveille in the manner of Britten's 'Dies irae', but are coupled (from R65:9) with a dance on three tom-toms; and the soloist does not mourn her lover, but instead proclaims her incest, to the vulgar accompaniment of a woodblock. Similarly, in 'Look, Madam' the vocal line expresses laughter in the form of a striking motif (Example 6a) that the composer was to transfer to his subsequent Thirteenth String Quartet (1970). Britten's depiction of death in the context of the First World War is not without a shockingly grotesque aspect, as in his setting of Owen's 'The Parable of the Old Man and the Young' – an inversion of the Biblical story as well as of his *Canticle II: Abraham and Isaac* (1952) – and Britten's two soldiers themselves laugh in the face of death (Example 6b); it is, however, consistently informed by a profound sense of compassion. It is indicative, for example, that

Britten chose not to follow Owen in setting 'Strange Meeting' in hell;[54] and that the composer inscribed Owen's words 'My subject is War, and the pity of War. / The Poetry is in the Pity' as an epigraph on the title page of the score.

In the Owen texts Britten selected for *War Requiem*, death is equated with sleep on three occasions: in his partial setting of 'Voices' in which 'voices of boys were by the river-side. / Sleep mothered them'; in 'Futility', in which 'Always [the sun] woke him, even in France, / Until this morning and this snow'; and, most extensively, the encounter with one of the 'encumbered sleepers' in 'Strange Meeting'. The sonority is distinctive: in the latter case, a contrast between sustained *pianissimo* chords marked 'cold' for the strings of the chamber orchestra (from R117 to R118) and the subsequent and highly expressive coda to which all the work's forces are added may imply that while the dead are granted sleep, the living must not forget the cause of their death. A parallel treatment is seen in Shostakovich's 'De Profundis' movement (no. 1) in which death is described in terms of perpetual sleep. The movement is an *adagio* with the dynamic marking *(p)p*, and the absence of cellos and percussion as well as the pronounced roles for violins and double basses contribute to a whispering and emotionally sterile effect in contrast to the colourful imagery of the poem. It is possible that the representation of death as sleep in the symphony was influenced by Britten; certainly, the double bass glissandi may be a reference to the opening of Britten's *A Midsummer Night's Dream* (1959–60), a work Shostakovich first heard in Berlin in November 1961 and greatly admired.[55] On the other hand, the composer may also have drawn from his recent 'Gorod spit' ['The city sleeps'], the third of *Seven Romances on Verses by Alexander Blok* (1967), as well as on the Soviet tradition of representing war dead as asleep.[56]

Britten's engagement with death in *War Requiem* is, in a sense, one-dimensional, in the context of war and violence. Shostakovich's symphony, on the

Example 6 (a) Shostakovich, Fourteenth Symphony, from 'Look Madam';
(b) Britten, *War Requiem*, from 'Dies Irae'

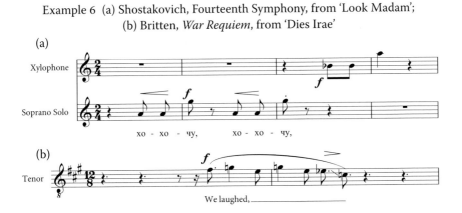

other hand, depicts death in a wider variety of contexts – and with a variety of characters, both male and female. Edison Denisov explains this aspect of the work, together with a number of allusions to Shostakovich's earlier works, in terms of Webern's description of *Das Lied von der Erde*: 'It is as if pictures of a life, most likely lived to excess, are passing in front of a dying man.'[57] Indeed, if *War Requiem* can be viewed as the consummation for Britten of the Dance of Death motif, with the exception of the reworking of material from *Canticle II* in the 'Offertorium', the works cannot otherwise be compared in this respect. Furthermore, the three longest settings in the symphony – 'Loreley', 'The Suicide' and 'At the Santé Jail' – seem to have been important to the composer in terms of autobiographical reference. Shostakovich's setting of 'Loreley' is striking for its compassion and operatic in its scope; and it is possible that the composer saw the sorceress, as well as the unnamed protagonist of 'The Suicide', in a comparably sympathetic light to the heroine of *Ledi Makbet Mtsenskogo uezda* [*Lady Macbeth of the Mtsensk District*], whose revision as the rehabilitated *Katerina Izmailova* Shostakovich had completed as recently as 1963. Moreover, Galina Vishnevskaya recalls that Shostakovich listened with 'deep self-absorption and apparent agony' to 'The Suicide' during rehearsals; and its intensity of expression may reflect the suggestion of some biographers that the composer seriously contemplated suicide on at least two occasions earlier in his life.[58] 'At the Santé Jail', on the other hand, depicts the spiritual death caused by imprisonment, in a melodramatic setting of a text which draws on Christian imagery of the Passion and Crucifixion, just as Britten's setting of Owen's 'At a Calvary near the Ancre' identifies the sacrifice of men at the front with the figure of Christ on a war-damaged Calvary. This depiction of spiritual death had a striking contemporary resonance: not only is the vocal line from R105 to R107 reminiscent of Sviridov's setting of Mayakovsky's 'Conversation with Comrade Lenin' in his *Pateticheskaia oratoriia* [*Pathetic Oratorio*, 1959], a work Shostakovich regarded as servile, Elizabeth Wilson sees the metaphor of a 'living death' as 'a poignant symbol for the unjust incarceration of a whole generation of Shostakovich's contemporaries'.[59]

Both *War Requiem* and Shostakovich's Fourteenth Symphony represent a response by their composers to 'eternal problems' of particular concern: *War Requiem* to war and violence, and the Fourteenth Symphony to death, remembrance and the immortality of creativity. The symphony can also be seen as a response to Britten's own 'anthology' vocal works such as *Spring Symphony* and *Nocturne*. It follows *War Requiem* less in terms of formal structure and musical language than in its selection of unconventional poetry employed within an apparently conventional context – a vocal cycle described as a symphony as opposed to a statement of Christian liturgy subverted by the texts of an anti-war poet. In both cases this accentuates an essentially pessimistic message, albeit one couched in humanist terms. Both composers drew upon Western motifs of the Dance of Death, the *Dies irae* and, most strikingly, the representation of death as sleep and in the context of the First World War. Where the works can be distinguished is not in terms of the serenity detected by some at the conclusion of *War Requiem* as opposed to the unambiguously bleak conclusion of the symphony, but rather the extent to which the latter work – particularly in its use of percussion and self-quotation – can be viewed as a response to death in its widest significance and as a reflection on the composer's own long creative life. The symphony should therefore be viewed alongside both Shostakovich's avant-garde pre-1936 compositions and the works of the last decade of the composer's life. Britten, on the other hand, was only to make such a statement with regard to his own work 13 years after *War Requiem* and at the very end of his creative life in his *Third String Quartet* (1975).

Notes

1 The chief articles are: Eric Roseberry, 'A Debt Repaid? Some Observations on Shostakovich and his Late-period Recognition of Britten', in *Shostakovich Studies*, ed. David Fanning (Cambridge: Cambridge University Press, 1995), pp. 229–53; and Liudmila Kovnatskaya, 'Shostakovich and Britten: Some Parallels', in *Shostakovich in Context*, ed. Rosamund Bartlett (Oxford: Oxford University Press, 2000), pp. 175–89.

2 Britten's tribute to Shostakovich, written in 1966, which subsequently appeared in a Russian collection of essays on Shostakovich (Moscow: Sovetskii kompozitor, 1967). Typescript source held at the BPF and reproduced in *PKBM*, pp. 300–1.

3 Letter from Shostakovich to Britten, Moscow, 15 October 1966, trans. Keith Grant; condensed English translation of press interview with Shostakovich in May 1968 cited in Boris Schwarz, *Music and Musical Life in Soviet Russia, 1917–81*, enlarged edition (Bloomington: Indiana University Press, 1983), p. 483; and letter from Boris Tishchenko to the author, St Petersburg, 21 May 2008, trans. Ivan Ivanov.

4 Letter from Britten to Shostakovich, 1 June 1970, and Shostakovich to Britten from Moscow, 16 June. Britten's copy of the score is inscribed: Дорогому Бенджамину Бриттену / в знак глубокого уважения от / сердечно преданного Д. Шостаковича/ 1 XII 1969 Москва ('To dear Benjamin Britten/ as a token of profound respect from/a cordially devoted D. Shostakovich/ 1 XII 1969 Moscow') and was annotated by Britten in pencil prior to conducting the work at the Aldeburgh Festival of Music and the Arts on 14 June 1970. Donald Mitchell argues that the dedication 'forms part of the total conception', highlighting the centrality of 'O Delvig, Delvig!', an interpretation with which

Britten seems to have agreed. See 'Shostakovich and his Symphonies', in *The Twenty-Third Aldeburgh Festival of Music and the Arts, 1970*, pp. 9–10.

5 Roseberry sees the symphony as the 'complementary antithesis' to *Spring Symphony*, a setting of an anthology of twelve (as opposed to eleven) poems ('A Debt Repaid?', p. 244). However, neither this work, nor *Nocturne*, which contains Britten's earlier Owen setting, are mentioned in the correspondence between the two composers, nor are these scores among those of Britten possessed by Shostakovich.

6 Conversation with Marion Thorpe, 5 September 2008; and letter to the author from Rosamund Strode, 26 October 2007.

7 Letter from Shostakovich to Britten from the Waldorf Hotel, Aldwych, London, 5 December 1963, trans. Marion Thorpe. Shostakovich's score of *War Requiem* is inscribed thus on the title page: 'For Dmitri Shostakovich/my great/ colleague whom I/am proud to/call my/friend/Benjamin Britten/Moscow 1963.' This score is in the Shostakovich Archive in Moscow.

8 See letter from Shostakovich to Boris Tishchenko, Moscow, 23 August 1963, reproduced in A. Ardova, trans., *Letters of Dmitri Dmitriyevich Shostakovich to Boris Tishchenko with the Addressee's Commentaries and Reminiscences* (St Petersburg: Kompozitor, 2001), p. 6. Whilst Shostakovich refers to *War Requiem* in this letter as 'almost a great work', Tishchenko feels that the qualification reflects the characteristically qualified way in which the composer spoke about music he profoundly admired; letter to the author, 21 May 2008. Indeed, according to Mstislav Rostropovich, Shostakovich regarded *War Requiem* as the greatest work of the 20th century. See Alan Blyth, *Remembering Britten* (London: Hutchinson, 1981), p. 151. Elizabeth Wilson recalls that Rostropovich was fond of quoting Shostakovich's remark that he 'would have given anything to have written that phrase of five descending whole tones followed by five ascending ones.' He was referring to the theme sung by the chorus in the 'Agnus Dei' of *War Requiem*; letter to the author, 22 November 2008.

9 Letter from Britten to David Adams, Managing Director, Boosey & Hawkes Ltd, 27 November 1965.

10 *MCWR*, p. 23. For Britten viewing the 'easy success' of the work as 'an outrage and invasion of privacy', see George, Earl of Harewood, *The Tongs and the Bones* (London: Weidenfeld and Nicolson, 1981), p. 148.

11 See Benjamin Britten, 'Freedom of Borough of Aldeburgh' (1962), and 'A Tribute to Wilfred Owen' (*c.* 1963), in *PKBM*, pp. 217–9 and p. 221.

12 Philip Reed, 'The *War Requiem* in Progress', in *MCWR*, pp. 20–48 at p. 29.

13 See Britten, 'Freedom of Borough of Aldeburgh', p. 217, and Benjamin Britten, 'Speech on Receiving Honorary Degree at Hull University' (1962), in *PKBM*, pp. 214–6 at p. 215. See also *BBAA*, p. 12. For Shostakovich's artistic credo, see Richard Taruskin, *Defining Russia Musically: Historical and Hermeneutical Essays* (Princeton: University Press, 1997), p. 496.

14 Richard Taruskin, 'Shostakovich and Us', in *Shostakovich in Context*, ed. Bartlett, p. 24.

15 See Dmitri Smirnov, *My Shostakovich* (2004) on homepage.ntlworld.com/ Dmitrysmirnov (accessed 3 October 2007); and Schwarz, *Music and Musical Life in Soviet Russia*, p. 493. On the other hand, Alexander Ivashkin notes that all three poets' work was readily available in Russian translations under the Khrushchev 'thaw' of the 1960s, and maintains that Lorca and Apollinaire were officially sanctioned (conversation with the author, 23 February 2008).

16 See Isaak Glikman, *Story of a Friendship: Letters of Dmitry Shostakovich to Isaak Glikman, 1941–75*, trans. A. Phillips and with a commentary by Isaak Glikman (London: Faber, 2001), pp. 158–66.

17 Letter from Shostakovich to Glikman, 19 March 1969, *ibid.*, pp. 160–1.

18 See Taruskin, *Defining Russia Musically*, p. 482; and Elizabeth Wilson, *Shostakovich: A Life Remembered*, 2nd edition (London: Faber, 2006), pp. 487–9.

19 Letter from Sir Duncan Wilson to Britten, 9 October 1969.

20 See M Yakovlev, ed., *D. Shostakovich: O vremeni i o sebe* (Moscow: Sovetskii kompozitor, 1980), p. 314; and Glikman, *Story of a Friendship*, p. 304.

21 I am grateful to Dr J. P. Devlin for amplifying the literary contexts of the Lorca, Apollinaire and Rilke texts and the poets' biographical details.

22 A fairly complete translation of this talk is given in Laurel Fay, *Shostakovich: A Life* (Oxford: Oxford University Press, 2000), p. 261.

23 Levon Hakobian, *Music of the Soviet Age, 1917–87* (Stockholm: Melos Music Literature, 1998), pp. 233–8. Hakobian also regards Lutosławski's *Paroles tissées* (1965), Stravinsky's *Requiem Canticles* (1966), and Penderecki's *Dies Irae* (1967) as influences on the work.

24 Alexander Ivashkin from a conversation with Irina Shostakovich (discussion with the author, 23 February 2008).

25 Letter from Sir Duncan Wilson to Britten, Moscow, 9 October 1969.

26 Titles of movements are cited as in the 1970 Musikverlag Hans Sikorski edition.

27 Shostakovich groups the movements: 1–4; 5–6; 7–8; 9–11. See Wilson, *Shostakovich: A Life Remembered*, p. 474.

28 Letter to the author, 21 May 2008.

29 *Ibid.* See also L. Grigoryev and Yakov Platek, eds., *Dmitry Shostakovich: About Himself and His Times*, trans. A. and N. Roxburgh (Moscow: Progress Publishers, 1981), pp. 290–1.

30 H. van der Groep, 'An Interview with Rudolf Barshai' (21 April 2002) on www. dschjournal.com (accessed 1 February 2008).

31 Conversation with Donald Mitchell, CBE, 20 September 2007. For the evolution of Britten's religious views, see his diary entry for 11 April 1936 and the report of Britten's statement to the Local Tribunal for the Registration of Conscientious Objectors on 28 May 1942, cited in *MRLL*, vol. 2, p. 1046.

32 Glikman, *Story of a Friendship*, pp. 293, 301, 306.

33 For contrasting views on this element of *War Requiem*, see Alec Robertson, 'Britten's War Requiem', *Musical Times* 103/1431 (May 1962), p. 308; and *MCWR*, p. 77.

34 When questioned on the 'sweetness' of *War Requiem*'s final pages in an interview with Charles Osbourne in 1963, Britten responded defensively: 'I can't see any great defect in sweetness as long as it's not weakness.' See 'An Interview', in *PKBM*, pp. 244–9 at p. 246.

35 Donald Mitchell, 'Violent Climates', in *MCCC*, pp. 188–216 at p. 211.

36 See Kathleen Mitchell, 'Edinburgh Diary 1968', in *On Mahler and Britten: Essays in Honour of Donald Mitchell on his Seventieth Birthday*, ed. Philip Reed (Woodbridge: Boydell Press/Aldeburgh: BPF, 1995), pp. 193–212 at p. 207; and letter to Britten from Sir Duncan Wilson, Moscow, 10 July 1969.

37 See, for example, the letter from James Blades to Britten, 23 April 1963, and Britten's undated postcard in response. Britten's early appreciation of the possibilities of percussion was stimulated as much by his film, theatre and radio work between 1935 and 1939 as from Shostakovich's compositions; indeed, his diary entry for 26 January 1934 describes the *Suite* from *Nos* as 'very amusing and exhilarating – but I shouldn't be surprised if it were found to be uneventful and even conventional with all the glitter taken off'. BBD.

38 Edison Denisov, *Udarnye instrumenty v sovremennom orkestre* (Moscow: Sovetskii kompozitor, 1982), p. 175. For Shostakovich's renewed appreciation of *Nos* at the time of the symphony's composition, see Laurel Fay, 'The Punch in Shostakovich's Nose', in *Russian and Soviet Music: Essays for Boris Schwarz*, ed. Malcolm Hamrick Brown (Michigan: UMI Research Press, 1984), pp. 229–43.

39 Boris Tishchenko, 'Remembering Shostakovich,' *DSCH Journal* 23 (2005), pp. 7–10 at p. 9.

40 Roseberry, 'A Debt Repaid?', p. 253.

41 The letters from Britten to Shostakovich on 1 June 1970, 26 September 1970 and 10 January 1972 contain simple expressions of gratitude and admiration; and the programme note for the 14 June 1970 Aldeburgh performance was written by Donald Mitchell rather than by Britten. In a letter from Britten to Henri Temianka on 13 September 1971 Britten writes 'how exactly [Shostakovich] expresses what he wants in his music. He is a very great composer and it is a wonderful symphony'.

42 Conversation with Eric Roseberry, 31 March 2008.

43 Mitchell, 'Violent Climates', p. 207. See also Kristian Hibberd, 'Shostakovich and "Polyphonic" Creativity: The Fourteenth Symphony Revisited' (due to be published in *Shostakovich Studies 2*, ed. Pauline Fairclough, 2010) for an analysis of this aspect of the symphony in the light of Bakhtinian 'polyphony' and the 'carnivalesque'.

44 Michael Kennedy, *Master Musicians: Britten* (London: J. M. Dent & Sons, 1981), p. 224.

45 'Malagueña', in common with the preceding 'De Profundis', is taken from *Poema del cante jondo*, written mostly during the 1920s but not published in

the USSR until the 1960s. Britten does not seem to have possessed a score of the Musorgsky work, but heard Galina Vishnevskaya's performance at the Aldeburgh Festival on 6 July 1961. Vishnevskaya believes that Britten conceived the soprano part of *War Requiem* for her as a result of this recital and she detects the influence of Musorgsky in those passages in *War Requiem* that contain very wide intervals. See E. Thomas Glasow, ed., *Mstislav Rostropovich and Galina Vishnevskaya: Russia, Music and Liberty, Conversations with Claude Samuel* (Portland: Amadeus, 1995), p. 57.

46 At R14 Britten has annotated his score (now held at the BPF) of the symphony 'with swing!!' See also Arved Ashby, 'Britten as Symphonist', in *MCCC*, pp. 217–32, which observes Britten's appreciation of 'the irony of purposefully banal material', p. 223.

47 Tishchenko, 'Remembering Shostakovich', p. 9.

48 'Britten in Rehearsal' included in the remastered reissue of the 1963 recording of *War Requiem* (Decca, 1999).

49 Schwarz, *Music and Musical Life in Soviet Russia*, pp. 476–96. For the further importance of the 'The death of the poet' motif as a means of contemporary reference following the Russian Civil War, see Marina Frolova-Walker, *Russian Music and Nationalism from Glinka to Stalin* (New Haven: Yale University Press, 2007), p. 57.

50 Wilson, *Shostakovich: A Life Remembered*, p. 465.

51 'Britten in Rehearsal'.

52 David Fanning, 'D. Shostakovich: works, 1953–62', *Grove Music online* (accessed 17 August 2008).

53 Mitchell, 'Violent Climates', p. 208.

54 *MCWR*, p. 74.

55 See, for example, Shostakovich's letter to Britten on 20 June 1965.

56 For an artistic example of the latter tradition, see Aleksandr Deineka's *The Shot-down Ace* (1943). In bars 5–6 Hakobian also detects an allusion to the opening words 'I can sleep no more' from *Ledi Makbet Mtsenskogo uiezda* [Lady Macbeth of the Mtsensk District] (1930–2); *Dmitri Shostakovich: opyt fenomenologii tvorchestva* (St Petersburg: Dmitri Bulanin, 2004), translated for the author by Hugh Lunghi, p. 376.

57 Letter from Anton Webern to Alban Berg, 23 February 1911, quoted in Denisov, *Udarnye instrumenty*, p. 168.

58 See Galina Vishnevskaya, *Galina: A Russian Story* (London: Hodder & Stoughton, 1984), p. 400; and Wilson, *Shostakovich: A Life Remembered*, pp. 243, 381.

59 Wilson, *ibid.*, p. 465; Hakobian, *Music of the Soviet Age, 1917–87*, p. 230.

4 *Six Metamorphoses after Ovid* and the Influence of Classical Mythology on Benjamin Britten

George Caird

On 14 June 1951 at 4.30 pm a concert was performed on The Meare at Thorpeness in Suffolk by the Cambridge University Madrigal Society under the direction of Boris Ord. The concert included a selection of English madrigals, Jacobean part-songs and 20th-century music, including the first performance of Benjamin Britten's *Six Metamorphoses after Ovid* (1951), op. 49, for solo oboe, played by Joy Boughton. From this relatively informal première the *Metamorphoses* quickly became established as one of the most important pieces in the oboe repertoire, offering the player a wonderful range of expressive and technical opportunities. The work is a suite of miniature portraits mainly in ternary form, which paint the characters and metamorphic stories of six immortals from Ovid's great poem, the *Metamorphoses.*

Described at the time as 'a real open-air piece written by way of relaxation during the creation of *Billy Budd*',[1] the *Metamorphoses* might appear on first acquaintance to be an inconsequential item in the composer's output. However, Britten's choice of Ovid as his muse is significant. The *Metamorphoses* is illustrative of an overarching theme that had an important but hitherto largely unrecognized effect on the composer. Britten's interest in classical mythology was encouraged by some key influences, including the novelists Hermann Melville and E. M. Forster, the poet W. H. Auden and Britten's lifelong companion Peter Pears. This absorption reached its peak in the late 1940s and early 1950s after the composition of *The Rape of Lucretia* (1946) and culminated in the creation of *Billy Budd* (1951) and the *Metamorphoses*. I will suggest that Britten's interest was more than passing, and indeed bears comparison to the importance in his repertoire of the Christian tradition.

I shall also consider the significance of the instrumentation of this piece. The choice of unaccompanied oboe to illustrate Ovid's texts may reflect a view that the work concerns the *individual*, or the responsibility of individual moral choice. Yet the use of the oboe also draws attention to its classical associations, particularly with Bacchus, and thus is an aesthetic and symbolic contrast to Apollo's lyre.

To use Ovid's *Metamorphoses* as inspiration for a solo instrumental work is original, and is evidence of the very particular approach the composer had towards his chosen texts throughout his career. Britten's literary horizons had widened quite considerably during the 1930s under the (at the time) all-pervasive influence of Auden,[2] who clearly developed Britten's interest in the classics. Paul Kildea comments further on the sense of 'otherness' the two artists shared;[3] Auden later made use of classical mythology to illustrate the pain and separation from society of the artist in his poem *Musée des Beaux Arts*: 'About suffering they were never wrong, / The Old Masters: how well they understood / Its human position'.[4]

Boris Ford also makes the point that poetry mattered greatly to the composer: 'Rosamond Strode has said that he never travelled anywhere without packing an anthology'.[5] It could be, then, that Britten had his copy of a selection of Ovid's works in the Everyman edition with him when he visited Vienna with Pears at the beginning of April 1951, six weeks before the first performance of the *Metamorphoses*.[6] In fact Pears was himself a further literary influence on the composer. He had been a classical scholar at Lancing, and, despite an early departure from Oxford University, had a lifelong interest in the classics, poetry and literature. Even at school he had become aware that his emotional development had resonances with classical thought: 'I realized … that the love I had discovered belonged to Classical times of Greece rather than to Christianity of today.'[7]

This remarkable comment by Pears mirrors two important themes running through Britten's life and work: the Christian tradition and classical mythology. Donald Mitchell has seen Britten as

> a peculiarly thematic composer. I am not thinking of the fertility of his melody or of the prominent role that themes and thematic organisation play in his music, but of themes in a broader sense – concerns, commitments, attitudes and sources of stimulation which have been long-standing preoccupations and which are variously reflected in his art.[8]

Graham Elliott draws on this view in his exposition of Britten's 'spiritual dimension',[9] further referring to Auden's idea of 'parable-art' as a major component of Britten's output: 'there must always be two kinds of art, escape art, for man needs escape as he needs food and deep sleep, and parable-art, the art which shall teach man to unlearn hatred and learn love.'[10] Elliott makes a strong case for the Christian theme running through so many of Britten's works from his liturgical music to the canticles, church parables and *War Requiem*. But perhaps an equal, or almost equal, case can be made for classical mythology which pervaded Britten's work from *Young Apollo* (1939) to *Phaedra* (1975).

Young Apollo, for piano and string orchestra, is another example of an instrumental work based on classical mythology. Britten took his inspiration from the closing lines of Keats's 'Hyperion', which includes a ravishing section in which Clymene, Phaeton's mother, makes music with a seashell. More importantly, the poem ends with Apollo being addressed by memory (Mnemosyne):

> Thou has't dreamed of me; and awaking up
> Did'st find a lyre all golden by thy side
> Whose strings touched by thy fingers, all the vast
> Unwearied ear of the whole universe
> Listen'd in pain and pleasure at the birth
> Of such new tuneful wonder. Is't not strange
> That thou should'st weep, so gifted?[11]

A few years after *Young Apollo*, Arnold Whittall notes, Britten wrote incidental music for Edward Sackville-West's radio play *The Rescue*, based on Homer's *Odyssey* in 1943.[12] This was followed by, and possibly influenced, Britten's acceptance of Eric Crozier's idea for an opera with a classical subject, *The Rape of Lucretia* (1948) which offered

> a small-scale yet strongly dramatic narrative in which a virtuous, sensitive individual is traumatically violated and driven to self-destruction.
> … Britten's acceptance of the Lucretia story is logical enough, given its direct association with his favoured theme of the conflict between the vulnerable and the vicious.[13]

Ronald Duncan makes the further comment that Britten was interested in seeking *universality* in classical literature: 'What is important is that it (Lucretia) has become a European legend. A legend contains universal truth, whereas history at its best is often only accurate in fact.'[14] That Britten chose to place the classical Lucretia story within a Christian framework is – *pace* Elliott – a telling example of the two concurrent influences running through Britten's works.

Classical literature makes an appearance, albeit through the mouth of a fictional character, in *Billy Budd*, an opera in which the titular character also has a surprising connection to Apollo. E. M. Forster's prologue for Captain Vere reveals the Captain's learned disposition:

> I am an old man who has experienced much. I have been a man of action and fought for my King and Country at sea. I have also read books and studied and pondered and tried to fathom eternal truths.

Much good has been shown to me and much evil. The evil has sometimes been absolute. And the good has never been perfect.

Later on (Act I scene 2) Vere makes a direct reference to the classical period
and to the universality of its tales: 'Plutarch – the Greeks and the Romans –
their troubles and ours are the same. May their virtues be ours and their cour-
age! O God, grant me light to guide us all.' This reference to Plutarch does
not come directly from Hermann Melville's original novella, but was created
by the librettists to flesh out the character of Captain Vere. Nonetheless, two
passages in chapter 7 of the novella are the pointers to Plutarch: 'his [Vere's]
bias was toward … books treating of actual men and events no matter of what
era – history, biography' and 'in illustrating of any point touching the stirring
personages and events of the time he would be as apt to cite some historic
character or incident of antiquity as he would be to cite from the moderns.'[15]

Vere's erudition is in fact an extension of Melville's own character and
approach to his writing. By any standards, Melville was a highly literary writer.
Billy Budd, his last work, is full of references – to Montaigne, Thomas Paine,
Voltaire, Diderot, Andrew Marvell and many more. It is almost as though
Melville needed to demonstrate his immense knowledge as well as his vol-
canic imagination. It is important for this discourse that in the first chapter
of the story, Billy is greeted on board with his travelling chest with the words
'Apollo with his portmanteau',[16] a reference to the writer's own researches in
Matthew Arnold's *On the Study of Celtic Literature* which revealed that the
Celtic equivalent of *Apollo*, 'Hu', was known also as 'Beli' and 'Budd'.[17]

Through the 1940s and 1950s, then, classical literature played a significant part in several of Britten's works and this interest doubtless influenced
his choice of Ovid as inspiration for the *Metamorphoses*. It also appears as
if Britten was particularly drawn to the character of Apollo, or to Apollonian
forces. Britten returned to the Nietzsche-inspired theme of Apollo in his last
great opera, *Death in Venice*. Clifford Hindley traces the connection between
'the intellectual quest for formal perfection (through an Apollonian order of
self-discipline) and, on the other hand, the Dionysian forces which emerge
from passion and the submission to collective feeling' in Britten's portrayal of
the relationship between the writer Aschenbach and the young boy Tadzio.[18]
The relationship between the artist, signified by Apollo yet who observes the
more Dionysian forces of passion, is highly significant to the debate on the
Metamorphoses.

The piece for solo oboe was written during a break from *Billy Budd* in the
summer of 1951. Work most likely started after the première of Britten's and
Imogen Holst's realization of *Dido and Aeneas* on 1 May 1951, although in

Britten's diary from 28 to 29 March of 1951 there is a sketch of the opening of the 'Niobe' movement.[19] It is possible that the 'universal' appeal to Britten of classical literature played some part in the construction of this work based on Ovid's monumental poetic creation. In his *Metamorphoses* Ovid sets out in 15 books of incomparable poetry a complete cosmos of understanding on human nature from the creation of the world to the deification of the Emperor Augustus, encompassing a vast range of human relationships, and asserting that the fundamental nature of existence is change, or metamorphosis:

> My vessel is launched on the boundless main and my sails are spread
> To the wind! In the whole world there is nothing that stays unchanged.
> All is flux. Any shape that is formed is constantly shifting.
> Time itself flows steadily by in perpetual motion.[20]

In choosing his texts, Britten seems to have concentrated on characters signifying particular relationships; these are taken from Books I (*Pan and Syrinx*), II (*Phaeton*), III (*Echo and Narcissus*), IV (*Bacchus and the daughters of Minyas*), V (*Arethusa*) and VI (*Niobe*). The metamorphoses in this volume represent a rich selection from the original 15 books in the renowned translation in rhyming iambic heptameters (attributed to Arthur Golding) in the 16th century. This selection includes the six stories in Britten's work in close proximity to each other: *Pan and Syrinx, Phaeton, Echo and Narcissus, Bacchus, Arethusa* and then *Niobe* as part of the story of *Latona*. The characters of Britten's final selection are encapsulated in his appended subtitles:

> Pan, who played upon the reed pipe which was Syrinx his beloved
>
> Phaeton, who rode upon the chariot of the sun for one day and was
>   hurled into the River Padus by a thunderbolt
>
> Niobe who, lamenting the death of her fourteen children, was turned
>   into a mountain
>
> Bacchus, at whose feasts is heard the noise of gaggling women's tattling
>   tongues and the shouting out of boys
>
> Narcissus, who fell in love with his own image and became a flower
>
> Arethusa who, flying from the love of Alpheus the river god, was
>   turned into a fountain

The six stories chosen by Britten illustrate relationships which caused a fundamental change to take place. Each movement in his work narrates a story that indicates certain characteristics of human nature. In this set, the story of Pan and Syrinx opens with the obvious connection to music but also demonstrating a man-woman relationship of unrequited love. The story of Phaeton follows, exploring the tensions of a father-son relationship as the sun-god's son crashes the chariot of the sun into the River Padus. This is followed by a mother–children story in that of Niobe, whose pride led to the multiple killings of her seven sons and seven daughters by Apollo and Diana. The story of Bacchus is perhaps the most complex of Britten's choices for his cycle, with the multiple metamorphoses including the transformational effects of drinking, the power of change over women, and the metamorphosis of the daughters of Minyas into bats. The fifth story is that of Narcissus, who fell in love with his own image and was turned into a flower, a tale of self-love, or self-discovery. And finally the sixth story of Arethusa returns us to a man–woman relationship, with Arethusa falling from the clutches of the pursuing river god, Alpheus, and being turned for eternity into a waterfall near the harbour at Syracuse.[21]

That Britten chose to depict a series of relationships and transformations through the use of a single instrument, without even piano accompaniment, suggests that a particular expressive point was being made. Edwin Roxburgh has commented on the 'harmony' of the work: the 'backcloth' of implied triads which are present in each of the movements.[22] As such, the single instrument *implies* the presence of other characters – and other supporting chords – while representing a story told from the perspective of a single subjectivity. However, it is not just significant that the stories here are 'told' by a single instrument. It is the choice of the oboe itself which requires further discussion.

The circumstances surrounding the composition of the *Six Metamorphoses after Ovid*, together with a discussion of the work's two main sources – the composition sketch and fair copy – have been documented elsewhere.[23] For the purposes of this discussion, however, it is appropriate to look at why Britten chose the oboe for this extraordinary work.

Britten seems to have had a particular attraction to the oboe from his early days as a professional composer. He included the oboe in his early wind sextet (1930) and wrote his Phantasy Quartet, op. 2, for the greatest player of the day, Leon Goossens, in 1933. His letter to Sylvia Spencer in 1935, during the composition of *Two Insect Pieces*, illustrates the composer's commitment to understanding the possibilities of the instrument;[24] and the tantalizing comment that an orchestrated suite, based on these works, was on the way is especially of interest.[25] The *Temporal Variations* followed in 1936, a clear reaction to the rise of totalitarian power in Germany and a work of compelling strength.

It is significant that Natalie Caine, who performed the oboe part in the première of the *Temporal Variations*, remembers Britten regretting that oboists seemed unable to play as raucously as she he would wish, particularly in the *Oration* movement.[26] Sarah Francis believes that Britten did not see the oboe as 'limited in range',[27] and certainly not superficial as some commentators such as Frank Howes clearly did on reviewing the first performance of the *Metamorphoses*:

> It is a slight but pretty idea for its setting. The oboe's tone carries well in the open air. Miss Boughton is an accomplished artist, instrumental accompaniment could not easily be managed in mid-Meare and something unpretentious, faintly pictorial, goes well with the imaginative word-painting of Weelkes and his madrigalist contemporaries.[28]

The idea of writing for a single unaccompanied instrument is of course not unique to Britten. The character pieces for recorder, *Der fluyten lust-hof* by Jacob Van Eyck, and Telemann's *Fantasien* for solo flute are early genre works for comparison, while Britten may have drawn influence from Debussy's *Syrinx* for solo flute (1913) and, perhaps more tenuously, from Stravinsky's *Three Pieces* for solo clarinet (1919). The fact that Britten chose the same Ovidian story as Debussy for his first metamorphosis, 'Pan', is interesting in itself and appears to be in keeping with the classical tradition of reworking old mythical stories as exemplified by Virgil's and Ovid's use of Homer.[29] *Syrinx*, originally called *La Flûte de Pan* and written for Gabriel Mourey's play, *Psyche*, was only rediscovered in 1927 and Britten may have been aware of Marcel Moyse's first recording of this seminal work.

Britten may also have known of the syrinx itself (bound rows of tube reeds) and its relationship to the flute in Debussy's solo work. But he may also have been drawn to the qualities of the equally ancient single or double-reeded aulos which, argues Linda Ardito, represented the opposite of the sensitivities of Apollo's lyre and was associated with 'the Dionysian cult and accompanied dance, poetry, song and drama in rituals of praise for Dionysus (Bacchus), god of wine, fertility and mysticism'.[30] Ardito goes on to say that Apollo's string music had a therapeutic power, whilst 'the aulos, with its characteristic shrill and powerful sound, could draw its listener into the dark depths of the Dionysian realm where the elemental, random and impulsive mingle'.[31] Frank Mulder associates the aulos with expressing 'ecstasy, emotion and unreason' in his programmatical analysis of the *Metamorphoses*.[32] Furthermore, the aulos was associated with mourning, according to Boethius, and was used to accompany Greek tragedies. The choice of oboe for the work could, therefore, be more to do with the weeping of Niobe and the central theme of Bacchus' story.

Ranging from the oboe's lowest note, *bb* (for the depths of Phaeton's plunge) to high *f'''* for the last flicker of a bat's wing at the end of 'Bacchus' (a semitone advance on the range of the *Phantasy Quartet*), the oboe's characteristics are completely and remarkably understood. Britten makes the instrument capture the dazzling allure of 'Pan', the expressive despair of 'Niobe', and the beauty of 'Narcissus' whilst also bringing energy and even danger into 'Phaeton' and 'Bacchus'. He asks the performer to play exquisitely quietly (in 'Niobe' and 'Narcissus' especially) and also raucously and brazenly ('Phaeton' and 'Bacchus'). Sarah Francis reports that Britten asked Boughton what was difficult to play on the oboe, and all that she told him – $a\sharp'$ to b' trill, downward slurs, etc. – he included. Britten obviously wanted to push the instrument to its limits.

Alongside the 'Dionysian' instrument of the oboe, however, the presence of Apollo can also be discerned in this work. He was connected with Hyperion, the sun god (*Young Apollo*), competed with Pan (Ovid, XI, 155–76), was Phaeton's father (I, 751–9), killed Niobe's children (VI, 205–56), was compared for beauty to Narcissus (III, 421) and, had a sister, Diana, who protected Arethusa. All of Britten's characters – in this work as well as in other pieces – play out sub-Olympian themes of love and change, along with Byblis who fell in love with her twin brother, Iphis, a girl brought up as a boy and later betrothed to a girl, Myrhha who fell in love with her father, Pygmalion who fell in love with his statue, and Phaedra who attempted to seduce her stepson, all more related to Bacchus than Apollo, though Apollo seems always present as an overseer of these tales. While working on the great triangular struggle in Captain Vere between the good of Billy and the evil of Claggart, could Britten have also thought about the relationship between the rationality of Apollo and the irrationality of Bacchus, between the lyre of Apollo and the pipe of Pan and between the adjudicator Apollo and all those relationships and metamorphoses as represented by Pan, Phaeton, Niobe, Narcissus and Arethusa?

Britten's *Metamorphoses* is an apparently insignificant work written for 'relaxation' during the composition of *Billy Budd*. While generally received well by critics it was often treated as a 'trifle' ('slight but pretty') rather than a work promising any lasting impact, and as something principally for oboe enthusiasts (although the same critics acknowledged Britten's skill in writing for the instrument).[33] However, it could also be said that the piece represented, or summarized, several preoccupations of the composer that were present throughout his life, namely the references to classical literature, the portrayal of 'universal' elements in music, and the attraction to the expressive potential of the oboe. Britten was a purposeful composer – rarely writing anything that was not inspired by an occasion or a person – and the pieces in *Metamorphoses*, while brief, demonstrate a seriousness of intention and a thoughtful response to the poetic and symbolic qualities of Ovid's work. The juxtaposition of this work's associations with Bacchus, or Dionysus, and the Apollo figure (the Beli/

Budd) of the opera he was working on concurrently lends further piquancy to the choice of instrument here, possibly suggesting to players to emphasize the work's 'Dionysic' elements in performance. Finally, the piece is proof that Britten could compress the most startling range of expressivity and characterization into the smallest of forms. As John Amis wrote, following the première:

> It seems that the more unlikely the proposition is, the more successful Britten is; give any other composer these subjects and he would demand an hour or two of your time, a full symphony orchestra, chorus, Ondes Martenot and heaven knows what else. Give Britten one oboe and ten minutes and you get something delightful, stimulating, and, from the point of view of the publisher and oboists the world over, something useful.[34]

After many years of absorbing classical literature, and during a year in which he appeared to have 'studied and pondered ... eternal truths', Britten managed beautifully to distil his preoccupations into 'ten minutes' in the open air.

Notes

1 Donald Mitchell and Hans Keller, eds., *Benjamin Britten: A Commentary on his Works from a Group of Specialists* (Westport, CT: Greenwood Press, 1952), p. 211.

2 See Paul Kildea, 'Britten, Auden and "Otherness"', *MCCC*, pp. 36–53 at pp. 38–40.

3 *Ibid.*

4 W. H. Auden, 'Musée des Beaux Arts' (1940), in *The Oxford Book of English Verse*, ed. Christopher Ricks (Oxford: Oxford University Press, 1999), p. 608.

5 Boris Ford, Introduction to *Benjamin Britten's Poets*, ed. Ford (Manchester: Carcanet, 1994), p. xii.

6 A. Golding, trans., *Ovid's Metamorphoses* (London: J. M. Dent, 1943). The BPF has two copies of *The Selected Works of Ovid* in the Everyman series.

7 Christopher Headington, *Peter Pears: A Biography* (London: Faber, 1992), p. 15.

8 Donald Mitchell, 'The Church Parables (I): Ritual and Restraint', in *CPBC*, pp. 211–4 at p. 211.

9 Graham Elliott, *Benjamin Britten: The Spiritual Dimension* (Oxford: Oxford University Press, 2006), p. 38.

10 W. H. Auden, cited in *ibid.*, p. 39.

11 John Keats, 'Hyperion', in *Keats' Poetical Works* (Oxford: Oxford University Press, 1999), pp. 36–53.

12 Arnold Whittall, 'The Chamber Operas', in *MCCC*, pp. 95–112 at p. 96.

13 *Ibid.*

14 Ronald Duncan, *Working with Britten: A Personal Memoir* (Devon: Rebel Press, 1981), p. 58.

15 Hermann Melville, *Billy Budd, Sailor and Other Stories*, selected and edited by Harold Beaver (Harmondsworth: Penguin, 1967), p. 340.

16 *Ibid.*, p. 326.

17 Harold Beaver, 'Note', in *ibid.*

18 Clifford Hindley, 'Eros in Life and Death: *Billy Budd* and *Death in Venice*', in *MCCC*, pp. 147–64 at pp. 157ff.

19 See George Caird, 'Benjamin Britten and his *Metamorphoses*', *The Double Reed* 29/3 (2006), pp. 73–99 at p. 78.

20 D. Raeburn, trans., *Ovid's Metamorphosis* (Harmondsworth: Penguin, 2004), XIV, pp. 176f.

21 Britten and Pears had had a holiday in Sicily in September 1950, and this is possibly pertinent to the choice of the final tale of *Metamorphoses*.

22 Cited in Caird, 'Benjamin Britten and his *Metamorphoses*', p. 76.

23 See *ibid.*

24 *MRLL*, vol. 1, p. 369.

25 Lloyd Moore, liner notes to *Simple Symphony/Temporal Variations* (Naxos, 1993).

26 Natalie Caine, '*The Temporal Variations*', *Double Reed News* (n.d.).

27 Sarah Francis, 'Joy Boughton – A Portrait', *Double Reed News* 26 (n.d.), pp. 4–7.

28 Frank Howes, 'Aldeburgh Festival', *The Times* (16 June 1951).

29 For more on this subject see Fritz Graf, 'Myth in Ovid', in *The Cambridge Companion to Ovid*, ed. Philip Hardie (Cambridge: Cambridge University Press, 2002), pp. 108–21. Mervyn Cooke has observed that *Syrinx* can be seen as part of a French tradition of using Greek myths as subject matter, and cites Roussel, whose stage works include *Bacchus et Ariadne* and *Aeneas*. Personal communication to author.

30 Linda Ardito, 'The Aulos: Symbol of Musico-Medicinal Magic', *The Double Reed* 22/2 (1999), pp. 67–72 at p. 67.

31 *Ibid.*, p. 67.

32 Frank Mulder, 'An Introduction and Programmatical Analysis of the *Six Metamorphoses after Ovid* by Benjamin Britten', IDRS, *The Double Reed* (n.d.), pp. 67–74.

33 See John Amis, 'The Aldeburgh Festival', *Musical Times* 92/1302 (August 1951), pp. 368–9; unattributed author, review of sheet music, *Music and Letters* 33/4 (October 1952), pp. 365–6; and Wendell Margrave, Review of sheet music, *Notes,* second series, 10/4 (September 1953), p. 673.

34 Amis, 'The Aldeburgh Festival, p. 369.

5 Britten and the Cinematic Frame

David Crilly

In the mid-1930s Britten was beginning to make his mark as a promising new-comer. He had developed some degree of individuality under the guidance of Frank Bridge, whom Britten was always to cite as the most significant single figure in terms of establishing a meticulous technique. The *Sinfonietta* of 1932 was evidence of an emerging maturity – he won the Farrar Prize for composition at the Royal College of Music for the second time in that year, and the *Quatre chansons françaises* of a few years earlier (1928) had already demonstrated Britten's enthusiasm to seek out and absorb a wider frame of stylistic reference. But there were signs, too, that Britten was entering something of a creative *cul-de-sac* and required new impetus before the next steps in his artistic development might be taken. In 1934 he wrote to Grace Williams, 'I cannot write a single note of anything respectable at the moment, and so – and on the off chance of making some money – I am dishing up some very old stuff (written, some of it, over ten years ago).'[1]

But during 1935 and 1936 Britten's direction as an individual, a thinker and as a composer was set, and events of that year were to establish the basis of a compositional aesthetic and political sensibility that persevered and continued to grow right up to and including the composition of *Death in Venice* some 40 years later. In January 1936 Britten's diary opens with this optimistic entry, marking a change in fortune and direction for the young composer:

> 1936 finds me infinitely better off in all ways than did the beginning of 1935; it finds me earning my living – with occasionally something to spare – at the GPO film unit under John Grierson and Cavalcanti, writing music and supervising sounds for film[2]

The final phrase is particularly significant, since Britten's role was not to be merely provider of incidental music, but rather to integrate sound into the fabric of the visual dramatic narrative – a role that would require a more detailed knowledge and understanding of the film-maker's craft. It is worth remembering, too, that the 'talkies' – films that could include speech, precisely timed music and sound effects – were a relatively new phenomenon and so any work in this area was likely to be both experimental and pioneering. But Britten was no stranger to film before taking up his post with the GPO Film Unit. At that time, film had as its primary role a mission of entertainment through romantic escapism and fantasy, and we know from the pocket diaries that Britten kept throughout his teens that he had become something of a cinema aficionado, regularly going to see stars of the screen such as Greta Garbo *et al*. Rather than being merely a passive observer of film, he regularly commented in his diaries about the effectiveness of various elements of the film's composition, essentially providing both an *aide memoir* and a stylistic critique. His library of scores and books on music also contained a number of novels that had been turned into films he had recently seen, together with copies of plays he had seen performed, and we can note in this the tendency in Britten to seek out the experience of the visualization of the spoken or written word.

Britten's first commissions during the early part of his time with the GPO were to compose music for *The King's Stamp* (1935) – a documentary that traced the history and production of postage stamps – which resulted in a through-composed score lasting around 20 minutes, together with *The Way to the Sea* (1936), a kind of *Whitsun Weddings* film, celebrating by way of a train journey the electrification of the London to Portsmouth line. There are features of this music that will have particular resonance in the forthcoming debate, such as the fragmented and quickly shifting pastiche and pseudo-archaic passages reflecting the brisk juxtaposition of contrasting images in the film, and I will return to highlight one particularly prophetic aspect of this music later in the discussion. But Grierson had embarked upon a much more experimental project; a film called *Coal Face* (1935), which had nothing to do with the Post Office, but rather took as its subject the far less comfortable topic of the poor working conditions of coal miners.

John Grierson, although originally from Scotland, had spent his formative years in America researching the psychology of propaganda, and particularly the power of the press, film and media in the process of forming and direct-ing public opinion. Grierson's fundamental principle of documentary – at that time a newly emerging form – was that the actor could be replaced by the 'original' actor; that is, that the story of an individual in society could best be told by that individual, rather than mediated through dramatic interpretation and representation. In this regard, Grierson's stance is similar to that of the Soviet propagandist Dziga Vertov, who dismissed the kinds of films produced in Hollywood as nothing more than bourgeois excess. Grierson gathered polit-ical kindred spirits, artists and other experimental film makers around him at the GPO in 1933, including Alberto Cavalcanti, Basil Wright, Stuart Legg and (for Britten) the hugely influential Paul Rotha, who echoed Grierson's philoso-phy of the documentary, saying

Real and creative thought must be about real things. Let cinema explore outside the limits of what we are told constitutes entertainment ... Let cinema attempt film interpretations of modern problems and events... Let cinema recognise the existence of real men and women, real things and real issues ...[3]

At the Unit Britten also encountered the artist William Coldstream and, most crucially, W. H. Auden, by whom he would at first be intellectually and socially intimidated, but who was to provide, through the discussions and collaborations that followed, the ideological and artistic spur he needed. Auden, too, was a committed socialist and the theme of the individual in society and the concept of citizenship recur throughout his writing, both poetic and polemic. Art was certainly a significant element of left-wing political discourse, and Grierson brought under his wing a potent mix of emerging thinkers and creative artists to provide the intellectual framework for the Unit.

Earlier in his career Grierson had been a member of the EMB (Empire Marketing Board), an organization dedicated to the promotion of British unity and British world trade, and in 1929 he wrote, produced and directed his first EMB film, *Drifters*, which charts the lives and tough working conditions of North Sea herring fishermen. This event is significant in the current debate on two counts: first, it is, once again, indicative of the intense socialist *milieu* into which Britten was to become immersed in the years to come, but perhaps more significantly because the film's first showing was, by coincidence rather than design, in London on a double-bill with Sergei Eisenstein's seminal and controversial work, *The Battleship Potemkin*.

Eisenstein's film has its place as a potent example of social and political commentary of the period, but is more significantly remembered for its revolutionary technique of composition and its attempt to create dramatic metaphor through the juxtaposition of cinematic 'frames'. The use of film as a means of storytelling had previously been mostly representational; that is, the camera functioned simply as the eye of the viewer, and often from one location, almost in the same way that an audience member might watch a play in a theatre in being able to see the whole scene the whole time. Eisenstein, on the other hand, sought to exploit the potential of the editing process and in so doing to experiment with the emotional responses that might be generated through the self-conscious collision of contradictory material. For example, in *Potemkin*, the famous 'Odessa steps' sequence serves to articulate the principle. Rather than seeing the whole action unfolding in a single shot, the audience first sees the chaos in the area, with crowds running in all directions – cut then to a close-up of the feet of soldiers marching, rhythmically and relentlessly down the Odessa steps – cut to a close-up of a distressed mother, trying to protect her child, with the pram teetering dangerously close to the top of the seemingly never-ending steps – cut to the soldiers who fire indiscriminately into the crowd – cut back to the injured mother who falls against the pram, forcing it to tumble over the top of the stairs.

In this dramatic narrative, the individual shots in themselves have no meaning. It is in their juxtaposition, or rather to use Eisenstein's term, their 'collision', that meaning arises as they 'explode' into a concept. The collision of the image of the machine-like efficiency of the military with the vulnerable images of mother and child generate the meaning: the oppression of the individual by the state. The idea of collision is central to the principle of cinematic montage, and the act of perception arises not by witnessing these conflicting images in succession, but rather by experiencing a kind of internal representation of successive images on top of one another. The process is fundamentally Hegelian (and, by implication, Marxist) with the conflicting frames of thesis and antithesis combining to form the synthesis which constitutes the emotional response of the audience.

In his recent *A History of Film Music*, Mervyn Cooke notes, referring to the work of the GPO Film Unit, that 'Grierson's own work was significantly influenced by Eisenstein's montage techniques'[4] and this is particularly evident in the aforementioned *Coal Face*, which was also to be the first collaboration between Britten and Auden. The fact that Grierson was alive to the possibility of generating a powerful dramatic message, without necessarily involving traditional dramatic narrative, is clear from the recollections of one of the unit's directors, Stuart Legg, recalling some 40 years after the event that Grierson had provided him with 'a lot of material to cut which has been shot in coal mines. He asked me to make it into a two-reeler. This was the beginning of *Coal Face*, because when it was cut, I somehow managed to make it look like a film.'[5] In fact, none of the footage used for *Coal Face* was shot with the intention that it would be used for the film, but was rather a collection of 'remnants' and archive footage from past projects.

Initially, Britten's involvement in the project appears to be something of an afterthought, since he was brought in to try and unify the fragmented nature of the piece by providing a continuous, though shifting, musical backdrop to the work after the editing process was complete. This, then, is Britten's first creative encounter with a self-conscious piece of montage-style film-making.[6] The levels of 'thesis' and 'antithesis' within the film are clearly delineated with the miners and their families and communities starkly at odds with the harsh machinery of their industry. The opening stages of the film highlight the world of the mine, supported by Britten's bare and angular music, brutally rhythmic and repetitive. Images of machine and man are quickly juxtaposed so that the miners lose their human identity – as though they become part of the machinery around them. As they rise from the pit to rejoin their families the music gives way to a 'heavenly choir' to reflect the contrast between the communal and industrial landscapes.

The overtly socialist message is never far from the surface, and the statistical information about the industry – the number of tons of coal mined, the number of annual fatalities – are intoned in an impersonal and robotic fashion. There is collision here, too, with the mechanistic and relentlessly impersonal depiction of the workplace palpably far removed from Auden's reflection on the spirit of the miner:

> O lurcher-loving collier, black as night,
> Follow your love across the smokeless hill;
> Your lamp is out, and all the cages still;
> Course for heart and do not miss,
> For Sunday soon is past and, Kate, fly not so fast,
> For Monday comes when none may kiss:
> Be marble to his soot, and to his black be white.

The contrast between the industrial and social are spelled out literally and metaphorically in black and white, though it is noteworthy that although Auden, Britten, Grierson and others at the Unit regarded themselves as part of an emerging socialist consciousness, it is also true that they remained firmly outside that social group. Paul Kildea notes that neither the meter nor language of the poem are simple, and also that the poem contains classical (and specifically Shakespearean) allusions which, rather than reflecting the view of the miner are actually those of 'an educated, literary, middle-class anthropologist'.[7] This didactic tone is also present in the opening stages of *The Way to the Sea*, in which the narrator chants, 'We pass the areas of greatest congestion, the houses of those who have the least power of choice'. Nevertheless, and despite the often pulpit-like oration of the narration and Auden's poetry, *Coal Face* exhibits a powerful and somewhat expressionistic confluence of music, image and spoken word, and this formula was to be retained for the next collaborative project, *Night Mail*, which merits further scrutiny in the current discussion, not least because Britten was involved in its production from the outset.

Like *The Way to the Sea* and *Coal Face*, the subject of *Night Mail* (1936) reflected, in line with the ethos of Grierson and Rotha, the exposition of the everyday. The film tracks the overnight journey of mail from London to Scotland, and marvels at the technology, speed and modes of communication

illustrated by the workers. Again, ideas are generated using cinematic montage. For example, early in the film we see a shot of a worker moving to a telephone – cut to an outside moving camera shot panning across a telegraph
pole and wires – cut to another worker picking up a telephone. Thus the
idea of communication over a distance is conveyed. It is the closing section
of the film, however, which transmits the most powerful imagery, as Auden's
rhythmically propelled text is underpinned by Britten's driving score, and it is
Britten's almost ekphratic depiction of the movement and energy of the train
which is particularly prophetic. The poem begins with the wonderfully evocative 'This is the night train, crossing the border, bringing the cheque and the
postal order', but Britten's score has already set up the rhythm of the distant
train, steaming through the countryside (Example 1). Within a few bars the
train has drawn nearer and the full, repetitive rhythmic pulse of the machinery
is clearly evident (Example 2).

Two other moments from this section warrant illustration as Britten effectively portrays the steady climb up a hill, followed by the easier descent on
the other side. The marked contrary motion followed by opposing glissandi
in Example 3 almost visually depict the contrary movement of the engine
parts, but the chromatic rise from A♭, through A♮, B♭, B♮ and C also reflect
the increased struggle of the engine, until the next pitch in the sequence, C♯,

Example 1 Britten, *Night Mail*, beginning

Example 2 Britten, *Night Mail*, excerpt

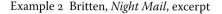

Example 3 Britten, *Night Mail*, excerpt

becomes the third of A major for the expansive string melody on the words 'Dawn freshens. The climb is done'.

In themselves, these details may not seem particularly momentous, but we see here the work of an apprentice and the emergence of a technique which reaches its fruition in scenes such as 'The Journey', from *The Turn of the Screw* (1954), with its dislocated percussive accompaniment that clearly mirrors the jarring movement of a carriage over uneven ground; or the first interlude from *Peter Grimes* (1945), wholly evocative of the swell and sounds of the dawn tide; and also the masterful passage from Act I of *Death in Venice* (1973) (from R28) at which point the reverberation of the engines powering the ship which is to take Aschenbach to Venice growl into action. This ability on the part of the composer to reflect and evoke the locale of the action stems directly from his cinematic experience during the 1930s. Not only does this ability enable the listener to acquire a marked sense of place, it also allows Britten to draw particular attention to strategic moments when our focus is directed elsewhere.

The opening of the second act of *Peter Grimes*, for example, provides a conspicuous illustration of the principle of cinematic cross-fading in Britten's work. The stage directions make clear that there are two points of visual focus in the scene: Ellen and the apprentice, John, are in the foreground sitting on a breakwater, while members of the Borough congregate in and around the church. (It is clear, too, that Britten was particularly conscious of the need for spatial separation of action. Later in the scene, stage directions in the published score indicate that 'Boles and Keene walk down the street. They stop for a moment to listen'; but this is actually a replacement for the original directions in the sketch score which emphasize the split-screen effect with, 'Behind closed doors or half-open windows – Auntie, Ned and Boles have been watching'.)[8] These discrete areas are articulated musically, too, since the open and bright D major music, associated with Ellen, is at odds with the tritonally and semitonally opposed peal of the church bells on A♭ and E♭. This effect of physical disconnection is further amplified when the remote sonority of the church organ interjects on E♭ major. This deliberate setting up of two areas of action allows, in what follows, the effect of frequent shifts of perspective similar to the shifts in depth of field on a camera lens, which enable the perceiver to alternately focus upon the foreground and background of a particular dramatic scene.

Through the scene our attention is constantly being drawn from one perspective to the other – from foreground to background – and as the scene unfolds it becomes clear that the church chorus is providing an ironic commentary upon the events unfolding in the foreground. The two planes of activity eventually create a kind of 'call and response' which parallels the relationship between the Rector and the congregation. The following exchanges elucidate this process:

> *Ellen*: John, you may have heard the story of the prentice Peter had before;
>> *Chorus: And shades of night return once more*
> *Ellen*: But when you came I said, now this is where we make a new start.
>> *Chorus: Amen*
>> *Rector: Father, we have erred and strayed from thy ways...*
> *Ellen*: There's a tear in your coat...
>> *Rector: And we have done those things we ought not to have done.*
> *Ellen*: John, what are you trying to hide?
>> *Rector: O Lord open our lips!*
> *Ellen*: A bruise... well it's begun
>> *Rec/Chorus: ... As it was in the beginning, is now...*

In Act I scene 3 of *The Turn of the Screw* we can spot another example of this 'call and response' dramatic construction. Once again the stage directions indicate two discrete areas of action, as the main characters of the scene – the Governess and Mrs Grose – are located on the porch at Bly, but are, significantly, witnessing and commenting upon events taking place inside the building through a low window. Both are shocked to learn that Miles has been expelled from school due to an unspecified 'injury to his friends'. The speculative dialogue which follows becomes increasingly tortured and chromatic, leading to an ethereal high tremolo on strings (with viola, cello and bass playing in high register) on the notes Eb, F and G. (The use of the major second as a dissonance and as a means of effecting dramatic stasis had become, by the mid-1950s, a Britten fingerprint.) The 'depth of field' shifts abruptly to the children 'playing quietly together' in the room within and the gently lilting 'Lavender's Blue' in a starkly contrasting G tonality (Example 4a).

Each phrase of the nursery rhyme is articulated by a response from Mrs Grose and the Governess which is at odds with it both tonally and metrically. The harmonic context of the duple-time passage is summarized in Example 4b. The F♯/C♯ opening dyad could not be further removed from *Lavender's Blue*, being (like the church bells in *Grimes* discussed above) both tritonally and semitonally opposed, though their music, taken in isolation, is not at all discordant and consists entirely of open fourths, fifths and thirds (with the almost omni-present major second making a couple of appearances). As the scene unfolds, though, and their resolve that Miles must be innocent hardens, their ending E♯ is rethought as F♮ for the final, and unified, 'it is all a wicked lie', resolving onto the G of the nursery rhyme (Example 5).

The process is, perhaps, made clearer with the use of a simple visual model. Figure 1 is a cube – or rather, represents a cube. The fact that it is not actually what it appears to be is rather obvious, though not insignificant in the current discussion, and we are reminded of Donald Mitchell's comment on the in-built ambiguity of Britten's music and 'its capacity to surprise … its conspicuous turnings of convention on its head while, at the same time, seeming to conform to convention, to sustain tradition, [which] is a paradox typical

Example 4 Britten, *Turn of the Screw*: (a) from Act I, scene 3;
(b) harmonic context of the duple-time passage

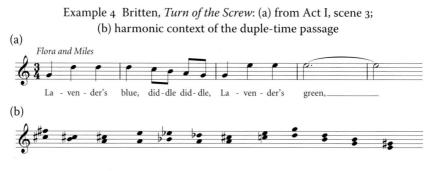

Example 5 Britten, *Turn of the Screw*, from Act I, scene 3

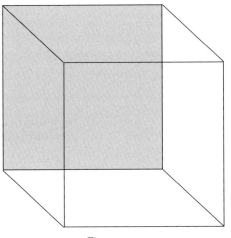

Figure 1

of Britten'.[9] But in looking at the image we are able to perceive a cube, even though we know it is not really there. Furthermore, we can see that one side of the cube is shaded. But is the shaded side of the cube at the foreground or the background of the image? The answer, of course, is that it is both – or either – depending on how we choose to attend to the image. We are able to see the image in one way and then shift our perspective to see it in another. Ludwig Wittgenstein referred to this ability within us to perceive one 'scene' from different perspectives as 'aspect change' (though he used the famous duck-rabbit drawing) and Britten exploits and directs our shifting perspectives within key moments of his operas in order to manipulate and direct our attention, and to articulate a precise dramatic point. As with Eisenstein's cinematic montage technique, dramatic meaning is generated by the collision of opposing images which explode into a concept.

Act II scene 2 ('The Bells') of *The Turn of the Screw* reveals a more complex illustration of this mode of expression, involving shifting perspectives in which a single scene is viewed from differing interpretative viewpoints before coalescing into all interpretations presented simultaneously. The scene opens vividly and triadically with a clear statement of F♯ major (the orchestral bells, depicting the church bells on a 'bright' Sunday morning, maintain an F♯ pedal through the bulk of the scene). The opening statement from the children reinforces the tonic, though the inclusion of an E♮ in the orchestra that supports the vocal line is unsettling and only serves to sour what appears to be a perfectly innocent scene (Example 6). The children, though, take this up, and their next phrase opens with a *f* and accented E♮ for '*Bless* ye the lord' – which turns out to be somewhat ironic – and it is clear that things may not be as straightforward as they might at first appear.

Example 6 Britten, *Turn of the Screw*, from Act II, scene 2

Indeed, while the children's material continues with the triadic and prayer-like material of the opening, the sonorities which punctuate this passage create a nebulous and vague impression, and it proves difficult to detect a feeling of harmonic movement in any traditional sense. Example 7 summarizes the harmonic shifts that occur between the start of the scene and R30. We might notice, too, the register and chorale-like movement of the parts, reminiscent of the heart-stopping moment towards the conclusion of Berg's Violin Concerto, at which a chorus of clarinets, variously exploiting the sumptuous chalumeau range of the instrument, introduce the Bach chorale *Es ist genug* which draws the piece to a close. Britten's admiration of Berg is well documented and it is quite possible that Britten sought to imply or imitate the sonority of the church organ here in the same way.

The 15 chords that underpin this section of the opera create a relatively dense harmonic texture which negates or corrupts, rather than supports, the harmonic implication of the children's phrases. The nature of the dissonance, however, is largely diatonic, resulting from suspension and accented appoggiatura, rather than any Bergian influence. This harmonic language

Example 7 Britten, *Turn of the Screw*,
harmonic shifts from beginning of Act II scene 2

actually reflects something much more familiar in English music, and although the effect is aurally different, the same mechanism can be seen in the music of Vaughan Williams and Gerald Finzi. (The diatonic dissonance in, for example, *Dies Natalis*, is achieved entirely in this way.)

So, in the opening section we have a depiction of innocence and musical clarity, soured by the inclusion of E♮ (the flattened seventh of the mixolydian mode) and by the largely non-functional chorale-like shifting in the strings. Mrs Grose's entry at R30 finds her seemingly oblivious to any clouds on the horizon as she enters boldly in B major, thus rendering the souring E♮ diatonic and neutralizing its disquieting effect (Example 8a). Such is her enthusiasm to brighten the mood, her next phrase pushes the harmonic implication further, cadencing on (what is for her) the secondary dominant of C♯ (Example 8b). Her enthusiasm is short-lived, however, as her final cadence embraces the E♮ to cadence on F♯ mixolydian – ironically to the phrase 'How sweet they are together' (Example 8c). Her change of emphasis may be evidence that she is determined to put a brave face on the situation, or perhaps reflects her concerns for the mental health of the Governess. (Her next phrase is, 'Come Miss, don't worry, it will pass'.) Indeed, Mrs Grose's increasing desperation as the scene develops is reflected in the lurching, vertiginous harmonic shifts which underpin her plea 'They're so happy with you, You're so good to them' as her

Example 8 Britten, *Turn of the Screw*, from Act II, scene 2

attempts to move the music back to the reassuring F♯/B territory are utterly negated by the tritonally opposed C major material in the strings (Example 9).

At this point the Governess appears almost in a trance, and responds only monosyllabically until, at R53, she takes Mrs Grose to one side to insist, now in an urgent A♯ minor, that the children are not playing but are 'talking horrors'. Their seemingly Christian prayer of 'Praise him and magnify him forever' has given way to 'O ye dragons and snakes, worms and feathered fowl;' now more suggestive of pagan incantation and ritual.

We have in this scene, then, a single occasion – the walk to church on a Sunday morning – witnessed from three distinct musical and dramatic perspectives. Our focus shifts, or is directed, from one stance to another as in turn the protagonists are foregrounded then recede into the background as another perspective takes precedence. This dramatic montage serves not only to introduce, but also to prepare us for what becomes the achingly beautiful climax of the scene (from R40) at which point all three musical strands collide tonally, rhythmically and dramatically, with the flowing triple-metre melody of the Governess at odds with the fragmented and increasingly desperate pleas from Mrs Grose that all will be well, sung over the continuing off-beat and metrically shifting incantation of the children. The orchestra, too, operates almost as a fourth level of discourse with an extensive and expansive chorale-like passage, dynamically shifting from *pp* to *f* and back again in just a few bars.

One consideration, of course, is to what extent this process was part of Britten's conscious thinking. While it is clear that in *Coal Face*, *The Way to the Sea* and *Night Mail* Britten was alive to the influence of Eisenstein and cinematic montage, it is also true, or at least could be argued, that Britten was merely responding to a given stimulus, rather than being a driving force behind its creation. But an examination of the early drafts of the libretto for *The Turn of the Screw* reveal that the stratified layers of meaning in the scene discussed above were not the work of Myfanwy Piper, but were rather insisted upon by Britten himself. Plate 5 shows the original typescript received from Piper, covered in alterations and annotations in Britten's hand. Piper's original

Example 9 Britten, *Turn of the Screw*, from Act II, scene 2

conception began the scene with the entrance of Mrs Grose – 'Oh Miss, it is a bright morning to be sure'. On the right-hand side of the page the letters A and C indicate that something is to be inserted at these moments. Plates 6 and 7 are the additions, written by Britten, to be added to the scene, demonstrating clearly that it was Britten rather than Piper who instigated the various strata of dramatic action.

One further characteristic of the scene, which adds dramatic weight and which is exploited elsewhere in Britten's stage works appears at the beginning of the scene; that is, the reiteration of the Latin mnemonic, '*O amnis, axis, caulis, collis, ...*' which first appears in 'The Lesson' in Act I. The reappearance of the earlier material serves to articulate the significance of the children's pseudo-Christian incantation, in that we are reminded that the apparent innocence encountered initially was fleeting and ephemeral, and that its seemingly cheerful and light-hearted tone is deeply ironic. The idea of play functions to create an air of disquiet in the scene – much in the same way that *Lavender's Blue* operated earlier, but more significantly it also introduces the notion of 'flashback' as a dramatic device.[10]

The principle of cinematic flashback is, perhaps, most effectively exploited in the closing scenes of *Peter Grimes*, and especially at the point at which Grimes' mental state has deteriorated to the brink of collapse. He wanders the beach in darkness and fog while the Borough folk, reduced now to nothing more than a lynch-mob, hunt for him. In his delirium he imagines himself back in the time before our story began, on the ill-fated journey with the first apprentice. As in other scenes already discussed, our focus shifts from Grimes to the mob, concealed by darkness, but evident in their distant choral interjections. In a short series of outbursts Grimes calls to mind earlier times, first his forlorn desire, filled with pathos, to go back in time – to 'turn the skies back and begin again', echoing his 'Pleiades' reverie in The Boar during the storm. This prompts a grotesque and now macabre rendition of a phrase from the round 'Old Joe has gone fishing' though now Grimes himself has become 'the catch'. Following another interjection from the mob Grimes laments the loss of Ellen ('my only hope is held by you') recalling an all too rare moment of tenderness between them, before his final collapse and recognition that all is lost, with a brief return to the moment at which he struck Ellen and the words, 'And God have mercy upon you'. The reiteration of these musical fragments does not represent a musical reprise, of course, but rather has a purely cinematic and dramatic function; that is, to remind us of the full significance of earlier exchanges which now reach their zenith, and also to enable us to 're-frame' these actions and events and to see the ironic significance of their initial utterance.

As with 'The Bells' from *The Turn of the Screw*, Britten was not wholly reliant upon his librettist and appeared more than prepared to make alterations to suit his dramatic needs. In fact, as Philip Brett noted, Britten revised this scene with the help of Ronald Duncan – librettist for *The Rape of Lucretia* (1946) – while Britten stayed at his home in Devon in February 1945.

> The Britten–Duncan replacement tells the story of the opera in the music of the opera, recalling the inquest, the evil message of the posse ('bring the branding iron and knife') the soliloquy and the round in the pub, and the friendship and betrayal of Ellen, culminating in the symbolic capitulation to society.[11]

Indeed, Britten acknowledged Duncan's contribution in a letter to him dated 24 February 1945, which goes on to indicate that the structure of the piece was not something that responded to the demands of the libretto, but which was rather in a state of constant flux, prompted by Britten. He wrote:

> This is written in enormous haste and in Joan Cross's dressing room at the Opera House! (I am in the middle of the opera and all its consequences now) … We are having a terrific time with Grimes – and Peter and I are pretty well re-writing his part. Montagu agreed to the new mad scene, and I kept your part in it fairly quiet, altho' I murmured that you helped us abit! [*sic*][12]

Having already marked the influence of cinematic montage from the 1930s on the scenes previously discussed it comes as no surprise that we are also able to trace Britten's awareness of the dramatic potential of flashback in the earlier work. In Britten's first project for the GPO Film Unit – *The King's Stamp* – the simple and memorable march of the title music recurs at strategic points within the film; first when Friedmann completes the design of the stamp, then again as we see the actual printing of the stamp and are able to examine the finished article, and finally when the Jubilee stamps appear in the Royal philatelic collection. This was perhaps Britten's first use of cinematic flashback which, in a thorough discussion of this work, Philip Reed also describes as his 'recollection technique'.[13]

Throughout Britten's compositional life the elements of contrast, ambiguity and collision remained at the core of a compositional aesthetic based upon the principles of Eisenstein's cinematic montage. But it is important to recognize that the tensions and subsequent meanings generated by this technique do not come about simply through the unapologetic juxtaposition of unlike material. The nature of a dramatic 'frame' is that it is defined both in terms of its interpretation as an element of discourse, and also by its total relationship with other frames which precede and follow it. Indeed, it could be argued that the frame does not have meaning outside of this system of dialogic relations. Moreover, the frame will carry with it a number of codes which may operate outside its normal sphere of reference, and the combination of frames, and the image they create, will be determined by the reading of a range of cultural codes, and not just by an understanding of the highly coded structure and syntax of musical signification. Throughout the preparation of the operas it is clear that Britten relied upon – whether via Kenneth Green's initial stage designs for *Peter Grimes* or the meticulously planned details of the libretti – a clear and highly detailed visual narrative upon which to centre his music, and this elucidation of the working methods of Britten only serves to amplify Donald Mitchell's contention that,

> the assurance, expertise and confidence ... that marked *Peter Grimes* must strike one not as qualities conjured up out of the air but as manifestations of techniques that had been prepared over a long period in the often gruelling environment of the film studio, cutting room or theatre pit.[14]

Notes

1 *MRLL*, vol. 1, p. 319.

2 *MRLL*, vol. 1, p. 400.

3 Paul Rotha, *Documentary Film*, third edition (London: Faber, 1952).

4 Mervyn Cooke, *A History of Film Music* (Cambridge: Cambridge University Press, 2008), p. 274.

5 Elizabeth Sussex, *The Rise and Fall of British Documentary: The Story of the Film Movement Founded by John Grierson* (Berkeley: University of California Press, 1975), p. 29.

6 For a further discussion of the use of Eisenstein's montage technique in Britten's music see my 'Britten and Owen: an intertextual reading of the War Requiem', in *Phrase and Subject: Studies in Literature and Music*, ed. Delia Da Sousa Correa (Oxford: Modern Humanities Research Association and Maney Publishing, 2006), pp. 178–92.

7 Paul Kildea, 'Britten, Auden and "Otherness" ', in *MCCC*, pp. 36–53 at p. 48.

8 Paul Banks, ed., *The Making of Peter Grimes*, vol. 1 (Woodbridge: Boydell Press, 1996), p. 61.

9 Donald Mitchell, '*Peter Grimes*: Fifty Years On', in *The Making of Peter Grimes: Essays and Studies*, ed. Paul Banks (Woodbridge: Boydell Press, 1997), pp. 125–65 at p. 125.

10 I am indebted to Colin Matthews, who first pointed out this aspect of the music to me.

11 Philip Brett, '*Peter Grimes*: The Growth of the Libretto', in *The Making of Peter Grimes: Essays and Studies*, ed. Banks, pp. 53–78 at p. 71.

12 *MRLL,* vol. 2, p. 1242.

13 Philip Reed, 'The Incidental Music of Benjamin Britten: A Study and Catalogue Raisonné' (PhD dissertation, University of East Anglia, 1987), p. 61.

14 Donald Mitchell, *Britten and Auden in the Thirties: The Year 1936* (first published 1981; Woodbridge: Boydell Press, 2000), pp. 30–1.

6 Storms, Laughter and Madness: Verdian 'Numbers' and Generic Allusions in Benjamin Britten's *Peter Grimes*

Jane Brandon

Just before the close of the final act of *Peter Grimes* (1945) Peter is left alone in his hut wailing in hallucinatory horror, his rejection from the Borough community underlined by the cries of the persecutory off-stage chorus calling his name, convinced of his guilt in relation to the death of his latest boy apprentice. In a mad scene of chilling intensity, Peter relives the music that accompanied his downfall. His fevered, fragmented recitative thematically recalls his visionary hopes, the inquest, Ellen's affection (the agent of his failed salvation) and the vindictive, prejudicial voices of the seafaring society. Suicide is, apparently, the only option; a fate made more poignant by the obliviousness of the villagers who return apparently unchanged to their daily routine as the curtain falls.

Writing about the libretto of *Grimes* in 1945, Desmond Shawe-Taylor suggests that it was such generic scenes as the mad scene that drew Britten to George Crabbe's poem as possible operatic material. He describes the libretto's

> rapid and dramatic action, full of atmosphere, of vivid country characters, and of genre pictures of a kind ideally suited to musical treatment. There is a pub scene with the storm growling outside and bursting in whenever the door is opened; a sunny Sunday morning on the beach with matins drifting through the open church door as a background to dialogue; a dance at the Moot Hall, with an unseen band.[1]

That Britten, too, considered these scenes as significant structural and musical elements is underlined by the fact that the early draft scenarios of the work include generic titles for many of these sections.

Grimes is also notable for its number opera construction. Britten himself famously suggested that he had adopted the 'practice of separate numbers'[2] in the work, and many commentators have viewed this allusion to 19th-century and earlier practice as a problematic and even conservative element in the score.[3] Further, these number opera conventions (the division of scenes into discrete dramatic units, often marked by clear scene-changes and set-piece forms such as arias, ensembles and choruses) and generic scenes (stock scenes employed to set the mood or articulate dramatic action, for example storm scenes, dance scenes and mad scenes) also resonate with specifically Italianate and Verdian models.[4] Yet, though Britten's handling of numbers and generic scenes resonates with Italian practice, the work often reveals more about Britten's innovations than his reliance on tradition.

This exploration of *Grimes* will move from consideration of the genesis of the libretto and the generic and number opera allusions in the large-scale planning of the work, to analysis of a collection of Britten's generic scenes placed alongside possible models taken primarily from Verdi's *Macbeth*, *Rigoletto*, *La traviata*, *Aïda* and *Otello*: the storm scene (Act I scenes 1 and 2), the laughing chorus (Act II scene 1 and Act III scene 1) and the mad scene (Act III scene 2).

Britten and Verdi

Peter Pears observed that his work with the Sadler's Wells Opera company during 1942–3 was 'all food for *Grimes*'.[5] The Verdian repertoire of that season included *Rigoletto*, in which Pears played the Duke, as well as *La traviata*, in which he played Alfredo. Britten wrote glowingly of the opportunity that these performances offered him and even attended *La traviata* over twelve times:

> I had a great piece of luck, and that was that I was able to go to rehearsals and performances of virtually the whole of the repertoire of the Wells at that time. I had friends who were singing in the company and as I was planning 'Grimes' and actually writing it, I made use of the opportunity of getting to know the repertory extremely well. I learned a tremendous amount, particularly from … 'Traviata' … and 'The Barber of Seville'.[6]

(In addition, the repertoire included *La bohème*, *The Bartered Bride* and *The Magic Flute*.) Earlier, in 1938, Pears had a walk-on part in *Macbeth* with Glyndebourne Opera, which Britten enthusiastically attended, and the composer's letters reveal that he was an ardent admirer of *Otello*. He had obtained scores of all of these Verdian works by the early 1940s. Britten acknowledged the importance of past works to his own compositional project in a telling interview with Donald Mitchell in 1969.

> I couldn't work alone. I can only work really because of the tradition that I am conscious of behind me. And not only the consciousness of the musical tradition, but the tradition of painting, and architecture, and countryside around me, people around me.[7]

It appears that Verdi, along with a large collection of other musical 'voices' – we may note Purcell, Mahler, Stravinsky, and Berg amongst others – played a significant role in shaping Britten's conception of operatic practice.

A 'number' libretto and large-scale structure

Britten famously observed in the introductory booklet to *Peter Grimes*' first performance at Sadler's Wells in 1945 that he was 'especially interested in the general architectural and formal problems of opera, and decided to reject the Wagnerian theory of "permanent melody" for the classical practice of separate numbers that crystallize and hold the emotion of a dramatic situation at chosen moments'.[8] More specifically, it seems that Britten embraced the idea of Verdian number structures in his works for similar reasons. He observed in 1966: 'I was particularly influenced by the sectional division of the operas which Verdi used all his life – working on different dramatic layers rather than the one slope up and down that other composers have used.'[9]

Britten's working practices suggest that decisions concerning operatic form were pivotal in the early stages of libretto writing. Eric Crozier recalls:

> All I knew of him suggested that he thought first of each new composition in terms of forms, that these notions of form generally became clearer in his mind, and that it was prolonged consideration of the formal units and relationships among them that finally gave rise to the melodies and harmonies that would express them most vividly.[10]

Similarly, Montagu Slater recounts that the libretto was constructed with numbers, and what Britten intriguingly called 'half numbers', very much in mind:

> [The libretto consisted of] 'four-beat half-rhymed verse', as conventional as possible and not too regular ... Then, as feelings rise, the momentary situation will be crystallised in an aria in any measure, sometimes rhymed and sometimes half-rhymed. At some places too we come to what the composer calls 'a half number'. An example of this is in the lines first spoken by Hobson and later repeated by Ellen [Act I scene 1]:
>
> > I have to go from pub to pub,
> > Picking up parcels, standing about,
> > The journey back is late at night.

And so on to the end of the paragraph. This, as you will find, without quite breaking away from the frame of the recitative develops a little tune of its own.[11]

These 'half-numbers' may well be understood as *scena* – half recitative, half arioso passages of action – suggesting adoption of a specifically Verdian technique.

That Britten conceived his opera in terms of numbers is evident from the first outline of the *Grimes* scenario, written by Pears on the ship the *Axel Johnson* on their journey back to England from America in 1942.[12] Not only is the scenario sketched in acts, scenes and numbers, which suggests generic allusion to wider 18th- and 19th-century practice, but set pieces such as the final chorus and ensemble (Act I scene 3 no. 18) resonate more specifically with 19th-century Italian conventions of large-scale form. Set-piece designations are also made, including arias (for example Act II scene 2 no. 26 for Ellen) and duets (for example Act II scene 1 no. 21 for Peter and Ellen). Furthermore, Pears introduces generic titles at this stage: no. 14 'Landlord starts drinking song', no. 35 'Grimes Mad Scene' and no. 37 'Ellen's Lament'. Thus, from the first stages of planning it appears that Pears and Britten were guided by number opera precedents to structurally and dramatically shape the work.

The centrality of generic scenes in the early stages of the opera's genesis is underlined by Britten's draft scenario, also from 1942.[13] Here, the action includes: 'Magistrate scene' (Prologue), 'Pub scene' (Act I scene 2), 'Church scene' (Act II scene 2), 'Ellen Lament' (Act III scene 1) and 'P. G.'s Mad Scene' (Act III scene 2). In an alternative version he also mentions a 'terrific court scene' for Act II – later incorporated into the Prologue – and Peter's demise amongst the marshes (an ending not adopted here, but which acts as a precursor to the Madwoman's distress at the close of *Curlew River* (1964)). Britten also proposes a 'rumour chorus'. In light of the number of conspiratorial choruses in Verdi (the songs of the courtiers in *Rigoletto* for example), it is tempting to suggest that the Borough community may be interpreted in this light.

Perhaps the most significant document relating to Britten's conception of the work in numbers and generic scenes, however, is his annotated copy of the libretto typescript, dating from September 1942.[14] Not only is the libretto divided into numbers – recitative, aria, duet and so on – throughout, but Britten adds detailed notes about the structure and character of the music he was about to write. These annotations range from descriptions of mood – 'mostly conversational (mood, quiet at first, gradually becoming more & more lively as storm increases)'[15] – to orchestration – 'over single percussion instrument'[16] – to structural descriptions – '(a set aria) quiet for Ellen'.[17] Britten marks set-pieces as well as what may be termed *scena con arioso*: 'mostly recitative with small set numbers interspersed.'[18] This use of scena sections to convey action resonates with that found in Verdi's middle and late works, which consists of loosely structured musical settings of 'speech-like' dialogue in moments of dramatic action or, in Harold Powers' terms, the 'kinetic' passages that link and prompt set-pieces, or 'static' phases.[19] There is a strong suggestion, then, that generic allusion to number opera is accompanied by specific allusion to Verdian scena techniques.

Britten's working processes, which were characterized by mapping out set pieces and taking into account generic possibilities in a detailed scenario before proceeding to collaborate in the drafting of the libretto also resonate with Verdian practice.[20] The Italian composer's correspondence with his librettists frequently demonstrates a concern for generic precedent at the libretto stage and often betrays a tension between the demands of singers and his wish to push these established forms to the limits. Letters between Verdi and Ghislanzoni during the genesis of *Aïda* are a case in point.[21] Other signs of Italian opera thinking in the *Grimes* scenario include the 'lively "patter"' designation for the sextet in Act I, redolent of Rossini, and the vocal casting – 'heavy' for Balstrode, 'light' for the Nieces, 'rhetoric[al]' for Boles and so on.[22]

Analysis of the score of *Grimes* reveals various levels of absorption or transformation of smaller-scale Verdian elements, as well as allusions to wider signs of the Italian and number opera traditions. They fall into three broad categories: near-quotation; allusion (both specific and generic); and 'assimilation'. These are joined by varying degrees of transformation (often through layering), parody, and subversion. Furthermore, Roger Parker proposes a useful model of operatic intertextuality – with an emphasis on audience reception – which identifies, in his words, operatic 'moments [that stray] into one another, confounding our sense of their separate fictional worlds.'[23] This observation refers specifically to the infusion of elements from *Il trovatore* into *La traviata* (works composed by Verdi in close succession). It is also pertinent here, however, as it suggests that dramatic and musical parallels may be experienced simultaneously with the work itself. Although the Verdian resonances that form the basis of the following discussion are more distant (both in terms of chronology and authorship), I shall argue that a similar co-existence of musical moments is implied by *Grimes*.

Storm scenes and society

In Britten's opera the chorus is unified by the adversity of the weather. As the gale is sighted (Act I scene 1) the solidarity of the community is defined in relation to the raging elements. Later, as it howls outside 'The Boar' (Act I scene 2 no. 1), their discourse in the warm interior is interrupted by the opening and closing of the door, marked by orchestral gusts of wind and lashing waves. Indeed, Britten was drawn to *Grimes* in part because of its sense of place, in which the atmospheric conditions are an integral part.[24] Moreover, due to Peter's position in the storm outside before his first 'real time' entrance, he is aligned with the tempest, the unknown and dangerous; he is revealed as literally out of 'place'. His affiliation with the weather, paradoxically, underlines his human alienation.

The storm scenes in *Grimes* allude to two of Verdi's most affecting storms: the opening of *Otello* and Act III of *Rigoletto*. The tempestuous opening of *Otello* is marked by tense tremolando figures, fluttering arpeggios and chromaticism, musical signs referring to the wider tradition of 'mimetic' storm representation. Britten wrote admiringly of this scene, saying, 'No one has ever made the orchestra roar so terrifyingly as at the beginning of *Otello*.'[25] There is a suggestion, then, that it may have been a conscious model. The 'roar' that Britten refers to may be attributed to the bass drums, gong and suspended cymbals that Verdi includes, as well as the famous organ cluster of three notes a semitone apart that lasts 255 bars, creating a constant moan beneath the unfolding action. The storm both frames and interjects in the foreground of the scene and, importantly for this discussion, it prompts a diegetic prayer for the chorus as they fear for the life of Otello at sea.[26] Furthermore, the storm itself is centralized here. The presence of the storm outside with Otello acts as a sign of the ruler's strength – emphasizing the distance of his later fall – as well as a sign of his wildness, suggesting the underlying recklessness of his tempestuous inner life.

Britten's first storm scene (Act I scene 1) is marked by sinister tremolo chords, at which Balstrode announces, 'look, the storm cone!'[27] It is followed by silence, a sign of mortality suggesting the very real danger that the villagers face. Generic musical gestures suggesting the ferocity of the storm abound as in the Verdi example. Britten's allusion to the wider operatic tradition is underlined by the orchestration, including punctuated timpani rolls, snare drum, cymbal, the dark sonorities of trombones (traditionally associated with death) and wailing woodwind. More specifically, Edward Sackville-West highlights a direct link between Verdi's and Britten's approach to orchestration: 'the orchestra used in *Peter Grimes* is, by operatic standards of the past sixty years, modest; it is, in fact, the orchestra of the later Verdi operas'.[28]

Other, more specific allusions to Verdi are also evident. As in *Otello* the chorus sings its own prayer for safety against the elements. Although the text is not explicitly religious it conveys the sense of pleading with a higher, even numinous, power.[29] The community defines its identity through strophic, diegetic song. This, as in Verdi, serves both to set the scene of the opera – the cold sea and the adverse elements – and to define the societal backdrop to the drama to follow. (In turn, this invokes the earlier precedents of *opera seria*, where the chorus plays a strong structural role, frequently alternating between 'menace and entreaty'.)[30] However, while the communal pleading of Verdi's chorus is indicative of an apparently unshakable solidarity, in *Grimes* we have already seen the bickering eccentricity of the Borough residents in the 'flash-back' to the trial that acts as the prologue. In Britten's work, therefore, society achieves only a transitory unity. These internal tensions are also deeply pro-phetic: if the Borough residents are united against the elements, it is only one step further for them to be united against one of their number; group hatred turned inwards rather than outwards.

Moreover, unlike the Verdian examples, the scene is a concertato, a chorus with complex layering of voices. It is also a synthesis of set-piece chorus and a scena as the chorus alternates between verses of diegetic song and recita-tive accompaniment to the action, reaching a striking climax of convergence. Furthermore, the scene is supported by insistent ostinato patterns that gradu-ally build towards a climax in a Stravinskian manner, for example the shifting and cumulative repetitions that characterize Britten's beloved *Symphony of Psalms* and *Oedipus Rex*; just one example of the multiple influences that run alongside those of Verdi. Paradoxically, the regularity of this accompaniment contributes to the affect of the storm's power and irrationality. Moreover, the irony when the opening of *Otello* and Britten's scene are placed side-by-side is great. When Otello arrives with his ship he is greeted with adulation and a victory chorus. When Peter arrives with his boat he is met with silence and reproach. Nowhere is the contrast between hero and anti-hero so strongly sig-nalled through the implications of these Verdian allusions.

In Britten's second storm scene in Act I scene 2, *Rigoletto* is more strongly evoked. Verdi's Act IV no. 17 storm is fully integrated into the action, weaving through the scene, at times dominating and at times acting as a backdrop to the drama.[31] Musical descriptions of the storm include tremolo string chords and piccolo arpeggios suggesting far off thunder and lightening, a wordless chromatic chorus suggesting the moaning wind, and woodwind staccato semi-quavers suggesting heavy rain. The embedded set-piece trio for Maddalena, Sparafucile and Gilda (dressed as a male beggar) is interrupted by the opening and closing of the door to the room – the very same external-internal tension found in Britten's scene. The interjections of the storm shape the structure of the scene, which consists of: (1) scena and storm; (2) trio; (3) storm interlude; (4) recommenced trio with Gilda's stabbing; (5) long diminuendo of storm music; (6) Rigoletto's triumphant recitative; (7) the Duke's 'Donna è mobile'; (8) flashes of lightening to reveal Gilda; and (9) final duet and Gilda's death. Moreover, the storm appears to play an integral part in the plot, both reinforc-ing the atmosphere through pathetic fallacy, and revealing Gilda's dead body at the close with two flashes of lightening. In *Grimes* the scene is also shaped

by the storm as the roar of the chromatic descents, *sf* shock chords and tremolando cluster chords with cymbal crashes intervene into the prevailing action
each time the door is opened.

Furthermore, the elements, this time the sea itself, punctuate Britten's work
on a large-scale. The famous sea interludes – six spans of purely orchestral
music – appear to serve at least four functions within the opera. First, they
describe the visual landscape in order to set the scene for the following action,
particularly in the third interlude prior to the church scene in Act II. Second,
they suggest 'interior' landscapes by exploring the emotional state of characters, for example the fourth interlude that describes the boy's suffering. Third,
they act as narrative sections, especially the fourth interlude. Fourth, they integrate non-representational processes into the work. As Christopher Morris
suggests, the interludes are poised between 'description' and 'absolute' motivic
working.[32] The headings that Britten added to the libretto sketch to describe
five of the sections underline his understanding of their multiple functions: (1)
'everyday grey seascape'; (2) 'storm at its height'; (3) marked prelude: 'sunny,
sparkling music' leading to the following church scene; (4) 'Boy's suffering
passacaglia'; (5) marked introduction: 'Summer night, seascape quiet'.

Aligning Britten's interludes with Verdi's instrumental music suggests
some generic allusions. Considering the instrumental music in Verdian opera,
David Kimbell suggests that orchestral sections – interludes as well as battles,
storms, dances – create the 'social frame'[33] of opera. Furthermore, they are
intimately linked with stagecraft, facilitating scene changes and providing visual spectacle and even accompanying pantomime. The emotions of the characters are also frequently implied by instrumental means. Such scene setting
is clearly suggested by the more pictorial of Britten's descriptions. Moreover,
the 'Boy's suffering passacaglia' suggests the musical exploration of an interior state. While Britten's orchestral passages frequently allude to Verdian uses
of the *intermezzo*, however, they also allude to Wagnerian interludes through
their denser play of motives. As well as containing 'themes of reminiscence',[34]
a typically Verdian use of 'obvious' motives to link dramatic action and to mark
character, Britten uses the interludes to link sections thematically, involving a
technique closer to leitmotiv and the 'art of transition'.

Laughter and vendetta choruses

Conspirators play a central role in a number of Verdian operas, including
Rigoletto and *Un ballo in maschera*. In the former, the cries of the conspirators
are both jocular and macabre; 'zitti, zitti moviamo a vendetta' ('silently, silently,
our movement to revenge')[35] becomes in Julian Budden's terms a 'gleeful
chorus'[36] and they recount their adventures to the Duke in Act II – 'scurrendo

uniti remoto vida' ('at night in the secret and undetected')[37] – with jocular cruelty. In *Un ballo* this mixture is emphasized still further in the Act II laughing chorus as the conspirators discover the unsuspecting Renato with his disguised wife. In contrast with more overtly threatening cries of vengeance, such as the chorus reaction to Alfredo's insult to Violetta in Act II of *La traviata*, Verdi often brings laughter into moments of menace, tracing a thin line between light-hearted fun and cruel mockery.

In *Grimes* too, the Borough community – themselves conspirators against Peter – laugh. In Act II scene 1 their *concertato* culminates in a cruel laughing chorus. This leads to the search for Peter in his hut and an intense march scene, 'Now is gossip put on trial',[38] as they mercilessly hunt down their victim. Even more cruelly, after the strains of the final dance in the Moot Hall fade away in Act III scene 1, a concertato again ensues involving a choral curse ('our curse shall fall on this evil day')[39] and cruel bursts of laughter before a ritual naming of their victim. These moments mark the trajectory of the tragedy, each time increasing in violence. By using laughter as a climax in two choruses, Britten invokes the Verdian models, but makes them even harsher. Indeed, this laughter with its powerful homophony is uttered with the diction of the emotive vendetta in *La traviata*. Thus in *Grimes*, laughter is 'elevated' almost to the level of a curse, a sign of ultimate contempt.

By the time the townspeople reach Peter's hut their hate-speech is such that we may imagine that they are close to killing Peter themselves in a feverish hunt to the death.[40] Britten thus transforms and exaggerates the ferocity of the conspirator genre, giving it a new persecutory intensity. Moving beyond the passion even of Verdi's military choruses, this denotes a show of force of a much more personal and venomous kind. It is anger directed inwards to a member of their community, rather than outwards. As E. M. Forster notes, 'Crabbe's Peter is an embodiment of the dark side of an uncaring and morally enfeebled society, whereas Britten's is the victim of that society and a symbol of its oppression.'[41]

Peter's mad scene

With the cries of the chorus we return once again to the mad scene. Peter is abandoned and rapidly losing his sanity. Like many Verdian *heroines*, he is left reeling, his thoughts a jumbled recollection of musical memories, misremembered fragments of his operatic past. There are some similarities between this moment and mad scenes for Macbeth and Otello, but we will focus first on its resonances with Donizetti's *Lucia di Lammermoor*.

The Act III aria for Lucia in Donizetti's *Lucia* is a quintessential example of the mad scene genre, which stretches back through the roles of Amina in

La sonnambula, Imogen in *Il pirata*, Elvira in *I puritani*, Linda in *Linda di Chamounix* and Anna in *Anna Bolena*.[42] That Britten knew the opera is clear from his article about E. M. Forster's portrayal of the piece in his novel *Where Angels Fear to Tread*.[43] The scene, as many others, involves copious amounts of coloratura between Lucia's stanzas, abrupt changes of tempo, sudden tonal swerves and unaccompanied song, which have been interpreted as the flights of fancy of a disturbed mind, either denoting a need for liberation[44] or of attaining it through music.[45] In *Lucia* the structure of the aria is clear, but the utterance is fragmented, recalling Lucia's wedding theme and her love theme as well as describing the horrors of the murder she has just committed. Her state of delusion is underlined by her attentive reaction to the many piccolo flurries, symbolizing birdsong, that punctuate the aria.

Peter's mad scene has a far looser structure, consisting of arioso-like utterance, swathes of which are unaccompanied. Yet, like the mad scenes in *A Midsummer Night's Dream* (1960) and *Curlew River*, it resonates with the musicalizations of madness described above. The fluidity of Peter's scene accentuates the 'stream of consciousness' nature of his musings and, like Lucia, he is haunted by themes he has heard previously, including fragments of the trial scene and 'Old Joe has gone fishing'. In an even more exaggerated way, however, his diction veers from tenderness to biting hatred, breaking the bounds of the form. And crucially, unlike the courtiers in *Lucia*, the chorus does not act as a constraining voice at the end of the aria, but sends Peter further into madness: suggesting perhaps that it is society that is the cause of his mental disturbance. Intriguingly, he is also aligned with hysterical characteristics: Britten describes him as 'demented, hysterical' in the draft scenario of 1944.

This provokes the question: what is Peter striving for? If Lucia's song highlights a desperate attempt to wrest free from the shackles of social convention and gender stereotypes, is Peter, too, rebelling against society in this sense? Indeed, he appears to be rebelling on many levels: he is protesting against the corruption and cruelty of his community, he protests against his own nature in a vicious tussle between love and hate, and he may even be seen to be protesting against his own gender stereotype. If *Grimes* is understood as an allegory of the homosexual condition, Peter is stepping into Lucia's role of the marginalized in society, a 20th-century version of the angst over sexuality.

If Peter takes a feminized role here, he also musically recalls the downfall of Macbeth and Otello, both of whom are haunted by their psyche. Macbeth's 'sword scene' in Act II displays his deteriorating mental state as he attempts to deal with the murder he has just committed, and Otello loses his wits before

Flauto.

Fl. II or Pic.

(143)

Side drum.

(143)

This composition was written by a lad of 12 years, in nine days: written in his very few spare moments snatched from the hourly routine of his "Prep" school (in the very early mornings for instance). He has only an elementary knowledge of harmony. Has had no instruction of any kind in Orchestration or counterpoint, a little in form. It is quite an original copy; no piano score written before. We thought it worth sending, if only for advice

9104001

A L

1 Britten, 'Ouverture', front page

2 Britten, *Poème* no. 4, first page

3 Britten, *Poème* no. 5, first page

4 Britten and Shostakovich. The photograph was probably taken during
the Festival of British Music in Moscow, March 1963.

ACT II.

Scene III.

The Churchyard ~~tomb, indication of church, bells children~~ *The lights fade in on the churchyard — with table tomb in indication of cloud*
~~skip on. Mrs. Grose and Governess follow immediately.~~
~~Children sit on tomb and are deep in each other.~~

Mrs. Grose.   Oh Miss, it is a bright morning to be sure.

Governess.   (absently) Yes.

Mrs. Grose.   Bright as the Sunday morning bells. I love the sound.

Governess.   Yes.

Mrs. Grose.   And what a pretty sight. It does me good to see them so
sweet together.

Governess.   Yes.

Mrs. Grose.   Come Miss, don't worry. It will pass I'm sure, they're so
~~happy with you, you're so good to them — we all love you Miss.~~

Governess.   Dear Good Mrs. Grose.- - - They are <u>not</u> playing, they are
~~talking of them — of Quint, and of Jessel. They are~~ talking honors.
~~horrors.~~

Mrs. Grose.   Oh! never.

Governess.   Why are they so charming? Why so unnaturally good? ~~Why do~~
~~they never speak~~ of those who have gone? I tell you they
are not with us, ~~they are not mine, not yours, they are his~~
~~and hers.~~ *but with the others.*

Mrs. Grose.   With Quint and that woman?

Governess.   With Quint and that woman.

Mrs. Grose.   But what could these ~~scoundrels~~ do?

Governess.   Do. They can destroy them.

<u>(B)</u>   ~~But you not feel them ... there,~~
~~everywhere ... had told them ... the Day ... Darkness.~~

~~Here Miles and Flora look up and ... and smile — Mrs. Grose is~~
Mrs. Grose is quick to feel that the children should not hear themselves talked about,
though Governess is almost too far gone to care, Mrs. Grose
bustles towards them.

Mrs. Grose.   Come — it is time we went in. Come to church, my dear, it
will do you good. Flora! Miles! Come along, dears!

D1

6 Britten's revisions to the libretto draft for *The Turn of the Screw*

Ⓐ

Chor 〕 (chanting) O sing unto them a new song: let the
rule 〕
(unseen) congregation praise Him.

O ye works & days: bless ye the Lord
(walking in — little choir-boys)
O ye rivers & seas & lakes; bless ye the Lord
O Amnis, axis, caulis, collis, clunis, crinis, fascis follis,
bless ye the Lord: praise Him & magnify Him for ever.

The children settle themselves in the tomb, as the Gov. & Mrs G
enter.

Mrs G. O miss - bright morning as h sun.
Gov (absently) Yes.
Chor 〕 O ye fowls of... & trees: praise Him
rule 〕
Mrs G: Bright on the Sunday morning bells. How I love the sound.
Gov: Yes
Chor 〕 O ye hills & towns : praise Him
rule 〕
Mrs G And the dear children. How sweet they are together.
Gov Yes:
Chor: 〕 O ye pastures & words: Praise Him.
rule: 〕 O ye frosts & fallen leaves; praise Him
O ye dragons & snakes, worms & feathered fowl: rejoice The Lord
Mrs G. Come Miss, don't worry. It will pass. I'm sure; they're so happy
with you. You're so good to them; We all love you, Miss.

                                                   P.T.O. Ⓕ

7 Britten's revisions to the libretto draft for *The Turn of the Screw*

Owen Wingrave · Henry James · Benjamin Britten · Piramont · David Myerscough Jones. 1969.

8 Set design by David Myerscough-Jones for the original television production of *Owen Wingrave*

the Venetian ambassadors, cruelly encouraged by Iago. These instances of madness, however, are both linked with guilt. It is because they have killed or plan to kill that they suffer from persecutory delusions. This brings into question Peter's culpability – is he persecuted by shame over his part in the previous deaths or by the fact that he was unable to 'save' the lives of the children in his care? This ambiguity is heightened in the mad scene as we are left with a fallen hero – a fallen hero who equally may or may not be to blame for his demise.

Placing scenes from *Grimes* alongside moments from Verdian opera, thus, not only illuminates the pervasiveness of this strand of influence on Britten's musical thought, but sets off fruitful resonances and reverberations that inform interpretation of the work, bringing to the fore the central issues of Peter's societal persecution, sexuality and guilt. We find further complex layers of resonance, here, ranging from generic allusion to the number opera tradition, Italian 19th-century opera and Verdian opera in general, to specific references to Verdi's works and direct modelling. Yet, it is what Britten does to challenge, deviate from and transform his allusions that tell most about his compositional individuality. In short, Britten's glances towards Verdian practice are perhaps most revealing when they challenge 'conventions' within the conventions themselves.

Notes

1 Desmond Shawe-Taylor, '*Peter Grimes*: A Review of the First Performance', in *Benjamin Britten: Peter Grimes*, ed. Philip Brett (Cambridge: Cambridge University Press, 1983), pp. 153–8 at p. 154.

2 Benjamin Britten, 'Peter Grimes' (1945), in *PKBM*, pp. 49–51 at p. 50.

3 See Michael Kennedy, *Master Musicians: Britten* (Oxford: Oxford University Press, 2001), p. 159; and Donald Mitchell, 'Peter Grimes: Fifty Years On', in *The Making of Peter Grimes: Essays and Studies*, ed. Paul Banks (Woodbridge: Boydell Press, 2000), pp. 125–65 at p. 151.

4 See Scott L. Balthazar, 'The Forms of Set Pieces', in *The Cambridge Companion to Verdi* (Cambridge: Cambridge University Press, 2004), pp. 49–68.

5 Christopher Headington, *Peter Pears: A Biography* (London: Faber, 1992), p. 125.

6 Benjamin Britten, 'Verdi – A Symposium' (1951), in *PKBM*, pp. 102–3 at p. 102.

7 Benjamin Britten, 'Mapreading' (1969) in *PKBM*, pp. 321–9 at p. 328.

8 Britten, 'Peter Grimes', p. 50.

9 Benjamin Britten, 'Britten Talks to Edmund Tracey' (1966), in *PKBM*, pp. 292–9 at p. 293.

10 *HCBB*, p. 201.

11 Montagu Slater, 'The Story of the Opera', in *Peter Grimes*, ed. Eric Crozier, Sadler's Wells Opera Books no. 3 (London: Bodley Head, 1946), pp. 15–26 at p. 20.

12 All libretto material referred to is held at the BPF. Termed L5 in Paul Banks, 'Bibliographic Notes and Narratives', in *The Making of Peter Grimes: Essays and Studies,* ed. Banks, pp. 167–228 at p. 175. I have retained Pears's spellings from his hasty sketch.

13 Draft scenario. Termed L6 in *ibid.*, p. 175.

14 Libretto typescript, held at the BPF. Termed L15 in *ibid.*, p. 177.

15 Libretto typescript (L15), p. 17.

16 *Ibid.*, p. 22.

17 *Ibid.*, p. 36.

18 *Ibid.*, p. 12.

19 Harold Powers, 'Making *Macbeth* Musicabile', in *Verdi: Macbeth*, ed. Nicholas John, English National Opera Guide 41 (London: John Calder, 1990), pp. 13–36 at p. 21.

20 Luke Jensen, 'An Introduction to Verdi's Working Methods', in *The Cambridge Companion to Verdi*, pp. 257–68 at p. 262. 'The next stage [in the composition of *Aïda*] ... was a more extended prose libretto of thirty-seven pages in Verdi's own hand. Indicated in the margin were the ways in which each passage was to be set – "lirico", "cantabile", "concertato", "recitativo", and so on.' Julian Budden, *The Operas of Verdi* (Oxford: Clarendon Press, 2002), vol. 3, p. 171.

21 Verdi to Ghislanzioni (16 October 1870): 'Develop this situation [duet for Amneris and Radamés Act IV] then as you think best, and let it be well developed, and have the characters say what they must without concerning yourself in the least about the musical form ... Of course if you send me a recitative from beginning to end, I would be unable to create rhythmic music, but if you begin directly with some rhythm and continue it until the end I will not complain at all. Just perhaps it should be changed so as to make a little cabalettina at the end.' Philip Gossett, 'Verdi, Ghislanzioni, and *Aïda*: The Uses of Convention', *Critical Enquiry* 1/2 (1974), pp. 291–334 at p. 313.

22 These quotes were taken from the libretto typescript of 1942 (see n. 14 above).

23 Roger Parker, *Remaking the Song: Operatic Visions and Revisions from Handel to Berio* (Berkeley: University of California Press, 2006), p. 13.

24 'For most of my life I have lived closely in touch with the sea. My parent's house in Lowestoft directly faced the sea, and my life as a child was coloured by fierce storms that sometimes drove ships on the coast and ate away whole stretches of neighbouring cliffs. In writing *Peter Grimes*, I wanted to express my awareness of the perpetual struggle of men and women whose livelihood depends on the sea – difficult though it is to treat such a universal subject in theatrical form.' Britten, 'Peter Grimes', p. 50.

25 Britten, 'Verdi – A Symposium', p. 102.

26 Verdi, *Otello*, trans. Walter Ducloux (New York: G. Schirmer, 1963), p. 13.

27 Britten, *Peter Grimes*, op. 33 (London: Boosey & Hawkes, 2003), p. 65.

28 Edward Sackville-West, 'The Musical and Dramatic Structure', in *Peter Grimes*, ed. Crozier, p. 30.

29 Verdi, *Otello*, p. 13.

30 Ivan Nagel, *Autonomy and Mercy: Reflections on Mozart's Operas*, trans. Marion Faber and Ivan Nagel (Cambridge, MA: Harvard University Press, 1991), p. 3.

31 Verdi, *Rigoletto*, trans. Ruth and Thomas Martin (New York, G. Schirmer, 1961), p. 195.

32 See Christopher Morris, *Reading Opera Between the Lines: Orchestral Interludes and Musical Meaning from Wagner to Berg* (Cambridge: Cambridge University Press, 2002). The argument is first mapped out on pp. 5–6.

33 David Kimbell, 'Instrumental Music in Verdi's Operas', *The Cambridge Companion to Verdi*, pp. 154–68 at p. 154.

34 Joseph Kerman, 'Verdi's Use of Recurring Themes', in *Studies in Music History*, ed. Harold Powers (Princeton: Princeton University Press, 1968), pp. 495–510. (This term is defined/discussed throughout the article, but first introduced on p. 496.)

35 Verdi, *Rigoletto*, p. 108.

36 Budden, *The Operas of Verdi*, vol. 1, p. 477.

37 Verdi, *Rigoletto*, p. 120.

38 Britten, *Peter Grimes*, p. 247.

39 *Ibid.*, p. 341.

40 See Philip Rupprecht, *Britten's Musical Language* (Cambridge: Cambridge University Press, 2001), pp. 52–62.

41 E. M. Forster, 'Two Essays on Crabbe' (given at the Aldeburgh Festival in 1948), *Benjamin Britten: Peter Grimes*, pp. 1–21 at p. 2.

42 Jonas Barish, 'Madness, Hallucination, and Sleepwalking', in *Verdi's Macbeth: A Sourcebook*, ed. David Rosen and Andrew Porter (Cambridge: Cambridge University Press, 1984), pp. 149–55 at p. 151.

43 Benjamin Britten, 'Some Notes on Forster and Music' (1969), in *PKBM*, pp. 316–20 at p. 317.

44 Catherine Clément, *Opera, or the Undoing of Women*, trans. Betsy Wing (New York: I. B. Tauris Publishers, 1997), p. 88.

45 Susan McClary, 'Excess and Frame: The Musical Representation of Mad Women', in her *Feminine Endings: Music, Gender & Sexuality* (Minneapolis: University of Minnesota Press, 2002), pp. 80–111 at p. 84.

7 Dramatic Invention in Myfanwy Piper's Libretto for *Owen Wingrave*

Frances Spalding

After the success of *The Turn of the Screw* (1954), almost 15 years passed before its librettist, Myfanwy Piper, again actively collaborated with Britten. Despite this lengthy gap in time, she never doubted that such an opportunity would arise, for Britten had indicated that he wanted to repeat their endeavour. He turned to her in 1967, when the BBC commissioned an opera specifically for television and which was sold in advance to twelve other international companies for simultaneous transmission.[1] With this opportunity to reach a very wide audience, he needed a story that would be, in his own words, 'both personal and powerful' and which would suit the medium of television.[2] He had been impressed by Henry James's *Owen Wingrave* when he first read it in 1954. There is in the Red House at Aldeburgh a complete set of James, but in addition Britten acquired volume 9 of Leon Edel's collected edition of Henry James, published 1962, and this appears to have been his working copy for *Owen Wingrave*. It is widely recognized that the tale became the vehicle through which he voiced his deeply held commitment to pacifism and his hatred of war,[3] beliefs exacerbated at this time by the invasion of Czechoslovakia and the continuation of the Vietnam War.[4] The story also offers a challenge to the conventions and traditions of militarism, especially those rooted in dynasties.

Britten first mentioned *Owen Wingrave* to his librettist on a visit to Fawley Bottom, the Pipers' home in Buckinghamshire. Piper not only recollected that he had spoken of it before, while writing his *War Requiem* (1961–2), but she also immediately understood its significance for him, for she had read all James's stories. Asked if she would do the libretto, her response was straightforward: 'I said yes. And that was it.'[5]

Behind *Owen Wingrave* lies the complicated history of Britten's uneasy relationship with television. It is sufficient here to mention that in 1952, having reluctantly sanctioned the American NBC Opera Company's televised version of *Billy Budd* (1950–1), which reduced the four-act three-hour opera to a 90-minute production, Britten thought it 'badly and desperately cut',[6] and was left profoundly suspicious of the medium. Things improved in 1960, when Peter Morley obtained Britten's agreement to an Associated-Rediffusion televised production of *The Turn of the Screw*.[7] This was the first full-length opera by Britten televised in Britain and also the first full-length opera ever seen on Independent Television. As the suitability of opera for television was thought highly controversial, a publicity brochure was produced carrying a synopsis and comments by those responsible for the opera. All felt a need to be persuasive, none more so than Piper. 'The work is a combination of strangeness and intimacy,' she writes of the *Screw*, 'and so for television, at its best in conveying both these, an obviously suitable subject. What surprises and delights is that ... the producer has made it seem as though it were specially created for the medium. ... It makes me realise [she concludes] how much can be done with the exuberant possibilities of television when they are used with tact and sensibility.'[8]

Two further productions for television were the 1966 *Billy Budd*, directed by Basil Coleman, and the 1969 performance of *Peter Grimes* (1945), directed by Brian Large in collaboration with Joan Cross. To avoid the two-studio system used in the first of these, and which separated the orchestra from the singers, Britten had persuaded John Culshaw, Head of Music Programmes at the BBC, that *Peter Grimes* should be filmed at the recently converted Snape Maltings. This lost him Coleman as the director, but it enabled Britten to be closely involved with the filming. It left him convinced that television opera had to retain a musical intensity that never lets up. At a late stage in the making of *Owen Wingrave*, which was directed by Brian Large and Colin Graham, he told Donald Mitchell: 'the drive forward of the music, the singing of the tunes, the elaboration of the ensembles, must never be forgotten'.[9] He also admitted that at this late stage he and Piper had added 'arias galore'.[10]

Britten's insistence on collaboration in the making of opera makes it difficult to be certain who invented what. But there is no doubt that in *Owen Wingrave*, as in *The Turn of the Screw*, certain crucial ideas for the dramatic development came from Piper. She herself has observed that all three libretti which she wrote for Britten were based on sophisticated texts, 'highly developed literary works' which, she observes, 'depend on the poetic build-up of atmosphere and of mental apprehensions, on accumulated moments of word-filled suspense, on evocations of the authors' belief in the active magic of places to give force to the stories that they tell.'[11] Though all three texts had presented difficulties, none, she claimed, was due to the richness of the original. 'The richness was, rather, a help.'[12] The chief difference between James's *Owen Wingrave* and his *Turn of the Screw* is that the former is much shorter. If compression remained at the heart of her enterprise as librettist, Piper also recognized that with *Owen Wingrave* there was more need to invent, to search for words and incidents that would give Britten the vehicle for his musical ideas and which would unfold, with a sure-footed inevitability, the drama of the tale.

She soon became aware, if she did not know of it at the start, as to how Henry James had arrived at his ideas for *Owen Wingrave*. In Kensington Gardens one summer afternoon, a 'tall, quiet slim studious young man' had sat near him and 'settled to a book with immediate gravity'.[13] Though James had no notion of how he would use this figure, the words 'Dramatize it, dramatize it!' suddenly rang in his ears. Then, in March 1892, he read Marcelin Marbot's memoirs of the Napoleonic wars. He became fascinated with the notion of hereditary military valour, and the way in which, alongside the tradition of personal bravery and honour, ran awareness of the ugliness, blood and carnage involved. This led to his conception of a different act of bravery: military recusancy and sacrifice; and out of this grew *Owen Wingrave*, which appeared in the Christmas number of the *Graphic* in 1892, was first published in book form in 1893, and in 1907 was transmuted into James's one-act play, *The Saloon*. In the course of this development, as Piper astutely observed, 'The peaceful young man in the twopenny chair took on the battle of all conscientious objectors against the pressure of righteous aggression.'[14]

Soon after work on this opera began, Britten observed that something was needed to precipitate Owen's outburst. At the start of James's story, Owen's mind is already made up and he visits Coyle, the tutor who is preparing him for Sandhurst, to tell him of his decision to withdraw from a military career. Britten wanted, instead, to begin with a lesson. Piper recollects him saying: 'I think it is important to establish the crammer's atmosphere before we break it up, and besides, I've thought of a nice way to do it musically!'[15] She therefore invented the scene in Coyle's Academy. In order to do this, she read widely, turning, as James had done, to General Marbot's memoirs, also going to the London Library for Clausewitz's three-volume *On War*, a systematic philosophical examination of war which had far-reaching influence on Western military thinking. Useful, too, was *The Story of a Soldier's Life*, a two-volume memoir by Field-Marshal Viscount Wolseley, whose ancestral inheritance was similar to Owen's. In general, Piper immersed herself in tales of the Napoleonic wars and of the Indian Mutiny. This reading not only gave her a better understanding of the vainglorious militarism of the Wingrave family and coloured the language that her characters use, but it also provided her with useful quotations. One example is a letter from Wellington to Lady Shelley which Piper copied into one of her notebooks:

> I hope to God I have fought my last battle. It's a bad thing to be always fighting. While in the thick of it I am too much occupied to feel

anything; but it is wretched just after. It is quite impossible to think of glory. ... I am wretched even in the moment of victory, and, I always say that next to a battle lost the greatest misery is a battle gained.[16]

This served her well in Act I scene 1. Here Letchmere, Owen's friend and fellow student, excited by Coyle's instruction on the Battle of Austerlitz, enthusiastically embraces 'the glorious luck of battle'. This moves Owen to condemn the military conception of 'glory' and to damn Hannibal, Caesar, Marlborough and Napoleon as 'Ruffians all'. 'And Wellington?' asks Coyle. Owen replies: 'Wellington, for all his warlike glory, remember what he said: "Next to a battle lost the greatest misery is a battle gained."' Elsewhere in the libretto, there is ample evidence of Piper's extensive reading: military metaphors come readily to hand and many of the words used resonate with additional layers of meaning and dramatic irony.

There were other places, aside from the opening scene, where Piper had to expand on James's story, which lacks the same build up of suspense and psychological ambiguity as *The Turn of the Screw*. James, for instance, gives no description of Owen's arrival and reception at his family's ancestral home Paramore. This is because his story is entirely told from Coyle's standpoint, and, in James's version, it is only a couple of weeks later, when Coyle and his wife, at Miss Wingrave's invitation, descend on Paramore that the reader learns that Owen looks five years older. '"I couldn't imagine that," said Mr Coyle, 'nor that the character of the crisis here would be quite so perceptible."' In her libretto Piper decided to invent the drama that lay behind that crisis. In the opera, as Owen approaches the house, his aunt (Miss Wingrave), Kate (his girlfriend) and her mother Mrs Julian, both dependents on the Wingraves, deliberately withdraw, for in their eyes Owen deserves no hero's welcome and must instead listen to the house and speak first to his ancestors, in the form of the family portraits. He therefore enters a silent house and, drawing on his military training, reflects: 'Good soldiers in a mist, we're told, keep silence – no friendly murmurs, no scream of pain betray their position to the enemy! How strange! Here in my own house I stand an enemy.'

Further glimpses into Piper's working methods and the progress of her libretto can be found in her notebooks. 'What is the military grace?' she queries, apropos the scene at the dinner table. She scans James's text carefully for telling words and phrases. The recurrence of 'scruples' gave her the word which becomes the focus of the scornful climax directed at Owen in the dinner scene, where, as before with the 'How dare you!' passage, the Wingraves and Julians unite in their stand against Owen and freeze into identical attitudes. 'One knows that there are people like these,' Piper wrote of the Wingraves, 'de-humanized by their own strict and immovable code.'[17] At the same time, she was aware that James had manipulated them in such a way that they were in danger of becoming caricatures. For this reason, as others have observed, she filled out the characters of Owen's military tutor, Spencer Coyle and his wife, giving to Mrs Coyle, especially, a depth of feeling that offers the necessary humane relief.

Her notebooks show her thinking about Kate and what factors may have shaped her character. 'Kate,' she writes. 'She has her own family circle – I mean her own ghosts.'[18] Yet in the opera she remains an unsatisfactory character, and she was, as Piper admitted, a source of argument between herself and Britten, as Britten loathed Kate so much he did not want to make her sympathetic. But to offset her obnoxious scorn of Owen, and to suggest the girl with whom Owen first fell in love, Piper devised a conversation between Kate and Owen in which they share memories of their childhood and exchange remembered images. She was trying to give Owen and Kate a life beyond soldiering and cowardice, a moment of possibility in which another sort of life is glimpsed. They reminisce together in the passage 'All our lives we've shared the same strange life / Here in this brave, old house / These silent rooms / the mist on the grass / owls in the dark / the broken branches in the park / the dry click-click of antlers', the final detail obtained from a neighbour's description of stags fighting in Stonor Park. Piper also tried to persuade Janet Baker, who sang Kate and never overcame her dislike of her, that she was a victim of circumstances. Even so, the young woman came across as 'bigoted, unimaginative and unsympathetic, black against Owen's white', as Piper herself has acknowledged.[19]

After a period of gestation, she began work on the libretto in March 1968, letting it take the form, for the most part, of heightened prose. It has to be remembered that, as with *The Turn of the Screw*, such work had to be fitted in between what Piper referred to in one letter to Britten as 'the fish and the laundry'.[20] Famous for her cooking, she fed many guests; among those who lunched at Fawley Bottom that year were Jennie Lee, the first Minister for the Arts. Geoffrey Jellicoe, the landscape designer, once carried a glass of sherry to Piper as she sat in the car outside the Woodstock Hotel in Oxford, composing.[21] Her first draft of *Owen Wingrave*, she admitted to Britten, was 'a depressing mixture of styles' and very verbose 'but', she adds, 'I feel that it is not right to try to prune and shape it now as I might prune away just the bit that you might find suggestive or even inspiring.'[22] She was aware, at this stage, that her approach was instinctively to think in terms of theatre, but before long both began to give more thought to the medium of television. BBC 2, though it had begun broadcasting on 21 April 1964, could not be obtained at Fawley

Bottom. This may explain why Piper found depressing the few things she had seen. But she was not averse to the medium, and now watched it with interest in order to discern its possibilities. Britten, on the other hand, did not own a television until 1973, when Decca gave him one for his 60th birthday. Piper tried to keep him up to speed. 'The popular programmes, the news and sport are very well done', she wrote: 'the awful mess are those that try to be a bit highbrow but still keep the million viewers.'[23]

Nevertheless both took the medium very seriously. Their first discussions, Piper claims, dwelt upon the visual, rather than the verbal presentation of dramatic points in this work,[24] and in one of her notebooks she lists 'Strong visual images in the actual story.' The opera begins with an emphasis on the visual, the camera focussing, one by one, on ten family portraits, before ending with Owen who appears in the scheme of things like an eleventh portrait. In addition, four orchestral interludes were devised, all with visual matter in mind. In the first, regimental banners 'wave brilliantly'. In the second, Owen reads aloud an extract from Shelley's *Queen Mab*, book IV, concerning the futility of war, while the screen shows a sequence of faded and tattered flags. A third interlude works as a transition from the London scenes to Paramore, the ancestral home, while the fourth allowed for preparation of the dinner scene, with servants silently bringing in silver and glass and lighting candles.

Wanting to make full use of the resources available, Piper and Britten took advice from those who had a technical knowledge of television. It was agreed that when the ghosts of the Wingrave boy and his father appear the colour film would revert to black and white, or rather a kind of sepia effect, which conveyed a sense of unreality and of another age. However, Piper became irritated by what she privately called the 'built-in TV mind'.[25] Publicly, in her essay for David Herbert, 'Writing for Britten', she regretted the mystique associated with this relatively new medium created by a closed circle of experts. She realized how those in television were uncertain of their audience, and, because of this, there was 'a tendency to overdo things, to underline them, so that the subtleties of which the medium is capable can easily be thrown away in the interest of making something, already perfectly clear, obvious.' Television, she concluded, was 'a mixture of inventiveness and crudity'.[26] At the Maltings, where *Owen Wingrave* was filmed, when it was time to do the ghost scene, they found a man busily spraying cobwebs onto every surface of the set, because in television at that time, 'Ghosts meant Cobwebs'.[27]

Both composer and librettist were keen to go beyond what could be achieved in a theatre and do things that could only be done with television or film. The use of close-up in order to convey interior thought has become a television cliché, but it has to be admitted that it works well in Act I scene 7, the dinner party scene, where general conversation is intercut with a moment of inner reflection and the tension between the spoken and the unspoken is at its height. The camera, by means of close-up, reinforces the change of mood in the music by shutting out the other characters as it isolates each head in turn. It is an example of Piper's bold adaption and her acute sensitivity to Britten's needs. Overall, effects were kept simple, as Britten was aware that this television opera would later be transferred to the stage. Nevertheless, the dinner party scene is more effective on film than in the theatre.

Piper had a more elaborate idea for the double scene in Act I, which was intended to expose a dichotomy. While Owen reads in the park – not Goethe's poems, as in James, but Shelley's 'Queen Mab' (as Piper realized, it is politically exactly what a young man like Owen would be reading) – Coyle goes to see Miss Wingrave in her London lodgings nearby to inform her of her nephew's decision. Piper wanted this split scene to be united by a single vision of horse guards, riding past in their red uniforms. Both Owen and Miss Wingrave were to be exhilarated by the sight, but after a few moments Owen transforms the vision in his imagination into a chaos of falling cavalrymen and horses. In retrospect, Piper admitted: 'it was a typical amateur's idea, over-elaborate and impractical'.[28] The television crew made no attempt to respond to this idea until the last minute and then fruitless hours were spent looking at film sequences of battlefields in Aldeburgh cinema, all, in Piper's recollection, on the wrong scale. Eventually the Royal Military Police Mounted Troop were filmed in black and white at Aldershot and a dim section was spliced into the final film. But the scene ends with Miss Wingrave's eye caught not by a vision of soldiers riding by, but by a conventional military print hanging on the wall.

In August 1968 Piper took her notebooks to Garn Fawr, a tiny cottage with a slurry roof, half buried into the hillside at Strumble Head, near Fishguard in Pembrokeshire. It had no amenities other than a breathtaking view, southwards down across fields and pastures to the rocky coastline and the sea's boundless horizon. Here not a sound can be heard other than the wind and birds. As she told Britten:

> Lovely peaceful conditions for working; no telephone, no people, not even children this time ... I'm finding everyday that problems in O.W. solve themselves. I don't mean the final expression of them because that is fluid of course – but little cross-currents, relationships – echoes – in particular I find a very strong identification of Owen and the murdered boy has taken over and left me feeling much happier about the Ghost's Story and the way to use it.[29]

As Claire Seymour has pointed out, the legend of the Wingrave Boy was originally intended to emerge in the course of a dialogue between Coyle and Owen.[30] But it appears that in Pembrokeshire Piper conceived of it as a ballad sung by the narrator at the start of Act II. 'I remember it took me ages to do,' she told Roderic Dunnett, 'ages and ages, and I worked on it a lot in the cottage in Wales, the whole of that ballad, the Wingrave Boy ballad'.[31] The tune returns at the end of the opera, when the final verse is sung, its final line echoing that in James's story.

Right up to December of that year Piper was still reading and rereading *Owen Wingrave*, together with the play *The Saloon*, and coming to new conclusions, finding in the latter a useful conversation between Coyle and Wingrave, as well as the description of the saloon, and Kate's red dress which she thought would work well on colour television. Aware that this play had been rejected by the Stage Society on Bernard Shaw's advice, owing to its abrupt ending and the fact that Owen's death means his noble intentions go unrewarded,[32] Piper remained adamant that more optimism would have been aesthetically wrong, unsuited to the psychology of the family. She was firm, too, in her belief that Owen's death does not invalidate the message of the tale. The hymn of peace in Act II scene 1, which she wrote for Owen, acts as a kind of coda to Britten's *War Requiem*. It is evident from the many drafts that it too caused much work before it was structured, as Arnold Whittall observes, like a psalm or canticle.[33] When set to Britten's music, it transcends conflict with a moment of great beauty that becomes the opera's climax.

In February 1970 at the Red House, Britten played through the whole of *Owen Wingrave* to Piper and she was greatly moved. The opera also benefited from superb casting, with Sylvia Fisher as Miss Wingrave, Janet Baker as Kate, John Shirley-Quirk as Coyle, Heather Harper as Mrs Coyle, Benjamn Luxon as Owen and Jennifer Vyvyan as Mrs Julian. In November 1970 Piper was present throughout the three-weeks rehearsal at the Maltings and the eight days filming that followed. Afterwards she wrote to Britten:

> I enjoyed every minute of 'The Month at the Maltings' in spite of the grind, tedium, frustration and the curious grandmother's steps of progress of TV production (or snakes & ladders if you prefer it). It was marvellous to hear the whole work grow and to get to know the singers and watch their enthusiasm – forbearance – not to mention yours. I do think it a great work and I am proud to be associated with it.[34]

She and John Piper returned to Aldeburgh on 16 May 1971, when *Owen Wingrave* was simultaneously seen and heard in 13 countries, to watch it with Britten and Pears, on a television set rented for the occasion. It pleased Piper still further when her younger son Sebastian telephoned to tell her he had been very impressed.

In later years her enthusiasm for this opera, in comparison with the other two she did with Britten, slightly receded. (In the 1990s, writing to friend, she admitted: 'I went last weekend to Glyndebourne and saw the first night of *Owen Wingrave* ' – not my favourite piece but full of good things all the same.')[35] Yet she had helped achieve a musical drama in which each incident and emotional development is carefully structured and finely dovetailed, one into the next, either by means of contrast or out of narrative necessity. Thirty years later a new television film of *Owen Wingrave* was made for Channel 4. But it is the original BBC 2 version, despite its slightly predictable sets, over-harsh studio lighting, and other limitations, that nevertheless best displays the dramatic power of this opera, as well as something of the tact and sensibility that Myfanwy Piper had desired.

Notes

1 *Owen Wingrave* was a co-production by the BBC and 12 other television stations: Belgische Radio en Televise (BRT, Brussels), Danmarks Radio (DR, Copenhagen), Jugoslovenska Radio-Televizija (JT, Belgrade), national Educational Television (NET, New York), Nederlandse Omroep Stichting (NOS Hilversum), Norsk Rikskringkasting (NRK, Oslo), Office de Radiodiffusion-Télévision Française (ORTF, Paris), Osterreicheischer Rundfunk-Fernsehen (ORF, Wien), Radio Èireann (RE, Dublin), Sveriges Radio Television (SRT, Stockholm), Swiss Broadcasting Corporation (SRG, Zürich) and Zweites Deutsches Fernsehen (ZDF, Mainz). Within a week of the UK broadcast, several of these stations broadcast the opera. Britten and Piper received royalties every time it was transmitted. I acknowledge here and elsewhere in this chapter a debt to Jennifer Barnes's book *Television Opera: The Fall of Opera Commissioned for Television* (Woodbridge: Boydell Press, 2003).

2 This he acknowledges in an interview which formed part of *An Introduction to Owen Wingrave*, a BBC television film for Music 2: Music Now, transmitted 9 May 1971 in advance of the transmission of the actual opera. Britten's commission fee of £10,000 went straight into the fund for the rebuilding of the Maltings, which had burnt down in 1969.

3 For an authoritative examination of this theme, see John Evans, 'Owen *Wingrave*: A Case for Pacifism', in *CPBC*, pp. 227–37. It is necessary also to acknowledge here that pacifism and homosexuality are linked themes in Britten's work, and that the Wingrave family's oppressive attempts to shape Owen in their own image resonate also with sexual politics.

4 After student protesters were shot at by police Kent University, Ohio, Britten kept a newspaper cutting of this appalling event among his papers.

5 Myfanwy Piper in conversation with Roderic Dunnett: typescript of interview, Roderic Dunnett archive.

6 As recorded by John Culshaw, 'The Making of Owen Wingrave', *The Times Saturday Review* (8 May 1971).

7 In 1955 Independent Television Authority service (ITA), the first commercial station, began broadcasting in Britain. It soon divided into a network of regional subsidiaries. Associated-Rediffusion was the first production company responsible for the London area.

8 Piper quoted in '*The Turn of the Screw* by Benjamin Britten', publicity brochure printed to commemorate the Associated-Rediffusion broadcast (W. S. Cowell Ltd, Ipswich, 1959). Copy at BPF.

9 From 'Mapreading', in *CPBC*, pp. 87–96 at p. 88. The interview took place in February 1969.

10 *Ibid.* p. 90.

11 Myfanwy Piper, 'Writing for Britten', in *DHOB*, pp. 8–21 at p. 8.

12 *Ibid.*

13 James documented the origin of the tale in his preface to *The Altar of the Dead*.'

14 Piper, 'Writing for Britten', p. 12.

15 *Ibid.*, p. 15.

16 Piper, notebook for *Owen Wingrave*, BPF.

17 Piper, in 'Writing for Britten', p. 13.

18 Piper, notebook for *Owen Wingrave*.

19 *Ibid.*, p. 14.

20 Piper to Britten, n.d. [January 1954].

21 See letter from Geoffrey Jellicoe to Piper, 14 May 1990, Tate Gallery Archives.

22 Piper to Britten, 7 March 1968.

23 *Ibid.*

24 Piper, 'Writing for Britten', p. 13.

25 Piper to Britten, 11 September 1970.

26 Piper, 'Writing for Britten', p. 13.

27 *Ibid.*, p. 13.

28 *Ibid.*, p. 14.

29 Piper to Britten, 19 August 1968.

30 *CSOB*, p. 289.

31 Piper in conversation with Roderic Dunnett, typescript of tape-recording. Courtesy of Roderic Dunnett.

32 Shaw was not alone in thinking James's ending too abrupt. Virginia Woolf also felt Owen's death too sudden: 'The catastrophe has not the right relations to what has gone before'. See Virginia Woolf, *Collected Essays* (London: Hogarth Press, 1966), p. 289.

33 Arnold Whittall, 'Britten's Lament: The World of Owen Wingrave', *Music Analysis* 19/2 (July 2000), pp. 145–66.

34 Piper to Britten, 10 December 1970.

35 Piper to Rhiannon and Alun Hoddinott, n.d. Courtesy of Rhiannon Hoddinott.

'The Minstrel Boy to the War is Gone' – Father Figures and Fighting Sons in *Owen Wingrave*

Arne Muus

Britten's *Owen Wingrave*, first broadcast as a television opera on 16 May 1971, is generally regarded as one of his weaker dramatic works and remains one of his least performed. In part this is due to a number of visual sequences, conceived by Britten and his librettist Myfanwy Piper specifically for the television première, which turned out to be ill-suited to the medium. Piper herself later conceded that the split screen and crossfades of the Horse Guards sequence (Act I scene 2), filmic rather than televisual in nature, were 'a typical amateur's idea, over-elaborate and impractical'.[1] These elements also create problems for stage productions of the opera. Although Britten clearly saw the future of the work on the stage and was planning to make 'certain adjustments'[2] to the televised version, *Owen Wingrave* eventually opened at Covent Garden on 10 May 1973 unchanged, presumably due to Britten's ill health and preoccupation with *Death in Venice*. Thus stage directors are left with a dramatic work that is scenically awkward.

Much harsher criticism, however, has been levelled at the subject matter of the work and at Britten's and Piper's portrayal of their operatic characters. Against the historical backdrop of the Vietnam War, early critics perceived *Owen Wingrave* primarily as a political statement, and subsequent writers continued to place the emphasis on the pacifist 'message' of the opera; Michael Kennedy, for instance, regarded the work as 'blatant propaganda'.[3] Even sympathetic reviewers admit that there are problems with the way that Britten and Piper argue their supposed point. First, Owen's attitude is considered intellectually inconsistent: 'A pacifist ought never say (as he does twice) "I'd hang the lot"',[4] as Stanley Sadie remarks. Secondly, the opera is said to neutralize the counter-argument, allegedly represented by the Wingraves and Julians, because it turns 'the Paramore contingent into cardboard devils'.[5] This 'contingent' includes Kate, whose cold and unsympathetic portrayal renders it unlikely that Owen would accept her challenge to sleep in the haunted room. And finally, the political message is at odds with, or at best unrelated to, the supernatural element of the opera. Donald Mitchell, in his sleeve-note for Britten's 1971 recording of *Owen Wingrave*, first put forward the 'two-story' idea, i.e. the notion that a 'public' pacifist story (Owen's stance against war) and a 'private' one (his fight against the ghosts of Paramore) co-exist in *Owen Wingrave*. This reading has pervaded discussion of the work ever since, usually as a point of criticism.[6] Commentators have pointed out that the dénouement of Britten's and Piper's opera, while representing a certain conclusion to the 'private' haunting theme, does not resolve the issue of 'public' pacifism and makes Owen's conscientious resistance seem futile.

Frequently these perceived shortcomings are traced back to the tale by Henry James on which the opera is based. James's *Owen Wingrave*, too, has been analysed predominantly in terms of its political significance; Leon Edel calls it 'the only "pacifist" story in all his fiction'.[7] There is no doubt that James held strong views against war, but his tale pre-dates the concept of pacifism (hence Edel's inverted commas), and the ideals of military heroism and bravery in battle which it evokes sit uneasily with later 20th-century notions of non-violence, as does Owen's fierce idea of justice: for one thing, he believes that all the great generals should have been shot.[8] James was clearly fascinated by military tradition and glory, as is evident from his perusal of the memoirs of the French general Marbot, and his notebook entries leave no doubt that he planned to endow Owen with a military mind: 'The idea should be that he fights, after all ... – acts the soldier, *is* the soldier, and of indefeasible soldierly race.'[9] All this does indeed make James's Owen a rather unconvincing advocate of pacifism, at least in the modern sense. Yet the evidence also suggests that the author never intended *Owen Wingrave* primarily as a political statement. In 1909 George Bernard Shaw famously rejected James's own dramatization of the tale, *The Saloon*, which the author had submitted for performance by the Incorporated Stage Society. In his letter to James, the socialist Shaw criticized the ending of the play and the message it conveys:

> It is a really damnable sin to draw with such consummate art a houseful of rubbish, and a dead incubus of a father waiting to be scrapped; to bring on for us the hero with his torch and his scrapping shovel; and, then, when the audience is saturated with interest and elated with hope, waiting for the triumph and the victory, calmly announce that the rubbish has choked the hero, and that the incubus is really the master of all our souls.[10]

In two telling replies James rejected Shaw's criticism, saying that in both *The Saloon* and the original *Owen Wingrave* aspects of artistic craftsmanship, such as playing with an idea and solving a dramatic situation, took precedence over any kind of 'encouragement', and it was not his intention to 'preach'.[11]

It might therefore be deemed bad judgement on Britten's part when he decided to base his pacifist opera on a narrative that, while undoubtedly reflecting James's anti-war stance, was neither in line with modern concepts of pacifism nor ever meant as an unequivocal creed against violence. However, Britten's opera is in fact just as far from being a clear-cut political statement as James's tale is. Britten and Piper did not simply fail to eradicate the soldierly and violent traits of Owen's character from the original; on the contrary they consciously underlined them both in the libretto and in the music.

In the very first scene of the opera Owen's fellow pupil Lechmere, who revels in the idea of fighting and cannot wait to go to war, sums up his enthusiasm in a quotation from Moore's *Irish Melodies*: 'The Minstrel Boy to the war is gone, / in the ranks of death you'll find him' (Example 1a). The first phrase, in the original tune, ends with an ascending major triad spanning an octave. Britten alters this so that the melody now rises by a diminished octave made up of a broken diminished triad plus perfect fourth (marked *x*). Not only does this distortion express the fallacy of Lechmere's ideas, but both the diminished triad and the fourth have also been introduced previously as military *topoi*: perfect fourth fanfares in the woodwind accompany Lechmere from his first appearance, and the opera opens with a 'call to arms' consisting of a stylized drum signal followed by a brass *reveille* that, like the Minstrel Boy tune, is

Example 1 Britten, *Owen Wingrave*, from Act I, scene 1

tainted by diminished harmonies in place of heroic major triads (Example 2). Diminished chords continue to dominate the harmonic structure right up to Lechmere's quotation.

Only a few moments later in the same scene – Lechmere has meanwhile left the stage on another emphatic statement of the diminished octave ascent on the words 'La Gloire c'est tout' (R23:−2)[12] – Owen confesses to his teacher Coyle that he 'can't go through with it' (Example 1b). The first four notes of his melodic line (marked y) are a transposed retrograde inversion of x; hence the corresponding chord, played simultaneously by the strings, is a transposed inversion of that formed by the pitches of x (compare X and Y, Example 1c). Given the pivotal role which these two pitch collections assume in the further development of the opera, as both melodic and harmonic elements, it is surprising that they have not been identified in any of the existing literature. Almost the entire following conversation between Owen and Coyle is based on transpositions of Y, and its relatedness to X is made perfectly clear in Coyle's subsequent arioso, which illustrates the teacher's momentary confusion: after a calm, diatonic section the tone changes noticeably and the orchestral accompaniment takes up Lechmere's 'Minstrel Boy' chord (R34), before switching to Owen's 'defiance' chord (R34:5) and finally presenting the two in direct juxtaposition (R34:9).

The interpretative significance of these mutually inverted chords lies in the fact that Owen, while opposing the idea of going to war and killing the foe, uses the same musical language as his antagonists and equally cloaks his defiance in 'military' diminished triads and perfect fourths. Britten's music thus

PRELUDE Example 2 Britten, *Owen Wingrave*, opening

cleverly suggests that Owen (Welsh for 'the young warrior')[13] is different but the same: even though he fights a different enemy, he is still a fighter. As in James's tale, this point is also repeatedly reinforced textually, for instance by Coyle's remark, 'Oh my dear boy, the pity is you are a fighter' (R161).[14] While the opera is very true to the original in this respect, the above diagnosis seems to conflict with the passionately pacifist statements that Owen delivers in the Hyde Park scene (Act I scene 2) and in his peace arioso (Act II scene 2 from R246). James's third-person narrative, which takes Spencer Coyle's point of view, provides no model for these soliloquies, and one might be tempted to assume that Britten and Piper got carried away with their political agenda when devising operatic monologues for their protagonist. Once again, however, this assumption is disproved by Britten's music: the string ostinato underlying the Hyde Park scene spells out another transposition of Y ($g–c'/eb'/f\sharp'$ at R43), thus hinting at the pugnacious aspects of Owen's defiance and creating a contrast to his pacifist pledge.

Like the vision of battle, blood and death into which Owen sees the passing Horse Guards transformed later in the scene, the military diminished triads and perfect fourths of his defiance chord seem to represent a trace of an underlying layer, a psychological disposition which is belied by his intellectual pacifism. Seen from this perspective, a discrepancy becomes evident between Owen's somewhat militant psychological imprint and the love of peace he professes, which may help to explain a good deal of the perceived inconsistencies in Britten's and Piper's *Owen Wingrave*. In fact their opera reveals a great amount of detail if read not as a political manifesto but as a psychological study of an adolescent mind that is torn between conscious ideals and subconscious formation or, in the words of a Stephen Fry witticism, between 'nurture' and 'Nietzsche'.[15] Using approaches borrowed from psychoanalysis, this essay offers a reading that places Owen's psychic formation as a 'Wingrave boy' at the centre of the work's dramaturgy and reconsiders its critical reception in this light.

In one of the notebook entries on his projected tale Henry James reminded himself that he 'mustn't make it "psychological"', but this may have been merely a private sneer at the readers of the *Graphic*, the magazine in which he was hoping to publish it: 'they understand that no more than a donkey understands a violin',[16] he added. James's *Owen Wingrave*, typically for the author, leaves us in doubt about the exact nature of the events and thus invites psychological speculation. An early critic to draw attention to this, Mary Sturge Gretton pointed out in 1912 that many of Henry James's tales, 'such as *The Beast in the Jungle*, *Owen Wingrave*, and *The Birthplace*, are not really concerned with the "supernatural" at all. They are brilliant presentations of rare and delicate but "natural" psychological experiences.'[17] Britten and Piper built upon and systematically amplified the psychological overtones of the original narrative. Owen's subconscious, as formed by 'nurture', plays a decisive role in the opera, and although G. B. Shaw understood the narrative to be political, he raised a significant and intriguing point in making the 'dead incubus of a father' responsible for Owen's fate.

It is striking and surprising that Owen's father, although long dead, features prominently in the opera. He is in fact introduced before Owen appears on stage or screen: at the end of the prelude to Act I his picture comes into view as the last of a series of military family portraits – an inspired opening idea prefiguring Owen's two addresses to these portraits later in the work.[18] For each Wingrave ancestor shown, the strings add another pitch of the chromatic scale to a swelling sustained chord; this reaches its eleven-note *fff* climax at the appearance of Owen's father (Example 3, R10), while the wind instruments suddenly erupt into a disjunct fortissimo sequence of pitches which Donald Mitchell characterizes as 'volcanically anguished'.[19] This is a formidable entry for a dramatis non-persona. Moments later Owen appears, looking 'like the last portrait' (Example 3, R11). His musical caption, at first glance, could not seem further removed from the explosive violence of his begetter. Yet there are points of connection. Visually, Piper's effective idea to let the protagonist appear literally in his father's place underlines their affinity. Musically, Owen's *pianissimo* unison D contrasts sharply with the loud dissonant chord that marks his father as the heir to a long line of military ancestors, but it also completes the twelve-note collections of this chord and of his father's disjunct pitch sequence. The tonality and melodiousness of Owen's 'peaceful' horn theme are diametrically opposed to the disrupted dodecaphonic tone row of his father, but at the same time the latter's final A acts as a dominant to Owen's D minor/major (and the lyrical horn cadenza turns out to be an extended and more diatonic variant of the twelve-note *reveille* from the opening bars of the opera – another hint at the protagonist's military psyche). Thus it becomes unmistakably clear that Owen is both very different from, and inextricably linked to, his father.

We are reminded of this in no uncertain fashion at the end of Act I scene 4 (R130:–2), when Owen turns to his father's picture with the words: 'Father! Father! You must understand. I am as resolute as you at Kandahar.' Once again the preceding address to the family portraits (from R129), a condensed version of the prelude, is based on a twelve-note sequence, played by the harp and strings. And once again the father's harsh eleven-note row sums up the underlying dodecaphonic structure and brings it to the audible surface, branding him the representative and focal point of a long and – by the sound

Example 3 Britten, *Owen Wingrave*, from Prelude

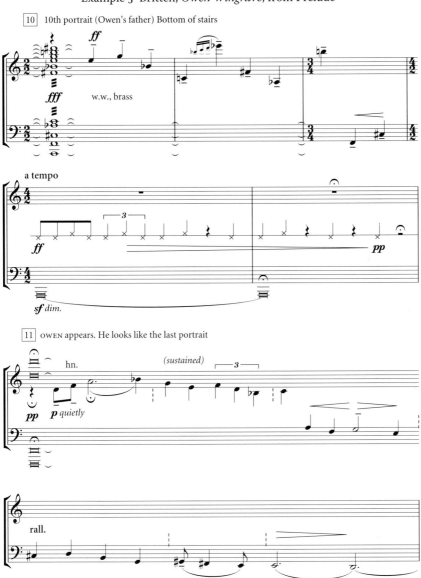

of it – clearly 'tainted' family history.[20] Owen's eventual exclamation, to this accompaniment, is as much an imploration as it is a self-justification, a strange mixture of protest and apology. One could almost detect a sense of guilt in the young hero's plea: in this revealing moment of clarity he himself proclaims he wants to follow in his father's footsteps, wants to be a fighter, but seems to feel he is failing. Yet if he is a pacifist, why would he strive for his dead father's ideal, especially when the music suggests it is less than noble?

In his fundamental essay on the theory of the self, *The Ego and the Id*, first published in 1923, Sigmund Freud proposes a model of how the self and the conscience are formed in the process of growing up, and his considerations open up a fascinating perspective on the protagonist's statements and behaviour in Britten's and Piper's *Owen Wingrave*. Freud's well-known basic distinction is between the id, the (largely unconscious) seat of instincts and passions, and the ego, the (predominantly conscious) realm of perceptions, reason and common sense.[21] Based on his clinical findings, he hypothesizes a third instance between these two, the so-called ego ideal or super-ego, which acts as a controlling force over the ego. While the ego, within the self, is representative of the external world, the super-ego is representative of the internal id; it reaches down to unconscious imprints and acts as their agent *vis-à-vis* the ego.[22] Particularly interesting in the present context is the source to which the super-ego is traced back: according to Freud it is formed by early-childhood object-cathexes and identifications, the strongest of which is with the father. Freud terms this the 'father-complex' since it represents one side of the oft-quoted and oft-misunderstood Oedipus complex: the male child will attempt to emulate the father in the desire to take his place but, realizing that this is impossible, will then internalize his character, substituting the object-relation to him and thus overcoming the complex.[23] Freud explains:

> Although [the super-ego] is accessible to all later influences, it nevertheless preserves throughout life the character given to it by its derivation from the father-complex – namely, the capacity to stand apart from the ego and to master it. It is a memorial of the former weakness and dependence of the ego, and the mature ego remains subject to its domination.[24]

Owen's ego, then, framed by his love of peace, could be understood to be under attack from his super-ego which preserves the paternal ideas of fighting and bravery; his conscious pacifist beliefs conflict with his unconscious pugnacious disposition which he cannot escape. This explains not only the violent traits of Owen's character and the continued presence of the defiance chord (*Y*) with its military diminished triads and perfect fourths, even when Owen sings of overcoming the detested family tradition. It also accounts for the further unfolding of events and for their tragic outcome. In his essay Freud is largely concerned with cases in which an overbearing super-ego leads to a sense of suffering in patients. In his analysis,

> The super-ego retains the character of the father, while the more powerful the Oedipus complex was and the more rapidly it succumbed to

repression (under the influence of authority, religious teaching, school-
ing and reading), the stricter will be the domination of the super-ego
over the ego later on – in the form of conscience or perhaps of an
unconscious sense of guilt.[25]

Britten's and Piper's hero seems almost a model case of what the psychoanalyst
describes: coming from an authoritarian household with strict moral standards, and having lost both his parents early and very suddenly, Owen would
have undergone a particularly abrupt and painful repression of the Oedipus
complex (and thus of the father-complex). All the stronger, in Freud's theory,
would be the authority of his super-ego over his ego and therefore, possibly,
his suffering arising from an unconscious sense of guilt, of his ego not being
able to live up to the super-ego's expectations. This is exactly the impression
we gain from Owen's encounter with his father's picture as described above,
and there is a sense throughout the opera that Owen, in his quest for peace,
is really looking for peace of mind. He is not merely using his father 'as an
example', and neither is this 'unthinking, yet instinctive use ... an ironic comment on his sterile upbringing and, perhaps, his own lack of imagination',[26] as
Michael Halliwell suggests. Owen struggles with the continuing influence of
a strict and commanding father figure, as becomes particularly evident when
he talks about his past and upbringing, first recounting his parents' fate in
Act I scene 3 (from R94), later describing how he was 'surrounded with love,
nursed in hope, spoiled with admiration' (Act II scene 1, R245). This is invari-
ably accompanied by mutations of the dodecaphonic martial chords from the
beginning of the opera (Example 2, bars 1–3), and there is in fact little sense of
loss or affection. Instead the music smacks of aggression and conflict.

Although Owen bids his past farewell in the second of these monologues
and rejects 'the man they planned to make of me' (sung on a transposition
of the Minstrel Boy pitch collection, X), his exorcism is bound to fail. As the
prelude suggests, he is very much a product of the Wingrave tradition, and the
paternal character deeply engrained within him, in the form of the super-ego.
Owen may revolt against and try to evade his past, but he cannot run from his
own self. The following peace soliloquy illustrates this ingeniously: although
largely diatonic and based on perfect major and minor triads, it is undercut by
another twelve-note sequence (as, amongst others, Peter Evans has shown),[27]
and its orchestration resembles that of the preceding martial chords, from
which it emerges organically. Once more, on a rational and conscious level,
Owen advocates peace while the music betrays the irrational fighting traits of
his unconscious, the legacy of the father.

Consequentially it is his overbearing super-ego that eventually seals the fate of the protagonist. The development leading up to this can be traced by what I have termed the defiance chord, *Y*. Its derivation from the distorted Minstrel Boy tune seems an especially pregnant idea in the present context, since Moore's text (never sung in full, but set by Britten in volume 4 of his *Folksong Arrangements* [1957]) begins with the words 'The Minstrel Boy to the war is gone, / In the ranks of death you'll find him; / *His father's sword he hath girded on*, / And his wild harp slung behind him [my italics]', and goes on to tell of the boy's death in battle. While derivations of *Y* abound in Act I,[28] they are largely absent from the beginning of Act II (with one notable exception, discussed below). Owen appears to have succeeded in laying his fighting ghosts to rest, at least temporarily. The pitch constellation only recurs when Kate arouses Owen's sense of shortcoming by calling him a coward (f''–d''–b'–$f\sharp'$, Example 4). With three stacked transpositions of *Y* (repeated a fifth lower, seven bars later, R271:5) the piano marks the dramatic resurgence of Owen's super-ego and its demand to prove his bravery. This accusation is a central moment in James's tale, too, emphasized by one of his characteristic ellipses, but it is voiced by the grandfather and occurs much earlier in the plot.[29] In the opera it becomes the trigger for Owen's demise. The reason behind his decision to accept Kate's challenge, however, is not his love for her or his resolve to prove his worth to her. She merely manages to stir up the most vulnerable part of his psyche: in responding to her provocation, Owen obeys the command of his imperious super-ego.

The only author to note the Freudian overtones of this scene, Jeremy Tambling argues that,

> as the choice between being a soldier and sleeping in the haunted room indicates, the issue is that of facing the Oedipal conflict, of exorcising the father, and asserting the right to self-determination, or of becoming a soldier and so accepting that domination from above and behind.[30]

In fact, by agreeing to sleep in the haunted room, the protagonist does not exorcise the father; on the contrary he 'acts the soldier' and submits to his will. Accordingly the martial chords from the opening bars of the opera (the call to

Example 4 Britten, *Owen Wingrave*, from Act II, scene 1

arms which has been haunting Owen throughout the entire work and which he had hoped to banish with his eulogy to peace) return for a last time and build up to a full-blown twelve-note chord on his words, 'now I alone must take it on, I must go in there' (R277).

All the above, in the Freudian analysis, occurs on the unconscious level; Owen is not actually aware of any of this except the feeling of guilt that results from the ego's futile struggle to satisfy the super-ego. There are, however, elements of the conscious that mirror the depths of his psyche, visible representations of Owen's self. 'Thinking in pictures ... stands nearer to unconscious processes than does thinking in words', says Freud, and therefore 'anything ... that seeks to become conscious must try to transform itself into external perceptions'.[31] In the case of *Owen Wingrave* these external perceptions take the shape of the 'house', Paramore, and the apparitions of the old Colonel and the young boy, whose legend it preserves. It is impossible for Owen to access or even confront that part of his self which torments him, so he projects it onto the house, which becomes a highly charged symbol of the accursed fighting spirit and soldierly tradition, and onto the figures of the father and son of the ballad from the beginning of Act II. Both elements are strong presences in James's narrative as well – to Coyle's question what it is that worries him Owen replies, 'Oh the house'[32] – but once again, Piper and Britten systematically underline and expand their role in the psychological drama.

Musically, the house and the revenants are introduced simultaneously in Interlude III (R98), when Paramore becomes visible on stage or screen. The house is characterized by a series of motivic phrases which combine melodic and harmonic aspects: in their horizontal form (played by the strings) they foreshadow the melody of the ballad in Act II, their vertical constellation (sustained woodwind notes forming chords) prefigures numerous later occurrences of similar chords, whose common denominator is a fifth with major or minor second above or below.[33] The revenants are represented by a passacaglia bass that is derived from the opening chords of the opera. Its significance is revealed early in Act II when Owen sings, to a transposition of the first phrase, 'Walking, walking – these two: the old man and the boy, for ever in each other's company' (R206:–2).

This last line hints at the nature and origin of the apparitions: father and son are inextricably bound to each other, much like the dominating force of the father figure is forever impressed upon Owen's self. The young boy and the old Colonel could be regarded as external concretizations of Owen's peace-loving ego and his violent super-ego, and indeed Britten and Piper insistently equate the protagonist with the boy of the ballad, and the old Colonel with the father. 'In particular I find a very strong identification of Owen and the murdered boy

Example 5 Britten, *Owen Wingrave*, from Prelude

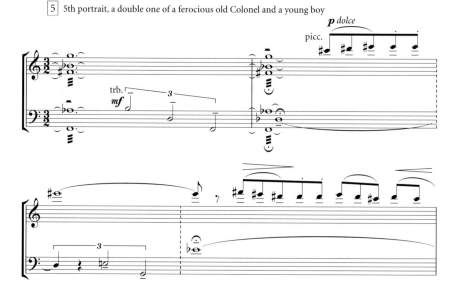

5 5th portrait, a double one of a ferocious old Colonel and a young boy

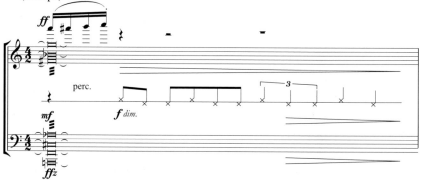

has taken over and left me feeling much happier about the Ghost story and the way to use it', wrote Myfanwy Piper to Britten on 19 August 1968.[34] Britten seems to have agreed. Already in the prelude to Act I, the appearance of a double portrait of Colonel and boy (Example 5) – rather than the single portrait of Owen's great-great-grandfather which James mentions[35] – is accompanied by a disjunct trombone theme covering all twelve steps of the chromatic scale, though not systematically, and ending on a low A'. Clearly connected with the ferocious Colonel, it anticipates the similarly shaped pitch sequence of Owen's father (see Example 3). The trombone entry is closely followed by a piccolo tune that, like Owen's theme at R11 (Example 3), stands out due to its diatonicism and evidently characterizes the boy. It is centred around $c\sharp''$, which is also the pitch it contributes to the sustained string chord (albeit three octaves lower), and which represents the leading-note to Owen's eventual d'', equally played by the piccolo.

The boy's tune and Owen's theme, now in inversion, are then brought into direct proximity during Interlude II (R64:–3) when Owen quotes the lines 'the thoughtless youth / Already crushed with servitude – he knows / His wretchedness too late...' from Shelley's *Queen Mab*, which Piper evocatively substitutes for James's original Goethe. This indicates that Owen and the boy share a tragic fate; they both suffer at the hand of an authority that is beyond their control. The parallel is enforced by details of the plot: whereas the original story gives no reason why the Wingrave boy had to die, the opera follows *The Saloon* in stating that the old Colonel struck him for having refused to fight.[36] Significantly, in the present context, the libretto does not make the Colonel the boy's grandfather as in James's dramatization, but explicitly identifies him as his father, thereby echoing Owen's relationship with his dead father, not with Sir Philip.[37] And finally the last of the Wingraves, in the tale, has already been disowned when he arrives at Paramore; in the operatic version, as in *The Saloon*, this verdict is postponed until later in the plot so that Owen can be tried behind closed doors, in a scene mirroring the punishment of his ancestor.[38] The locked room becomes a metaphor for the inaccessible depths of Owen's self in which he has to face the father.

After her nephew has been disinherited, Miss Wingrave declares that 'the renegade is now as if he had not ever been a member of our valiant family' (Example 6) – to the Wingrave boy's piccolo tune. There is no more doubt that history is repeating itself and that Owen is rejected in the same way as the boy of the ballad, eventually with the same disastrous consequences. This moment of emotional turmoil is marked by a repetitive, aggressive and semantically overdetermined orchestral accompaniment based simultaneously on pitch collections X ($c\sharp'$–e–g–c', in the trombones) and Y ($e\flat''$–c''–a'–e', in the

Example 6 Britten, *Owen Wingrave*, from Act II, scene 1

trumpets), and on the three martial chords from the start of the opera (with the first three quavers in the horns and trumpets derived from chord 1, the fourth and fifth from chord 2, and the tuba's bass G' representing the root of chord 3). Despite his apparent composure the external rejection has a profound effect on Owen because it reflects the super-ego's rejection of the ego within his unconscious. Like the Wingrave boy, his ego has failed the father. Owen later quotes this passage in his effort to exorcise the ghosts of his past (R244), and the analogy between himself and the boy does not escape him. In fact he emphatically identifies with him: 'He was my ancestor in ev'ry sense. For me it is not the past, but now', he tells Coyle at the beginning of Act II (R205:–3).

What unites them is their confrontation with an excessively strict and apparently loveless father figure. Freud describes the relationship between the constituent parts of the self in terms of love: to the ego, he explains, 'living means the same as being loved by the super-ego … The super-ego fulfils the same function of protecting and saving that was fulfilled in earlier days by the father.'[39] However, much like the old Colonel did not protect and save his son, Owen's overbearing super-ego denies his ego the love and approval it longs for.

In this sense Owen is very much a victim like his ancestor. That is why the boy of the legend, for him, becomes a strong external symbol of his ego's search for acceptance. His quest for peace is in fact a quest for love, for the love of the father figure. It is certainly no coincidence that the first arioso section of the great Act II soliloquy, a catechism of peace, concludes with the definition that 'it is the voice of love' (R252), delivered to the opening notes of the Wingrave boy tune. Yet since it is actually part of his self that he is up against, Owen is unable to walk away from the challenge of the father, as already mentioned: Kate's accusation will drag him back. His subsequent assertion, accompanied by a final and complete restatement of the old Colonel and boy themes from the prelude, is therefore telling but futile: 'Poor boy, you made your stand too young – but I have done it for you – for us all. Tell the old man, tell your fearful father, Your fate and his no longer frighten me. Tell him his power is gone and I have won, and at last *I shall have peace* [my italics]' (R258).

This Freudian reading of Britten's and Piper's opera does not explain how the hero meets his end in the haunted room – that much remains a mystery – but it helps to understand why he dies. If the ego, in order to live, relies on the super-ego's approval but the super-ego denies it this approval and instead exerts constant pressure on it, as in Owen's case, then the ego will eventually give itself up. As Freud puts it, 'It sees itself deserted by all protecting forces and lets itself die.'[40] Owen's death can therefore be regarded as a psychological consequence of his inner struggle. In this sense Owen Wingrave, despite his apparent intellectual maturity, is but a victim of circumstances, torn between his stern upbringing and a desire to be loved, and as helpless and vulnerable as the boy of the legend. This idea may have resonated with Britten, whose works are frequently concerned with innocent individuals that come up against a hostile environment by which they are spoilt or destroyed. The tragic tinge of the Wingrave boy's piccolo tune suggests as much, as does the choice of Moore's *Minstrel Boy* to denote Owen's fighting spirit. The sentiment is summed up by – of all characters – Sir Philip: his final exclamation 'My boy!' (R295:–2), an addition by Peter Pears,[41] for the first and only time in the opera displays the love that Owen failed to find, and the boys' choir underlines the point in the following ballad coda by resuming the story of the 'Wingrave boy'. This time they mean Owen.

Sir Philip's late acknowledgement of his affection for Owen raises the question what role the other residents of Paramore play in the drama. Are they really just stubborn, heartless caricatures? Piper's take on Kate was that 'she was as much a victim of her background as Owen, but lacked his opportunities to think again'.[42] If the above considerations concerning Owen's character development and psychological disposition are valid, then they indeed apply equally to Kate, whose background is similar, and who also lost her father at a young age. Her super-ego, too, would have established itself as an overbearing instance domineering over her ego, which in turn seeks to please the super-ego's authority. In other words her behaviour towards the pacifist Owen would equally be guided by unconscious processes rooted in her upbringing, and not by rational choices on the conscious level of the ego. This view is in fact corroborated by Britten's music. The woodwind lines and string chords that accompany Kate's introduction in Act I scene 4 (from R105) are exclusively comprised of major and minor triads, a remarkable occurrence in Britten's score which suggests a certain affinity with Owen. Only at R107, when she mentions the house ('It is too strong'), does one of the previously described Paramore chords ($eb'/bb'/c''$) break the sequence. The same happens again at R126. It is the house and the military tradition it stands for that speak through Kate at these points, and their musical presence hints at the influence of the super-ego which they helped to form.

Mrs Julian, too, is clearly a product of the soldierly tradition. The bitonal canon by inversion with which she is introduced (R101) is equally derived from the Paramore chords, and the same goes for the woodwind chords that conclude Miss Wingrave's phrases when she first appears in Act I scene 2 (R45). The entire household is musically portrayed as hostage to the past or, in Jeremy Tambling's words, as 'agents of the Father'.[43] Their harsh reaction to Owen's pacifism is not a sign of maliciousness or emotional cruelty but of the tradition that has pervaded Paramore and that, for fear of the militaristic super-ego, prevents them from expressing their love for Owen. In their attitude towards the heir of the house, they involuntarily replicate the strictness of their own education, which thus perpetuates itself through generations. Freud himself recognized this self-preserving character of moral teachings, and described them in his essay *Civilization and its Discontents* (1929–30). He argues that the development and education of individuals is reflected by the processes visible in human civilization, concluding that 'the community, too, evolves a super-ego under whose influence cultural developments proceed'.[44] And just like the individual, a group or society can suffer from a dictatorial super-ego, with similar consequences; he suggests that future sociologists embark on a 'pathology of cultural communities'.[45]

The prelude to Britten's opera, from this perspective, seems like a musical translation of Freud's theory: it traces the transmission of the soldierly ethos through the centuries, culminating in the intimidating violence of the father figure, and the super-ego which it enshrines. The political aspect of Britten's and Piper's opera thus emerges from the psychological. There is no evidence that, in their work, Britten and Piper consciously applied Freudian concepts, which have of course been much expanded since by authors such as Jacques Lacan and Julia Kristeva. Nevertheless the convergences between Freud's seminal ideas and *Owen Wingrave* highlight the fact that the opera is not primarily a pacifist statement. Britten's political views undoubtedly influenced his musical characterization, and the emphasis he places on the protagonist's innocence and boyishness makes his stand abundantly clear. Yet Owen is no figurehead of pacifism. In the first instance *Owen Wingrave* is a case study of the effect that a military upbringing and environment may have on the individual, and a story about fathers and sons. The 'political' and the 'supernatural' elements of the story are both mere facets of its psychological undercurrent. Equally there is no clear-cut distinction between the 'bad' family and the 'good' hero: they are all made of the same wood, and the Paramore personnel are as much victims of their situation as Owen is a fighter. His death does result from, and exposes, the underlying social and political structures of his environment, and in this respect he joins the ranks of Lucretia and Billy Budd, but as in these other Britten operas, the drama of the individual always takes precedence, and this is what makes us engage and sympathize with Britten's characters. Sir Philip's very personal catharsis, at the end, is therefore more of a resolution to the story than anything else – no concession of his misguidedness, but a glimmer of affection in a loveless place.

Notes

1 Myfanwy Piper, 'Writing for Britten', in *DHOB*, revised edition (1989), pp. 8–21 at p. 14.

2 Quoted in Alan Blyth, 'New Works from Britten', *The Times* (2 June 1971), p. 6.

3 Michael Kennedy, *Master Musicians: Britten*, revised edition (London: J. M. Dent, 1993), p. 235.

4 Stanley Sadie, 'Owen Wingrave', *Musical Times* 112/1541 (July 1971), pp. 663–6 at p. 665.

5 Winton Dean, 'Music in London', *Musical Times* 114/1565 (July 1973), pp. 719–26 at p. 719.

6 See Donald Mitchell, ' "Owen Wingrave" and the Sense of the Past', in *Cradles of the New: Writing on Music, 1951–1991*, ed. Mervyn Cooke, selected by Christopher Palmer (London: Faber, 1995), pp. 419–38 at p. 434; also Arnold Whittall, *The Music of Britten and Tippett: Studies in Themes and Techniques*, second edition (Cambridge: Cambridge University Press, 1990), p. 250; *CSOB*, p. 278; and Kennedy, *Britten*, pp. 234f.

7 Leon Edel, *Henry James: The Treacherous Years, 1895–1901* (London: Lippincott, Williams and Wilkins, 1969), p. 96. James's tale has attracted little attention in literary criticism but is more frequently discussed by music critics

in connection with Britten's opera: thus John Evans labels the tale an 'uncompromising expression of the pacifist views that James had held ever since the days of the American Civil War', and Warrack speaks of 'its intent as a pacifist tract'. John Evans, 'Owen Wingrave: A Case for Pacifism', in *CPBC*, pp. 227–37 at p. 230; John Warrack, 'Britten's Television Opera', *Opera* 22 (May 1971), pp. 371–8 at p. 371.

8 Henry James, 'Owen Wingrave', in *The Turn of the Screw and Other Stories*, ed. T. J. Lustig (Oxford: Oxford University Press, 1992), pp. 37–78 at p. 52.

9 Henry James, *The Complete Notebooks of Henry James*, ed. Leon Edel and Lyall H. Powers (Oxford: Oxford University Press, 1987), p. 68. See also p. 66 in the same volume and Edel, *Henry James: The Treacherous Years*, pp. 94f.

10 Leon Edel, 'Editor's Foreword', in *The Complete Plays of Henry James*, ed. Leon Edel (London: Rupert Hart-Davis, 1949), pp. 641–9 at pp. 642f.

11 See *ibid.*, pp. 644–6.

12 Performance figures and bar numbers refer equally to the vocal and study scores (London: Faber Music, 1977 and 1995).

13 See Jeremy Tambling, *Opera, Ideology and Film* (Manchester: Manchester University Press, 1987), p. 121.

14 Piper here conflates Coyle's original words 'Oh, you *are* a soldier; you must fight it out!' (James, 'Owen Wingrave', p. 61) with a telling phrase that appears later in the tale (p. 66): ' "Hang him, what a pity he's such a fighter!" he [Coyle] privately sighed – and with a want of logic that was only superficial.'

15 See Stephen Fry, *The Stars' Tennis Balls* (London: Hutchinson, 2000), p. 179.

16 James, *The Complete Notebooks*, p. 68.

17 Mary Sturge Gretton, 'Mr. Henry James and his Prefaces', *Contemporary* 101 (January 1912), pp. 69–78, quoted after Roger Gard, ed., *Henry James: The Critical Heritage* (London: Routledge & Kegan, 1968), p. 508.

18 The basic idea stems from *The Saloon* (in *The Complete Plays of Henry James*, p. 665); Piper certainly did not ignore James's own dramatization as several writers claim, e.g. Evans, 'Owen Wingrave: A Case for Pacifism', p. 229.

19 Mitchell, ' "Owen Wingrave" and the Sense of the Past', p. 421.

20 As before, Owen's D finally completes both his father's note row and the long-range dodecaphonic sequence in the harp and strings, with the penultimate $e\flat''$ acting as a leading-note.

21 See Sigmund Freud, 'The Ego and the Id', in *On Metapsychology: The Theory of Psychoanalysis*, trans. James Strachey, ed. Angela Richards (Harmondsworth: Penguin, 1984), pp. 350–401 at pp. 363f.

22 See *ibid.*, pp. 376, 390.

23 See *ibid.*, pp. 370, 373.

24 *Ibid.*, p. 389.

25 *Ibid.*, p. 374.

26 Michael Halliwell, *Opera and the Novel: The Case of Henry James*, ed. Walter Bernhart (Amsterdam/New York: Rodopi, 2005), p. 245.

27 See Peter Evans, *The Music of Benjamin Britten,* third edition (Oxford: Clarendon Press, 1996), pp. 515f.

28 In addition to the occurrences quoted earlier, transpositions of *Y* underlie Owen's protestation 'You'll never bring me round' (Act I scene 3, R80), the harp flourish when he enters Paramore (Act I scene 4, R 16:3), and the whole of Interlude IV (from R163), with the strings outlining the diminished triads and the harp and brass adding the fourth below (*tenuto* minims), to name but three examples.

29 'His grandfather had called him outrageous names. "He called me – he called me –" Here Owen faltered' (James, 'Owen Wingrave', p. 59) … 'He [Coyle] saw the moment after this when Owen was on the point of asking if he too thought him a coward' (p. 60). In *The Saloon*, Owen's reaction to the accusation is even stronger: 'Owen: *(Lashed as across the face; with a cry of pain and rage.)* A "coward"?' (James, 'The Saloon', p. 669).

30 Tambling, *Opera, Ideology and Film*, pp. 118f.

31 Freud, 'The Ego and the Id', pp. 358, 359.

32 James, 'Owen Wingrave', p. 61.

33 In fact, the first of these Paramore chords ($b\flat/f'/g'$) already occurs at the beginning of the Hyde Park scene (Act I scene 2, R43), where it alternates with the defiance chord (*Y*) in the rocking string ostinato, casting doubt on Owen's belief that with 'one little word: no!' he could be 'released for ever from all the bonds of family and war'.

34 Quoted in *CSOB*, p. 289.

35 See James, 'Owen Wingrave', p. 65.

36 See James, 'The Saloon', p. 658.

37 See *ibid.*

38 See *ibid.*, p. 654, and 'Owen Wingrave', p. 60.

39 Freud, 'The Ego and the Id', p. 400.

40 *Ibid.*

41 See Roderic Dunnett, 'A Collaboration Recalled: Myfanwy Piper talks to Roderic Dunnett', *Opera* 46 (October 1995), pp. 1158–64 at p. 1162.

42 Piper, 'Writing for Britten', p. 14.

43 Tambling, *Opera, Ideology and Film*, p. 116.

44 Sigmund Freud, 'Civilization and its Discontents', in *Civilization, Society and Religion: Group Psychology, Civilization and its Discontents and Other Works*, trans. James Strachey, ed. Albert Dickson (Harmondsworth: Penguin, 1985), pp. 245–340 at p. 335; see also p. 333.

45 *Ibid.*, p. 339.

9 Made You Look!
Children in *Salome* and *Death in Venice*
J. P. E. Harper-Scott

The Lust for Youth

Two operatic works with themes of more or less scandalous sexuality as good as bookend the 20th century. The first, acknowledged from the start as a problem work, is Strauss's *Salome* (1905); the second, whose sexual content, when it is admitted at all, has been bound up with recent queer studies, is Britten's *Death in Venice* (1971–3), which Clifford Hindley has read as a story of homosexual self-discovery in the specific form of 'a sublimated love of youthful male beauty along the lines of the Platonic philosophy'.[1] One purpose of this essay is to suggest that *Death in Venice* is more of a problem work than some scholars think it is; another is to examine its perhaps surprising relationship to a work whose aesthetic is radically different and therefore seems to resist the association.

The similarities in the plots of *Salome* and *Death in Venice* rest largely on the corrupting lust of a man for a much younger sexual object. In *Salome* the sexual focus causes the death of a man who refuses to look at her; in *Death in Venice* the sexual focus causes the death of the man who cannot stop looking at him. Strauss made his libretto by abridging Hedwig Lachmann's German translation of Wilde's play, and the telling of the Salome story is therefore Wilde's intensely decadent version.[2] Two men are sexually obsessed with Salome: a young Syrian (Narraboth) and her stepfather, Herod. She in her turn is evidently sexually obsessed with Jochanaan (John the Baptist), who is imprisoned in a cistern, as her father had been.[3] She uses her sexual power over Narraboth to command Jochanaan's release from the cistern; the prophet refuses to look at her, calling her the Daughter of Sodom among other things, but she promises that she will kiss his mouth. When he emerges from his feast, Herod pleads with Salome to dance for him, and she agrees on condition that he will grant her any request. He is happy to give her half his kingdom, and so when she has completed her dance of the seven veils she demands the head of Jochanaan. Reluctantly Herod obliges (while Herodias, his wife and Salome's mother, looks on smugly), and after a long monologue Salome kisses the lips of the severed head. At this, Herod commands her death, and she is crushed by the court soldiers' shields.

Death in Venice opens with a famous author, Gustav von Aschenbach, leaving his native Munich to seek inspiration in the South, and specifically in Venice. En route he encounters and is disgusted by an Elderly Fop, the first of a series of roles sung in Britten's opera by a single baritone, all of them playing parts that will lead Aschenbach to degradation and death. A Polish family at Aschenbach's hotel includes a boy 'of about fourteen', who is the perfect picture of Greek beauty.[4] Although Aschenbach hears reports of typhus (which the local officials try to suppress, fearing harm to the tourist trade) and has the opportunity to warn the Polish family to flee, he chooses instead to remain in Venice so that he can be close to the boy that he now knows from overhearing to be called Tadzio. He is infected, literally by typhus but figuratively by his lust for the boy. Tadzio acknowledges him twice, the first time causing Aschenbach to say 'I love you!' when the boy is safely out of earshot, and the second when his illness is so pronounced that after one last cry of 'Tadzio!' Aschenbach expires on the beach. (Since typhus is the symbol of the boy's effect, it is as accurate to say that the boy kills the man as it is in *Animal Farm* to say that Napoleon has a bigger meaning than just being a pig.)

These operas also share a common motivation in the dramatic symbolism of looking and veiling or concealing. *Salome*'s famous striptease with veils focuses the mind on the importance of seeing and being seen in the opera, but the nuanced symbolism of the veil in Wilde's drama, most of the details of which are retained by Strauss, stands at least as much for the relationship of artworks to truth or representation on the one hand and their own artifice on the other as it does to the covering and uncovering of physical nakedness. In this respect *Salome* (very plainly) and *Death in Venice* (more subtly) engage with a long-standing visual trope in art, not least in representations of the female figures of horrible temptation and emasculation, Salome, Judith, and Venus. The use of the veil in such artworks is both an invitation to gaze lustfully at what is being concealed and a sharpening of the viewer's awareness of the moral risk of that gaze.

'Salome' and the gaze

Lawrence Kramer's article on *Salome* in the *Cambridge Opera Journal*, recently reprinted as a chapter in his book on Strauss and Wagner, is a stimulating way in to the work.[5] His reading subverts the understanding of Salome as a 'personification of patriarchal fears of female sexuality, fears so disruptive that they compulsively play themselves out in a scenario of fetishism and castration'.[6] The drama is played out in two parts which also resemble the dramatic outline of *Death in Venice*: events leading up to a dance and revelation, and a second half dealing with the consequences, in *Salome*'s case of the decapitation of Jochanaan.

Salome's changing dramatic function is defined in terms of what Kramer, following Lacan, calls the male gaze. At first the gaze is directed towards her; until her dance she is passive to its penetrating domination, but while dancing she becomes a moving target for the male erotic gaze, impossible to fix on as a means of satisfying erotic desire.[7] But her relation to the male gaze operates in two separate spheres, first in this subjection to and later subversion of the gaze of Herod, her stepfather, who spends too much time looking at her, and second in her relationship to Jochanaan. As Kramer notes, she is the only character who directly relates to the prophet, and the basis for the relationship is her gaze: 'Salome desires to look, in her own right, from the forbidden masculine perspective, to take Iokanaan as the object of visual love.'[8] Eventually, Kramer suggests, her appropriated masculine gaze rebounds on her, as a ray of moonlight illuminates and then crushes her to death. I shall return to the moon imagery shortly.

The central moment of the drama is, of course, Salome's monologue with the head, her perverted *Liebestod*. Extended far beyond the proportionate weight it has in Wilde's original play, in Strauss this moment 'dilates' dramatic time and, Kramer notes, 'puts this dilation at the service of the gaze'.[9] It is here that the audience becomes implicated in the drama, taking on the character of Herod. The music becomes a 'phallic eye', holding her still, more for our eyes than our ears, Kramer suggests, and as we gaze on her, having obtained 'the unseen position from which to gratify scopic desire on the body of a real woman', we join in her debasement.[10]

Kramer writes that the musical handling of the all-consuming dramatic image of the gaze is achieved more by broad effect than structural process, but at the risk of contradicting himself he illustrates the connexion between one of Salome's identifying motives, an arpeggio figure in C♯, and the motive associated with Jochanaan's body (Example 1, a–b).[11] This second motive leads

Example 1   Strauss, *Salome*: (a) Salome's motive; (b) the Body motive

(a)

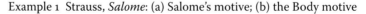

(b)

Nichts in   der   Welt   war so   weiss____ wie dein   Leib

Salome into an unaccustomed perfect cadence – on which more later – by breaking down her original motive in two sweeps, A and B, the first of which is a simple decoration, the second of which plays with the original rhythm. This 'collapse' of Salome into the body of Jochanaan signifies her longing for sexual union, and also suggests that it is this desire that kills her. As we shall see, a similarly elemental symbolic use of the function of the dominant has a rich hermeneutic significance in *Death in Venice*.

The dancing moon

One aspect of Kramer's reading that interests me particularly is his interpretation of Wilde's symbol of the moon, with which I disagree. The image survives intact in Strauss's opera, although another commentator on the work, Tethys Carpenter, claims that 'Strauss's moon is hardly more important than a conversational gambit'.[12]

The opera, like the play, introduces the moon in its second line, calling it, like Salome, a princess; from this moment on the two are dramatically twinned, and their fortunes parallel.[13]

THE PAGE OF HERODIAS
Look at the moon! ...

THE YOUNG SYRIAN
She has a strange look. She is like a little princess ... who has little white doves for feet. You would fancy she was dancing.

At the start of the fourth scene, Herod too is struck by the moon, but his reading is different. A critical reference to its nakedness is omitted in Strauss's libretto.

HEROD
The moon has a strange look to-night. Has she not a strange look? She is like a mad woman, a mad woman who is seeking everywhere for lovers. [She is naked too. She is quite naked. The clouds are seeking to clothe her nakedness, but she will not let them. She shows herself naked in the sky.] She reels through the clouds like a drunken woman. ...

HERODIAS
No; the moon is like the moon, that is all. Let us go within.

Salome, like the others, remarks on the moon in her second extended thought on stage;[14] tellingly, she thinks it is virginal ('The moon is cold and chaste. I am sure she is a virgin, she has a virgin's beauty. She has never defiled herself'). Considering this alongside the frequent description of Salome as little (dipping little lips into wine, possessing little teeth that will leave little marks in fruit that Herod can then finish off), it is clear that she is portrayed as a child – and not only that but the stepchild of Herod.

Wilde's recurring image of the clouds covering the moon like muslin veils, not present in Strauss, adds resonance to the pairing of the moon and Salome – who of course famously makes a feature of removing her veils, so uncovering her naked virginity in just the way that Herod thinks that the moon is doing. But even without this elaboration, the image of Salome and the moon as a mutually reinforcing pair is clear enough in the opera. The image of the dancing moon, elegant for Narraboth, drunken and louche for Herod, is the last important and obvious parallel with Salome.

Yet aside from being a symbol of Narraboth's and Herod's lustful gazing at Salome, and her desire to keep herself chaste (even if only for Jochanaan, for whom she clearly has a sexual longing), this obsessive interpretation of the moon serves to establish an important decadent trope: that knowledge comes through scopic contemplation, through the sensual appreciation of beauty, as readily as through the pure exercise of intellect. The moon means something to Salome, Narraboth, and Herod, however different their interpretations may be, because that is how things communicate meaning in the world. The wise learn by looking.

This is also probably the motivating thought of one of the least comfortable characterizations in *Salome*, that of the Jews. While Narraboth and Herod effectively worship Salome's beauty, and Salome worships her own chastity, all of these visible or capable of being tested visually, the Jews worship the invisible God, a belief which in decadent terms is unwise. Indeed, the foundation of their mistrust of Jochanaan is his assertion that he has seen God, whereas they hold inability to see God as the measure of piety. Herod, meanwhile, respects Jochanaan (despite the fact that he is clearly preaching against Herodias) because his love and insight are based on looking, on drawing intellectually from the appreciation of beauty.

One of the most often repeated lines in the drama is a variation on the sentiment that something dreadful is going to happen. Ultimately it seems that this terrible thing happens at the end of the opera, with the famous fall from Salome's last cadence, in C♯, to Herod's command to kill her, which stimulates the work's peremptory C minor close. Here the moon makes its last symbolic appearance. For Kramer it signifies the return of the phallic gaze to crush Salome, but I think it more likely, given the treatment of the image elsewhere in the opera, that it appears as a reminder and final confirmation of her virginity. All she does is kiss a man.

Before the kiss, Herod becomes very fearful, and begs his wife and attendants to hide with him inside the palace: 'something terrible will happen' ('Es wird Schreckliches geschehn'), he says twice. At this point Strauss gives three successive stage directions: 'the moon disappears' ('der Mond verschwindet'), 'it becomes dark' ('es wird dunkel'), and after Salome's last words, 'the moon breaks out again and illuminates Salome' ('Der Mond bricht wieder hervor und beleuchtet Salome'). Immediately before the third direction, Salome kisses Jochanaan's mouth, and in that moment Herod's fear leaves him. He commands Salome's death. The 'something terrible' that he had feared was not the judgement of the heavens on his lust for his stepdaughter, but rather his explicit sexual rejection by a child. In a moment, his sexual guilt is transferred onto Salome. She is the temptress, the moon who staggered drunkenly through the clouds during her perversely erotic dance of the seven veils. He switches from defendant to prosecutor and judge, and destroys the work's principal sexual monster.

The figure of the child

The child becomes a monster in *Salome* because she is sexualized in a manner that links *fin-de-siècle* misogyny to current constructions of the desirable. In two recent books James R. Kincaid establishes links between what he considers an erotic child in artistic contexts like *Salome* and *Death in Venice* and the very pressing modern concern with child molestation, making some uncomfortable claims along the way.[15] His starting point is the question 'Why do we tell tales of child abuse?', and he makes two assumptions: first that these stories 'are doing something for us', and second that they 'keep the subject so hot that we can disown it while welcoming it in the back door'.[16]

What Kincaid wants us to consider is that we have become so addicted to these stories that we no longer consider whether adults actually are sexually attracted to children. We have sexualized children while denying that we have done so, by an unfortunate conflation of cuteness with desire.

> We see children as, among other things, sweet, innocent, vacant, smooth-skinned, spontaneous, and mischievous. We construct the desirable [e.g. in adult women] as, among other things, sweet, innocent, vacant, smooth-skinned, spontaneous, and mischievous. There's more to how we see the child, and more to how we construct what is sexually desirable – but not much more. To the extent that we learn to see 'the child' and 'the erotic' as coincident, we are in trouble. So are the children.[17]

The origins of these forms of beauty are in Rousseau's vision of the Romantic Child, possessor of spontaneity, imagination, and closeness to God. For

Rousseau and for us, the child's qualities are mostly defined as absences: the child is '*free* of adult corruptions; *not yet burdened with* the weight of responsibility, mortality, and sexuality; *liberated from* "the light of common day"'.[18]

He perhaps overstates his case, but these observations demonstrate that the modern figure of 'the child' is to an extent a concept independent of age, more a manner of perceiving than a state of being, but something prized and deeply erotically charged. Ultimately Kincaid's claim is that we are all inculpated in the eroticization of children, and that we demonize the paedophile, telling endless stories about him, as a means of hiding our own guilt. In this sense we could say that for most of the course of *Salome* Herod is a type for ourselves, but that the turn of events in the closing pages converts him into the monstrous killer who perhaps characteristically – and here he stands diametrically opposed to our understanding of the Gothic story – blames the child for what has happened, transferring his sexual guilt like a rapist who blames a woman for being attractive.[19] In the case of *Salome*, we agree with him up to a point: the child has, after all, brought about the beheading of a holy man. Similarly, in *Death in Venice* Tadzio can seem to be presented as a sexually dangerous, corrupting, Salome-ish child.

Wagnerian process in Strauss and Britten

Before undertaking an analysis of Britten's opera to examine that claim, we should establish the links between details of Strauss's and Britten's musical techniques and the way that Kincaid believes that the full truth of some of our stories is being concealed. The most complex aspect of *Salome*'s structure is Strauss's alliance of tonal association with a basic tonal opposition of C and C♯, which, as for Wagner after *Tristan*, can each be considered as an amalgam of major and minor modes.[20] Tethys Carpenter expresses the basic relationship of the main associative tonal centres to the overarching opposition of C and C♯ as in Example 2a. Each key has an upper and lower third, corresponding to particular dramatic functions. C♯ and its relations belong to Salome, and C and its relations belong to whatever is opposed to her. When Salome seduces Narraboth and Herod, she adopts a timid A minor, flattening her C♯ keynote. When she obtains her desire, the unlocking of Jochanaan and then his beheading, she regains her C♯.[21]

C is principally associated with Jochanaan, although Herod also borrows it, as he borrows any key in his immediate surroundings. In this sense he is the opposite of Herodias, who has no associated key of her own but instinctively opposes whatever is around her tonally, reflecting her antagonistic character. Only in his final C minor death warrant is Herod ever decisively in his associated key. Jochanaan, meanwhile, tends often to turn his C towards its lower third, A♭. Craig Ayrey argues that A♭ has been principally associated with his mouth as opposed to his entire person, and that its final structural close into C♯ during Salome's monologue confirms the symbolic meaning of the opposition of C and C♯. Salome's desire in the opera is to be acknowledged as an individual, not as her mother's daughter, and to be the subject of Jochanaan's gaze, not Herod's. Although in life Jochanaan can refuse to acknowledge her by making himself blind to her by force of will, in death, and by translating his mouth, his kiss of recognition, into her own dominant, Salome is able to symbolically make him look at and acknowledge her.[22]

The tonal structure is more complex than this outline suggests, however, and as Example 2b shows, there are key centres in this opera on every chromatic pitch except F♯ and G.[23] The high incidence of chromatic tonicization at the deeper levels of structure accounts for Strauss's far greater willingness, in comparison to Wagner, to offer regular cadences. When tonal shapes unfold as patiently as they do in Wagner, a single perfect cadence per scene is possible; when they are so insecurely bandied about as they are in Strauss, frequent cadencing is required in order to establish any shape at all.

Among these additional key centres, D is associated with the pious blindness of the Jews in the minor mode, or the divine revelation of Jochanaan in the major. It can move easily in several directions. The absence of a strong structural G anywhere in the design means that, although Salome can turn A♭, enharmonically G♯, into the symbolic post-mortem gaze of recognition from Jochanaan, the world that is opposed to her, C, cannot gain similar strength through its own dominant. In any case, the unresolved final tension between Salome's C♯ and the C minor that destroys her seems to me entirely apt in dramatic terms, although Carpenter considers it a flaw in the design.[24]

However various the tonal centres in *Salome* are, they tend to coalesce, as Figure 2b shows, around the essential tension between C and C♯, and particularly around Salome's C♯, so that the opera's principal musical tension can be easily understood. A similarly straightforward tension narrates at the background level in *Death in Venice*, which, like *Salome*, engages with

Example 2 Strauss, *Salome*: the principal tonal relations

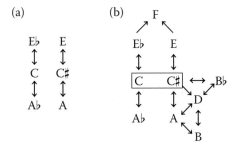

post-Wagnerian questions of tonal structure in opera, remarkable as that may seem so late in the 20th century, and in the face of Britten's known views on Wagner. In truth, Britten's opposition to the Wagnerian aesthetic operates more on the levels of form, genre, and harmonic palette than of structural tonal language. As in *Salome*, Britten's associated tonal centres pit the central character against harmful others. There is general agreement that the protagonist, the writer Aschenbach, has the associated key of E major, although he is also associated, particularly in the first act, with a meandering, serial-shaped but tonally tinged harmonic colouring that cannot so readily be pinned down. Tadzio, the Polish boy that Aschenbach falls in love with, and who is performed silently by a dancer, is generally in or spoken of in A major, where he is joined by the various characters – sung by the single baritone voice – who function as corrupting guides.

Disease and tonal association in 'Death in Venice'

Salome features in Mann's 1947 novel *Dr Faustus*, whose protagonist Adrian Leverkühn attends the notorious Dresden première. The character of Salome herself had featured in Oskar Panizza's 1894 play *Das Liebeskonzil*, where she is the devil's chosen means of spreading syphilis through the human race. Noting this, Hans Rudolf Vaget expresses the view that Salome had a mythical function for Mann as the creator of a sexual corruption that leads through a terrible disease to death – the embodiment, indeed, of a necessary link between desire and downfall.[25] This may help to explain why in Mann's neoclassical novella of intergenerational lust, Aschenbach's loitering in Venice during an outbreak of typhus leads him, through the seductiveness of the child who is the focus of his gaze, to the same deadly fate.

Britten's music charts the cancerous growth of the concupiscence that will overwhelm Aschenbach's personality in two ways: first, by subtle handling of the two associated tonalities of the opera, and second, by the manipulation of the gaze through the same trope of the dance that gives Salome her power. In the course of the opera the nature of subjectivity is questioned and even undermined, and the moment at which Aschenbach briefly pulls away the last veil covering his private emotional parts is a point of heightened engagement with the elusive meaning of the work.

At the opening, Aschenbach is the archetype of the subjective Romantic artist, engaging with the world at a studious remove, omniscient and aloof, guided by the pure processes of reason, and managing his writing through rigorous formal control. In his world, he is the centre. This makes him lonely, but it also makes him powerful and even in a sense immortal. As a subject he cannot be touched, reshaped, or distorted by another's views.

In the first scene Aschenbach presents himself in a characteristic monologue. The opening is emotionally cool for the most part, the effect enhanced by, as Philip Rupprecht notes, the 'unproductive' use of serial technique in its opening bars.[26] The first row (Example 3), which is announced in the first vocal line, rises to a melodic height that offers a major seventh before settling on the minor seventh from F to Eb. (The indecision between E and Eb is played out in subsequent pages.) The row is immediately brought back to its base through strict inversion. Yet its division into 4+3+5 notes, with the effect of fermata being stressed by the corresponding shift of repeating notes in the orchestral accompaniment, provides motivic material which can be used to suggest putatively tonal configurations – and, at least as important, groupings of three or four notes which are explored in various dramatic situations later in the work.[27] Of particular importance is the strong emphasis, enhanced by the only leap of the row, on E major, on the second rising third, from G# to B, and on the major and minor sevenths already mentioned. The second and third rows (Example 4), which are introduced orchestrally alongside the sung words 'I reject the words called forth by passion' (at R6 in the score), further deepen the emerging sense of E as a tonal focus for the opening scene. As they interlock contrapuntally their complementary fall and rise of two octaves apiece has the effect of articulating an arpeggiation of the modally mixed E tonic.

Example 3 Britten, *Death in Venice*, first row

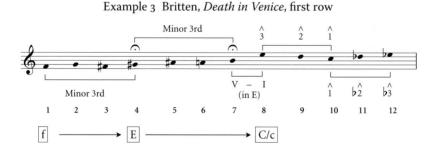

Example 4 Britten, *Death in Venice*, second and third rows

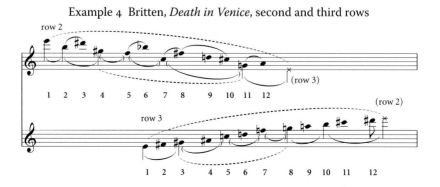

Example 5 Britten, *Death in Venice*, middleground sketch of opening

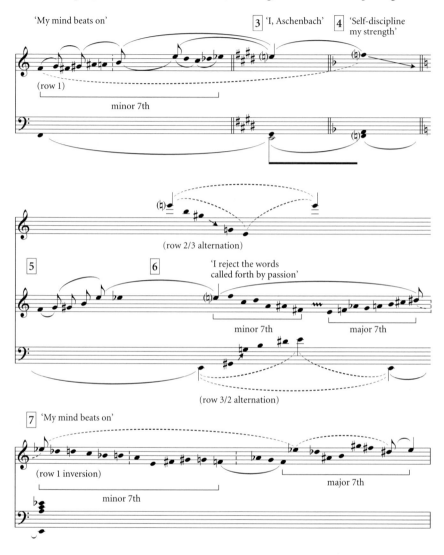

Example 6 Britten, *Death in Venice*, from Act I, scene 1

But it is as a larger unit that the opening scene most strongly establishes both Aschenbach's association with the E tonic, and the more complex way that tonal focus is presented (see Example 5). The first row, whose boundary interval is a minor seventh, is part of a rising motion that is expanded to a major seventh with the arrival of E-tonic brass fanfares for Aschenbach's first proclamation of his subjectivity at R3 ('I, Aschenbach'; within two bars the clash between *d♯′* and *e″* recalls the opening dispute between those notes). The score shows how, on the restatement of the row immediately before this, Aschenbach rises back through D♯ to an E – not the final D♭ and E♭ of the row – in preparation for his E major statement (Example 6). After nine bars the line has risen a semitone further to the modified repeat of this material on a kind of brief F tonic at R4, as Aschenbach explains that self-discipline and routine are his particular creative strengths. If E major is Aschenbach's key in the opera then it is a key essentially and importantly complicated by an F standing for the 'serial' component of his opening music, the starting point from which the tonicized E first arose. Also of interest in the E area is a figure unfolding the minor third from G♯ to B that will be central to the climax of the first act.

It is important to stress the two components of Aschenbach's character as expressed in the music. The text that comes at R3 suggests the E-component of Aschenbach's character – fame, honour, and the crucial subjective 'I' – while that at R4, the F-centred reminder of the starting point, the 'serial' aspect, quickly establishes that the Apollonian side of his artistic temperament, the urge to control and rationalize, is as essential as the music on E again at R6, for the 'words called forth by passion' and the 'easy judgement of the heart'. The E/serial duality of Aschenbach, as presented in this opening scene, is, then, a careful blend of what will increasingly through the opera be associated with the Dionysian and Apollonian, the chaotic and ordered, the passionate and the rational. What Arnold Whittall calls the opera's ' "modulat[ion]" from an initial twelve-note proposition to a modal "resolution" which seems both ambiguous and inevitable' is a move from the E/serial opening to the pure modal A (over a deep trilling A/G♯) of Tadzio's closing bars.[28]

Tadzio is introduced to music which soon provides the first moment of genuine tonal clarity in the work. Its A major has a defining mark of a rising melodic major seventh from A to G♯. At first sight, Aschenbach simply calls him 'the boy', but after a struggle to interpret the distant calls of his relatives, he correctly interprets his name as Tadzio (two bars before R98). Tadzio's music is increasingly coloured by the building up of a gamelan ensemble, until by R99, and the *largamente* marking, the Orientalism is overwhelming. Note the strong A major underpinning of this passage (Example 7a). The quiet restatement of Tadzio's theme which follows at R100 (Example 7b) fixes the

Example 7   Britten, *Death in Venice*, from Act I, scene 5

impression of his key. Philip Rupprecht notes that it is 'the first *root-position* triadicism of the entire opera'.[29]

We should not miss the significance of Tadzio's stage presentation, even though the tonal shape is our main concern. Britten makes Tadzio a spectacle for the audience, particularly in the Games of Apollo, his impressive show of physical prowess at the end of the first act, by not only giving him no words to sing but making him a dancer, his motions transfixing the eye. (Myfanwy Piper, the librettist, thought that the Games of Apollo should be danced naked, but the idea was ruled out.)[30] The only way we can relate to Tadzio at all is to look, and ideally to stare, at him. We are invited into Aschenbach's mind as much by that dramatic legerdemain as we are by the almost exclusive focus on Aschenbach's narrative voice – this opera comes as close as any to having a first-person narrator. If the opera works effectively on us, we begin to lose any sense of a distinction between Aschenbach and ourselves; his fascination with the boy and his loss of control become ours.

This unusual narrative situation may lead us to think, as Aschenbach arguably does, that beings and events in the outside world are merely aspects of his own character, denied all agency of their own. Tadzio's interest or otherwise in Aschenbach will then appear to be imaginary or spurious. Yet militating against this solipsistic reading is the experience in the opera house, where real human beings perform real actions that are presented in a realistic manner. Tadzio is not to Aschenbach as the ghost of Duncan is to Macbeth, not an imaginary figment but a real boy. It is essential to remember this, and to realize that it is part of Britten's artfulness to invite us to forget it: it is one of the ways we can avoid confronting one of the opera's most difficult figures – that of the monstrous child.

We shall return to Tadzio's A major; but what of his 'Orientalism'? Britten had often used the sound of the gamelan in earlier operas, notably orientalizing Quint in *The Turn of the Screw* (1954) and Oberon in *A Midsummer Night's Dream* (1960). In both cases men pursue boys – Quint, Miles; Oberon, the Indian boy that Titania wishes to keep for herself. But as Philip Brett notes, the gamelan music is applied to the 'wrong' party in *Death in Venice* – not the sexually dangerous figure of the older man, but the 'innocent' or 'nescient' figure of the boy. Brett summarizes his view of the Orientalism of *Death in Venice* by saying that it

> was dramatically apt, since the mind-driven Aschenbach through whom we perceive both Venice and Tadzio would be culturally conditioned to project them both in terms of the exotic, that which is Other. This Asian-derived music, then, opens up the meanings of the opera to

embrace the European philosophical discourse of Self and Other, and in turn to invoke the West's insatiable appetite for colonization – the same patterns of domination being apparent here as in classical pederasty.[31]

I think it unlikely that Britten intended a postcolonial critique in this opera; he had more original and dangerous concerns. What can be said more categorically is that in this presentation, Tadzio is the object of the gaze of the subject Aschenbach. By the simple but brilliant expedient of making Tadzio a dancer, Britten ensures that Tadzio is the subject of our gaze too. Safe in the darkened theatre we are invited to feast our eyes on him, and objectify him just as Herod objectifies Salome.

Like the voyeur in Sartre's vivid example of what he calls 'the Look',[32] Aschenbach is contented and safe while he objectifies the boy. The entire joy of their relationship comes, indeed, from its one-sidedness. But if the voyeur is caught watching, he suddenly switches from being an omnipotent, omniscient subject, and becomes the object of somebody else's Look. Being objectified in this way, Sartre suggests, causes him to feel shame. It is, in brief, why for Sartre 'hell is other people', and why human love is always painful: because it is based on a lover wanting a sexual object but being tormented when, as is inevitable, the sexual object demonstrates that it wants the lover as an object too. This desubjectifying of Aschenbach will indeed come by the end of the act, and the effect of all this looking will partly resemble the result of the tussle in *Salome*. Aschenbach neither loses his head nor kills his child obsession, but like Jochanaan the child's look will kill him, and once more, the audience is invited to entertain the thought that the child might be the monster.

The multivalence of opera

At the end of Act I, the last moment I shall discuss, Aschenbach is on the verge of explaining what his looking *means*. Expressing it in the most hackneyed terms, he says 'I love you', and spends much of Act II worrying the definition of this love. Till this point Aschenbach has mostly been the contemplating subject, the one who looks, but at the end of each act he experiences the piercing sensation of becoming the object of one of Tadzio's looks. The first occasion leads him to declare his love; the second, when the look is accompanied by a beckon which completes the objectification of Aschenbach as a child's plaything, immediately brings on the protagonist's death.

In an opera which sets Apollo against Dionysus, and Self against Other, the precise moment at which the switch is made, and the voyeuristic subject becomes the object of a second voyeur's gaze, is of critical importance. Tadzio's second look, the opera's fatal stroke, results in a resolution of the work into his own A major. Aschenbach's E major has expired. Whittall, Brett, and Rupprecht agree that in the moment of Tadzio's first look, the 'I love you', Aschenbach's E major begins to act as a dominant to Tadzio's A major – with the narrative effect either of allowing Aschenbach a strong moment of self-awareness as a homosexual (the traditional queer reading), or of demonstrating his growing aesthetic need for the boy.

But it is clear from our analysis of the opening scene of the work that Aschenbach's music is not merely centred on E. In tonal terms, the role of the 'serial' material is an important complication, and it has text associations with the Apollonian side of Aschenbach's character, the ordering, logical side which reins in excess of passion. (What seems to be in play here is an interrogation of the assumption that musical order in the 1970s is serial, or at least post-tonal, and tonality is a forbidden sensual indulgence.) So it is significant that this 'serial' component disappears at the end of the act. Important too, as Ruth Longobardi has recently suggested, is that the moments leading up to his confession are by no means as uncomplicated as the traditional readings might suggest. She writes that 'the plague motive [heard before 'I love you'], because it derives directly from a Dionysian realm that functions beyond the protagonist's point of view, erodes the psychological realism of this moment, superimposing on Aschenbach's experience a layer of mythical significance'.[33]

Longobardi notes that opera is a multivalent art-form, in which far from supporting the text or the singer, the orchestra can have an antagonistic role, which should be examined carefully for any hermeneutic reading. It is the lack of this objective commentating role that concerns Carolyn Abbate in her reading of Wotan's Monologue. The fact that the orchestra colludes with Wotan, never undermining his reading of the history of the *Ring* in the way it would do for other characters, leads her to suggest that this is a rare moment when music can *lie*.[34]

The multivalence in the present context is provided by the plague motive, a four-note motive marked 'y' on Example 8, which has been associated with the corrupting characters in the opera, and which makes itself heard menacingly in low brass instruments. Longobardi's essential insight here cannot be denied: at the same time that Aschenbach is building up to his confession of love (the moment when he is left utterly exposed by the sudden quiet from the orchestra – a symbolic dropping of the final veil, perhaps, as the curtain falls on Act I), the orchestra warns that the infatuation will lead him to death from a plague that has been making itself felt thematically throughout the first act. But something even more remarkable is going on which shows the junction between the binaries of Self and Other, Apollo and Dionysus.

Example 8 Britten, *Death in Venice*, Act I, scene 7 middleground sketch

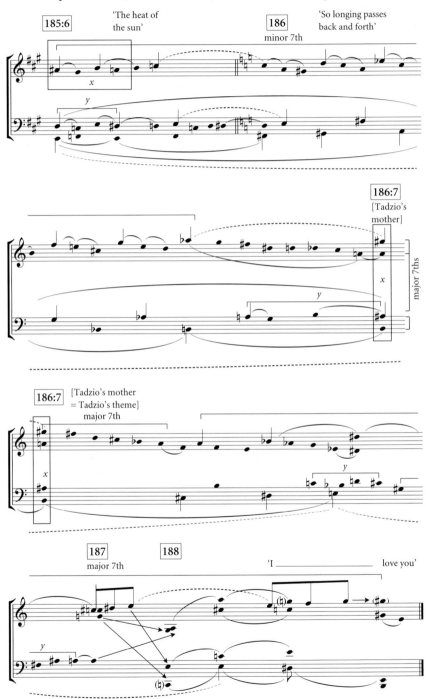

The trouble with the child in 'Death in Venice'

The crucial revelatory moment in *Death in Venice* is Aschenbach's 'I love you'; it has its effect by maximizing our experience of the switch between states of being, and so the existing readings of the work – whether as an autobiographical coming-out drama, a triumph of the appreciation of formal beauty over carnal lust, a critique of the West's relation to the East, or an abstract resolution of serialism to diatonicism or modalism – may all be partly concealing another possible rationalization that is lurking. The broader 'truth' of the opera, though we should be wary of so grand a term, may be in this case that Aschenbach, like us, is trying to hide something behind the story his first-person narrative voice wishes to tell, even after it has so honestly drawn our attention to his crisis of self-control.

Five bars before R186 we see the plague motive that Longobardi identified as having a disturbing effect, the motive marked 'y' in Example 8, helping to mark moments of arrival in this passage. It accompanies Aschenbach's suggestion that it is the heat of the sun that makes him feel ill, and forms the upbeat and downbeat to the arrival of Tadzio's mother, whose elegantly falling lines are a woodwind augmentation of Tadzio's percussive contours.

The moment of her arrival, seven after R186 (Example 9), is worth dwelling on for a moment. Here Britten piles up three major sevenths to form a chord that is derived from notes 4–7 of Aschenbach's original row, G♯, A, A♯, and B (see Example 3). These are the first four notes on route to the opening emphasis on E, the part of Aschenbach's row that is associated with his passion in the absence of his self-controlling intellect (boxed and mark 'x' in Example 8). They are also the first four vocal notes of the present passage, and the top third of the E major triad that closes the act. Their critical importance in drawing out the yearning and passionate side of Aschenbach's character is obvious: they verticalize the very idea of his passion and so locate its consummation with pinpoint accuracy. Recall that the association of Aschenbach with E major is too tidy, and misses something very important – the stripping away

Example 9 Britten, *Death in Venice*, from Act I, scene 7

here, with the removal of the 'serial' component of his associated tonal complex, of his rational self. The bass motions of this passage are from tonic E to dominant B, in stepwise motion until just before R187. Also notice a scalar rise in the tenor voice that is unable to decide whether to create an interval of a minor or major seventh with the bass. This dithering is another essential part of the Aschenbach row, from F to E/E♭, but now removed from its original context.

Dramatically the arrival of Tadzio's mother is the crux of the scene. As wordless here as her transfixing son, nevertheless she brings on Aschenbach's first catastrophe simply because she reminds him of the youthfulness of Tadzio. He is not a representation of a Platonic Form, a panacea for writer's block, but a barely pubescent boy whom it is agony to love – and a real one, too, not just an aspect of Aschenbach's solipsistic self, as I have already noted, though of course Aschenbach internalizes the situation. The mother's appearance makes Aschenbach feel essentialized as a monster; Tadzio's first glance makes him feel objectivized.

Aschenbach might say 'I love you', but the love he acknowledges in the remainder of the opera – a love of form, of artistic inspiration, or of the release from homophobic oppression, the love that the work's critics have acknowledged – may not be the fully honest expression of the love he actually feels. The moment that Aschenbach's nature becomes most clearly focused in the 'pinpointing' of his passion is also the moment when he sheds a vital part of his character, and in so doing runs away, afraid, from his own fundamental responsibility to shape that nature. The love at the end of this act is scandalous, and despite coming close to acknowledging it in these closing bars, Aschenbach and Britten never again bring it so close to the surface. The chaotic wellspring of Aschenbach's passion for an underage boy, which the popular media would reductively label his 'paedophilia', is henceforth hidden from view beneath the distracting alternatives.

But so what if Aschenbach is a 'paedophile'? Surely he dies, and (the popular media would go on to say) good riddance. But we cannot honestly claim that Britten says 'good riddance' too. Aschenbach dies the traditional death of the suffering *woman* in opera. In musical terms that Britten has established over several works (particularly, in this context, *The Rape of Lucretia* and *The Turn of the Screw*), he perishes because he is consumed by the lusting eye of an 'orientalized' other. The beautiful creature that Aschenbach and we have been staring at turns on us. Up till now we have been piecing together an understanding of the creative struggles of an artist torn between expression and form by adopting the decadent attitude – partly concealed by Mann's and Britten's neoclassical veneer – that knowledge comes from looking. Now at the moment when his physicality triumphs over everyone on the stage, in the ballet of the Games of Apollo, the scopophile object becomes a scopophile subject. He looks at Aschenbach. 'Ah! don't smile like that! No one should be smiled at like that.' No one should be objectified in that way by another. (Look at what happened when Jochanaan was objectified as a mouth after he had objectified Salome as the Daughter of Sodom.)

Yet Tadzio looks, and looks again, the second time with a beckoning that wrenches the last breath out of Aschenbach. To defend the claim that Tadzio has no agency here, a critic will have to explain away both the clear indications of the stage directions and the dramatic experience of seeing realistically portrayed human subjects on stage. Aschenbach is sick, and any failure on his part to acknowledge the possibility of other minds can be understood, but we should not make the same mistake. The destructive agent Tadzio may on the face of it seem simply to smile and be friendly, but the result of his actions, willing or no, is to objectify and essentialize another human being. Aschenbach loses his capacity to brood, to see the situation whole, and gives himself over to the ultimately fatal pursuit of lustful propinquity.

And that is, perhaps, the truth of this opera's closing scene. The figure more innocent in the closing bars is Aschenbach. It is, outrageously, Tadzio who is the more destructive pervert. Tadzio has corrupted the personality of the older man, reducing his enlightened complexity and rational control of his emotions to a purely carnal lust which overwhelms reason, compelling him to act against all sense by remaining in a plague-ridden Venice, and bringing the once-great figure of the artist to the humiliating depths of his death on the beach, mascara teeming down his cheeks.

Notes

1 Clifford Hindley, 'Contemplation and Reality: A Study in Britten's "Death in Venice"', *Music & Letters* 71 (1990), pp. 511–23, at p. 511. He expresses the thought still more delicately on the Platonic model in Clifford Hindley, 'Eros in Life and Death: *Billy Budd* and *Death in Venice*', in *MCCC*, pp. 147–64.

2 The lines connecting various late-19th-century retellings of the Salome story are traced in Lawrence Kramer, 'Culture and Hermeneutics: The Salome Complex', *Cambridge Opera Journal* 2 (1990), pp. 269–94.

3 A Freudian interpretation of what can be read as Salome's 'incestuous' love for Jochanaan is offered in Arthur Ganz, 'Transformations of the Child Temptress: Mélisande, Salomé, Lulu', *Opera Quarterly* 3 (1987), pp. 12–20 at pp. 17–19.

4 Thomas Mann, *Death in Venice*, trans. H. W. Lowe-Porter (Harmondsworth: Penguin, 1933), p. 30; Thomas Mann, *Der Tod in Venedig* (Frankfurt am Main: Fischer, 2007, orig. edition 1913), p. 30.

5 Kramer, 'The Salome Complex', and Lawrence Kramer, *Opera and Modern Culture: Wagner and Strauss* (Berkeley, CA: University of California Press, 2004).

6 Kramer, 'The Salome Complex', p. 271.

7 See *ibid.*, p. 274.

8 *Ibid.*, p. 278.

9 *Ibid.*, p. 281.

10 *Ibid.*, p. 282.

11 *Ibid.*, pp. 285–6, 289–90.

12 Tethys Carpenter, 'Tonal and Dramatic Structure', in *Richard Strauss: Salome*, ed. Derrick Puffett (Cambridge: Cambridge University Press, 1989), pp. 88–108 at p. 89.

13 In the examples that follow, the English text is the translation of Wilde's original French by his lover, Lord Alfred Douglas. The published text was probably modified by Wilde, but based on Douglas's work.

14 Both Narraboth and Herod have Salome as their first thought; Salome's first thought is to wonder why Herod will not stop looking at her.

15 James R. Kincaid, *Child-Loving: The Erotic Child and Victorian Culture* (New York: Routledge, 1992), and James R. Kincaid, *Erotic Innocence: The Culture of Child Molesting* (Durham, NC: Duke University Press, 1998).

16 Kincaid, *Erotic Innocence*, p. 6.

17 *Ibid.* Kincaid cites a study of desirability in 25-year-old women, which used a computer program to compare the appearance of children and women. It discovered that 'the ideal 23-year-old woman … had a 14-year-old's abundant lips and an 11-year-old's delicate jaw', with a child's prominent eyes and cheekbones. *Ibid.*, p. 18.

18 *Ibid.*, p. 13.

19 The most senior Muslim cleric in Australia, Sheik Taj Din al-Hilali, compared women who do not wear a full veil to 'uncovered meat' that will inevitably encourage rape by (it is implied) innocent men. His words were widely reported across the world in October 2006; see, for example, *The Economist* (26 October 2006), p. 1.

20 The most detailed analyses of *Salome* to date are still those by Derek Puffett, Tethys Carpenter, and Craig Ayrey in Puffett's Cambridge Opera Handbook to the work. See n. 12 above.

21 Carpenter, 'Tonal and Dramatic Structure', p. 96.

22 See Craig Ayrey, 'Salome's Final Monologue', in *Richard Strauss: Salome*, ed. Puffett, pp. 109–30 at p. 111.

23 This profligacy leads Carpenter to find the overall structure unsatisfactory. See Carpenter, 'Tonal and Dramatic Structure', pp. 97 and 107, where she writes that Strauss has 'miss[ed] the point of *Tristan*'s tonality in spite of his sophisticated adoption of its harmonic and instrumental style, just as, in the tone poems, he had missed the point of the sonata principle while filling

its outlines'. As recent studies by James Hepokoski have shown, Strauss's 'deformation' of the sonata plan is anything but a failure. See, for instance, James A. Hepokoski, 'Fiery-Pulsed Libertine or Domestic Hero? Strauss's *Don Juan* Reinvestigated', in *Richard Strauss: New Perspectives on the Composer and his Work*, ed. Bryan Gilliam (Durham, NC: Duke University Press, 1992), pp. 133–73; Hepokoski, 'Structure and Program in *Macbeth*: A Proposed Reading of Strauss's First Symphonic Poem', in *Richard Strauss and his World*, ed. Bryan Gilliam (Princeton: Princeton University Press, 1992), pp. 67–89; and Hepokoski, 'Framing *Till Eulenspiegel*', *19th-Century Music* 30 (2006), pp. 4–43.

24 I find it difficult to be sympathetic to her insistence in opera on a model of tonal coherence that works well in a relatively short instrumental movement but seems irrelevant in music on this scale. Even symphonic works of this period, and not only those by Strauss, operate according to different but still satisfying rules as compared to the archetypal Classical tonal plan she seems to expect.

25 Hans Rudolf Vaget, 'The Spell of *Salome*: Thomas Mann and Richard Strauss', in *German Literature and Music: An Aesthetic Fusion, 1890–1989*, ed. Claus Reschke and Howard Pollack (Munich: Wilhelm Fink, 1992), pp. 39–60.

26 Philip Rupprecht, *Britten's Musical Language* (Cambridge: Cambridge University Press, 2001), p. 249.

27 Noting that its four highlighted notes are F, G♯, B, and E♭, Rupprecht speculates on a possible reference to the *Tristan* chord (*ibid.*, pp. 249–50).

28 Arnold Whittall, *The Music of Britten and Tippett: Studies in Themes and Techniques* (Cambridge: Cambridge University Press, 1982), p. 261.

29 Rupprecht, *Britten's Musical Language*, p. 274.

30 Britten wrote that the idea was 'excellent, & could be wonderfully beautiful, Hellenically evocative', but 'I am worried lest the work might cause a certain interest that none of us really wants!' See *HCBB*, p. 339.

31 Philip Brett, 'Britten, Benjamin', *Grove Music Online* <http://www.grovemusic.com/>, 8.

32 Jean-Paul Sartre, *Being and Nothingness: An Essay on Phenomenological Ontology*, trans. Hazel E. Barnes (London: Routledge, 2003), pp. 276–326. Lacan, who derided Sartre, must have derived his 'Gaze' from Sartre nevertheless.

33 Ruth Sara Longobardi, 'Reading Between the Lines: An Approach to the Musical and Sexual Ambiguities of *Death in Venice*', *Journal of Musicology* 22 (2003), pp. 327–64 at pp. 333, 337.

34 Carolyn Abbate, *Unsung Voices: Opera and Musical Narrative in the Nineteenth Century* (Princeton: Princeton University Press, 1991), chap. 3.

10 From 'The Borough' to Fraser Island

Claire Seymour

Dear Benjamin Britten,

I enclose the synopsis for a libretto by Patrick White.

He has suggested that I forward it to you, since he would rather you wrote the opera than any other composer.

The Sydney Opera House opens in 1966 and the Elizabethan Trust Director, Stefan Haag, has asked White for a libretto in the hope that an opera could finally evolve for the opening.

I have shown it to K. Clark who feels that you might be interested.

Patrick White is now in London and will be here until the end of September. If you are interested I could bring him up to Aldeburgh one day for discussion.

I am most hesitant about approaching you an artist personally, but my admiration for his work is of the same order as I have for yours, so I hope you will not mind this informal approach.

Yours sincerely,
Sidney Nolan

So wrote the artist, Sidney Nolan, to Benjamin Britten on 8 August 1963.[1] Enclosed with the letter was a 21-page libretto synopsis, beginning with a cast list and followed by an account of the act and scene divisions, a brief description of each scene, including stage directions, clarifications of mood and atmosphere at the dramatic and musical climaxes, and some dialogue. The tale outlined was the history of one Mrs Eliza Fraser – a history which exposed the cruelty and hypocrisy of allegedly civilized worlds, and which explored the passage from innocence to experience, the revelation of repressed instincts, notions of betrayal and injustice, of imprisonment and freedom, through symbols such as the 'outsider' and the power, both physical and psychological, of the sea.

Eliza Fraser was a wealthy Scottish lady who, returning from Australia with her husband, the sickly Captain James Fraser, was shipwrecked off the Queensland coast on 21 May 1836. The Frasers boarded a leaky longboat, and after an arduous journey – during which Mrs Fraser gave birth to a still-born child – eventually reached Sandy Island, now renamed Fraser Island. Upon landing, the survivors encountered native Aborigines; a scuffle ensued and James Fraser, demonstrating uncharacteristic bravery, was among those killed. His wife subsequently spent ten weeks living among these 'savages'. The details of her escape are disputed, but one account records that she met with a deserting convict, Bracefell, who had himself been hiding in the bush for ten years. Together they made their way to Moreton Bay, whereupon Fraser, ashamed of her experiences and afraid of society's censure, reneged on her promise to plead for clemency for Bracefell, and threatened to hand him over to the authorities. Disillusioned and betrayed, Bracefell fled back to the bush; Mrs Fraser returned to civil society, and later remarried. Her new husband, Captain Alexander Greene, orchestrated appeals for her and her children, and the citizens of Sydney donated a generous sum to compensate her for her ordeal. She aroused much curiosity and admiration, and even exhibited herself in a booth at a show in Hyde Park.

Patrick White's attention had been drawn to this story of savagery and self-discovery by a retrospective of Nolan's work at the Whitechapel Gallery in London, in 1957. During a visit to the poet, Barrie Reid, in Queensland, Nolan had travelled to Fraser Island, an experience which inspired his first 'Mrs Fraser Series'. Reid described the paintings:

> For Nolan she was an emblem of a primary recognition of our environ-
> ment, our landscape which most of us still did not see accurately, our
> eyes still, somehow, misted by Europe ... in extremity Mrs Fraser had
> acted out our own submerged history, our own unexplored or hidden
> responses ...[2]

White wrote to Nolan, 7 June 1958, professing his interest and requesting more information: 'When you had the exhibition at Whitechapel Gallery, I read something about the woman, whose name I forget, who survived ship-wreck on the coast of Australia in company with a convict. It sounds like mate-rial I could use, and one day you must tell me more about her – although I have made a vow never to go further back in time than the last World War.'[3] In a preface to the libretto synopsis which was sent to Britten, White described the genesis of his ideas:

> I first heard of the Frasers and the convict Bracefell in 1958 when
> Sidney Nolan told me about the series of paintings he had done on that
> theme. I was very interested in the story, but did not think I could use
> it. Then a couple of years ago I decided to write a novel based on the
> Frasers, made a journey to Fraser Island where the survivors of the

<u>Sterling Castle</u> landed in 1836, did a certain amount of research on my return, and wrote half the book. I gave it up because I felt that too many Australian writers were preoccupied with the 19th Century, and that we should deal rather with our own times. However, I remember thinking the Fraser story made for opera.

White made his first visit to Fraser Island in mid-1961; and a letter to Geoffrey Dutton, written in September of that year, indicates that White had begun working on the Fraser story by this date. It was therefore at the forefront of his mind when, shortly afterwards, he was asked to collaborate on an opera for the inauguration of the Sydney Opera House, although he voiced his concerns about the whole project in a letter to Ben Huebsch (17 February 1963), in characteristically dismissive fashion:

> P. S. The Elizabethan Theatre Trust has asked me to consider writing the libretto for an opera to open the Sydney Opera House. I have an idea, but it will depend upon whether I can accept the composer. There are some truly dreadful ones at large.[4]

It was at this point that Nolan suggested Britten as a possible composer. Nolan's friendship with Britten had begun in 1951 when they were introduced by Kenneth Clark – Nolan's first patron, and a director of the English Opera Group – during the Aldeburgh Festival. Why did Nolan feel that Britten might be interested in this project, or that a shared sensibility might make for a successful collaboration between Britten and White? Some clues may be revealed by Clark's thought-provoking introduction to his book on Nolan's own work:

> Nolan deals his blows all around him with any instrument which comes to hand ... but there is no feeling of eclecticism, because all of these varying modes or styles are seized upon, almost unconsciously, as the most effective means of making an urgent communication. In this way Nolan's paintings seem to me to resemble ... the music of Benjamin Britten ... both are ready to assault, with a sort of reckless innocence, subjects which prudish men would have drawn back from, and in doing so have employed a bewildering range of instruments ... provided that, as a result, we are roused from polite indifference. ... their heroes are the odd men out – Peter Grimes and Billy Budd, Ned Kelly and Bracefell. And in both there is a quality that I find very hard to describe, except by saying that they are men of genius, but that in both their imaginations there is something very strange just over the horizon; something which may never reveal itself, but which gives, by refraction, a faint colour of menace to all their work.[5]

Much the same could be said of Patrick White. Here Clark identifies a shared sensibility which might explain Nolan's eagerness to encourage collaboration between Britten and White, sensing that they would both be sympathetic towards a theme which was integral to his own work. Indeed, White's 1975 novel *A Fringe of Leaves* (in which Mrs Fraser's history finally achieved published form) depicts an 'odd woman out', one reminiscent of Britten's 'outsiders' – most notably perhaps, Peter Grimes – whose experiences range through territory similar to that explored by Britten in his operas.

Inevitably, during Britten's long career as an opera composer, various projects and subjects were proposed, discussed, planned, only to be later rejected in the face of practical or financial circumstances, changing artistic ambitions or conflicting relationships. *The Canterbury Tales, Mansfield Park, Abelard and Heloise, Tyco the Vegan, The Tale of Mr Tod, King Lear* – even an opera on the subject of St Peter – lay in Britten's 'considered-abandoned-future project' pile. In spite of this, initially the prospects for a fruitful collaboration must have seemed promising.

Writer and composer, born one year apart, had much in common. Aged 13, White was sent to Britain to be educated at Cheltenham and subsequently Cambridge. As one of the 'Auden generation' he shared the left-wing ideals that were prevalent among artist-intellectuals of the 1930s. As an adult, he expressed pacifist ideals which echoed those expressed by Britten in *Owen Wingrave*:

> Passive resistance is of course fraught with danger … I personally feel that the dangers and suffering those who choose to practise passive resistance are bound to encounter are preferable to the moral seepage and contaminating ashes which will overwhelm those who accept the nuclear-holocaust their political leaders are preparing for them.[6]

Denying his origins and distancing himself from his family in Australia, White settled in London and, at the end of the decade, joined the artistic exodus from England, travelling to Europe. However, just as Britten had returned to his Suffolk roots after experiments in America, so White was drawn back to his Australian roots and resettled in Castle Hill in the 1940s.

Both Britten and White had long, stable relationships – with Peter Pears and Manoly Lascaris respectively. In Australia at this time, homosexuality was seldom tolerated; in his novels, White associates homosexual love with art and artistry. For example, in *The Vivisector* and *The Twyborn Affair*, sexual ambivalence is depicted as an essential human condition which is bestowed with religious significance, and physical love is a means of participating in a fundamentally religious experience which is closely identified with art and the imagination. White explained the way that his own experience had permeated his fiction:

> Of course, all artists are terrible egotists. Unconsciously you are largely writing about yourself. I could never write about anything factual; I only have confidence in myself when I am another character. All the characters in my books are myself, but they are a kind of disguise.[7]

Britten would surely have sympathized with White's account of the artist's duty.

> Artists of any kind, if they are to amount to anything, must be prepared to take risks, to jump over the precipice every day of their lives, in their attempts to illuminate and perhaps alleviate the human dilemma. Alternatively, you settle for security and the congealing comforts of tradition. No doubt this is why the creative artist in Australia has always been considered somewhat suspect. He troubles the spirit, the conscience, the dormant imagination of the average man.[8]

Moreover, the story of Eliza Fraser seems to have been rather more than a short-lived 'dinner-party idea'. Britten's profound attraction to, and interest in, the Australian landscape and history is confirmed by his ambition, revealed much later to Nolan, to compose a ballet with a similar setting and subject. In June 1990, at the 43rd Aldeburgh Festival, in conversation with Donald Mitchell, Nolan recalled a journey which he and Britten had made to the Barrier Reef in 1970, during an English Opera Group tour of Australia.[9] Describing the tragic suicide of a young friend who had hanged himself on the morning of his wedding, Britten told Nolan of his plans for a ballet, which would combine presentation of the typical life of an English boy, growing up and going to Oxford, with the life of a boy raised in an Aboriginal tribe, in order to demonstrate Britten's belief that 'Western civilization wasn't bringing up its children properly, and he felt that the Aboriginals in the past had [...] they reared their children to deal with life and be at one with it, and we hadn't done that.'[10] During this interview, Nolan described how Britten had opened up emotionally during the visit. Yet, when they returned to Cairns, his mood changed:

> Well, that's the end of that. Now ... [w]hen we get back to England I won't be like that any more. ... My destiny is to be in harness and to die in harness.[11]

Mitchell suggested that this 'tragic death of the friend who committed suicide ... [was] an example of a hidden experience, within Britten; and yet when he went to Australia and had the Australian experience, that was a way of unlocking that experience ... it would have found expression and perhaps mitigation through the writing of the ballet.'[12] Nolan's reply implies that he felt that Britten repressed his instincts, allowing them to surface only in his art: 'Well, he wanted to say it, and then he instantly wanted to have it locked back again. ... And that was the end of that. It could only be discussed again in the context of a work of art.'[13]

By the end of his life, the death of this young acquaintance seems to have become intimately interwoven with the Australian theme. The 'young friend' alluded to was Piers Dunkerley, who had died in 1959, at Poole, not Oxford, from self-administered poisoning – and not in his fiancée's home but after a heated discussion about their plans to marry (reported by the press on 11 June 1959).[14] In his study of Nolan's work, Brian Adams reveals that one idea was for Nolan's snake designs to be flashed on to the stage to fuse the contrasting Aboriginal and European elements of the story at the moment when the Oxford choristers and a tribal circumcision ceremony rite merged, forming a climax as the young Englishman and his bride-to-be underwent the rites of fire, water and sexual initiation.[15] It may be that Dunkerley's death, too recent a pain when the *Fringe of Leaves* proposal first surfaced, lay at the heart of the projected ballet, which could serve as a kind of expurgation.

The story of Eliza Fraser, as retold by Patrick White, is essentially a journey from innocence to experience, from ignorance to self-knowledge. This progression is prepared at the start, as two members of the settlement community discuss the rather mysterious Mrs Roxburgh – the protagonist's name being changed to Ellen Roxburgh, along with various other details, to make the characters, so White declared,[16] more psychologically interesting:

> 'I will tell you one thing,' Miss Scrimshaw vouchsafed. 'Every woman has secret depths with which even she, perhaps, is unacquainted, and which sooner or later must be troubled.'[17]

She continues, 'Ah ... who am I to say? I only had the impression that Mrs Roxburgh could feel life has cheated her out of some ultimate in experience. For which she would be prepared to suffer, if need be.' (p. 17)

Changing landscapes and cultures chart this passage from the innocence which is pre-experience, through suffering and degradation, to a knowledge borne of understanding and acceptance. Mrs Roxburgh's 'secret depths', paralysed by the inflexible, repressive society into which she marries, begin to surface in the European settlements in Australia and Tasmania, where brutalized systems are rigidly enforced to maintain control and preserve hierarchies among a community which includes convicted and suspected criminals. A visit to her miscreant brother-in-law, Garnet, awakens her desires; and during the subsequent shipwreck, the sea itself seems to liberate her primitive, and sexual, self. The placid, obedient Mrs Roxburgh of polite Cheltenham society, is ultimately transformed by her life among 'savages' into one who can acknowledge the darkness in man's soul and the depth of human suffering.

In his novel, White emphasizes Ellen's relationship to her native land. Miss Scrimshaw describes Cornwall as 'A *remote* country! ... Of dark people' (p. 12). Like Grimes's marsh-banks, Zennor, near Land's End, is a wild, harsh land, swept by wind and sea, and is literally 'separated' from southern England by a river – like the stretch of water which divides Fraser Island from the Australian mainland. Responding to the landscape of Van Diemen's Land, Ellen remembers her childhood:

> Often on such a night at Z.[ennor], a country to which I *belonged* (more than I did to parents or family) I wld find myself wishing to be united with my surroundings, not as the dead, but fully alive. Here too ... I begin to feel closer to the country than to any human being. Reason, and the little I learned from the books I was given too late in life to more than fidget over, tells me I am wrong in thinking thus, but my instincts hanker after something deeper, which I may not experience this side of death. (p. 92)

It is a sense of union with place that Peter Grimes shares:

> I am native, rooted here
> [...]
> By familiar fields,
> Marsh and sand,
> Ordinary streets,
> Prevailing wind.[18]

and one which both Britten and White themselves experienced. An oft-quoted passage from Britten's 1964 Aspen Award speech, clarifies his commitment to his native land: 'reading a most perceptive and revealing article about [Crabbe's 'Peter Grimes'] by E. M. Forster, I suddenly realized where I belonged and what I lacked. I had become without roots, and when I got back to England six months later I was ready to put them down ... I believe in roots, in associations, in backgrounds, in personal relationships. ... my music now has its roots in where I live and work.'[19] Similarly, White declared:

> When I came back from overseas I felt I had to learn the language again.

That is one of the reasons I work in Australia. I write about Australia …
I think it's a good thing to be close to one's roots … The essence of what
you have to say you pick up before you're twenty, really, so it ought to be
possible to go away and draw on that.[20]

In contrast, Ellen's scholarly, hypochondriac husband, Austin Roxburgh,
finds no joy or fulfilment in the land or seascape. On board ship, he observes:
'An infernal wind blowing from the wrong quarter caused her voice to flicker
like the landscape; the latter in no way appealed to him.' (p. 26) '[T]aught as
a boy to suppress emotion' (p. 132), he embraces the cerebral, rejecting the
physical, tactile and sensuous. As the couple reflect on 'home', Ellen notes,
'Mr Roxburgh will be the happier for laying hands on his books, myself simply
from having my own belongings around me. To make my home in the wilder-
ness!' (p. 78)

Similarly, the settlers such as Mr Stafford Merivale overlook 'the possibility
of a relationship with a landscape' (p. 8); and Mrs Merivale, who is 'an adept at
closing her mind to awfulness' (p. 9), is horrified by the lizards which inhabit
the scorched bush and reviles the golden teasel flower which Ellen takes with
her on board the ship, as a symbol to remind her of the beauty latent beneath
superficial ugliness. White's libretto synopsis clarifies the analogy between the
wild flower and Ellen's 'wild' nature:

Act 1: Sc. 2
contemplating flower
MRS ROX: *Its head so harsh, and wiry,*
 so fiery – passionate and noble.
MRS MERIVALE *yearns with some obviousness for the roses and*
 bluebells at Home:
MRS MER: … *for the things one need not be ashamed of,*
 where one knows for certain
 which people it is nice to know.

Mrs Merivale is a social 'type' – a Mrs Sedley or a Lady Billows – a self-
appointed protector of social and moral codes and conventions in this 'morally
infected' country. In the opera she wonders, *'Would you say she is a lady?' 'Not
quite'* replies her companion, Miss Sibilant, *'But she's doing very nicely';* which
prompts the tart response, *'Niceness is nicer when its bred, not learnt.'* The
strict rules endorsed by the settlement community embrace the justice system
and the Anglican church, and are reinforced by the imposition of a limiting
linguistic code. Characters such as Colonel Lovell embody a violent authority
which is based upon an unquestioning, misguided acceptance of 'duty' and

'honour' of the sort Britten also questions in *Owen Wingrave* and *Gloriana*. The society which stifles and hides its sexuality is the same society which judges this land of convicts and native Aborigines to be 'morally infected' (p. 73). Just as Britten reveals the hypocrisy of the Borough, which condemns Grimes yet turns a blind eye to its own inherent cruelties and depravities, so White attacks the duplicity of the settlers' self-righteousness, portraying their treatment of both the convicts and the Aborigines as unjust and pitiless. This is particularly so in the case of those such as Ellen's brother-in-law, in the light of the ambivalence ('unproved dishonesty', p. 71)[21] concerning the reasons for his own exile to the colonies.

Antagonistic to such snobbery and hypocrisy, Ellen finds herself sympathizing with the convicts:

> How much of the miscreant, I wonder, is in Garnet R.? Or in *myself* for that matter … If I am not all good (only my dearest husband is that) I am not excessively bad. How far it is to the point where one oversteps the bounds? I would like to talk to these miscreants, to satisfy myself, but do not expect I ever will. (pp. 79–80)

Moreover, the superficial religious observance of civilized society, epitomized by her mother-in-law's sterile words, 'Lord God of Hosts', is later exposed as meaningless by the genuinely spiritual message, 'God is Love'. These words, roughly scratched by the only other shipwreck survivor in a makeshift chapel at the settlement prison, recall Peter Grimes's angry rejection of the Borough's shallow religious practice, 'So be it! And God have mercy upon me!' (p. 105)

Austin Roxburgh and his mother have attempted to transform Ellen, to 'create a beautiful, charming, not necessarily intellectual, but socially acceptable companion out of what was only superficially unpromising material' (p. 54). The ignorant, crude Cornish girl, Ellen Gluyas, who longs for 'experience', becomes Mrs Austin Roxburgh, a respectable married lady forced to suppress her desires, both acknowledged and subconscious, by the civilized society of Cheltenham. However, in scene 4 of the opera scenario, on board ship, Ellen remembers her childhood:

The Deck of Bristol Maid, at sea. Movement of the ship. Sails. Slight fog

She recalls her childhood on the Cornish coast, and one occasion in particular when her father drove her to Tintagel and told her the legend of the place: how she had waited for a glimpse of what she hardly knew, in the little cove, with its intensely grey, brooding shores. All her life something has eluded her.

Her hopes for fulfilment of her desires through marriage have been disappointed:

> Just as she was to learn that death was for Mr Roxburgh a 'literary conceit', so she found that his approach to passion had its formal limits. For her part, she longed to, but had never dared, storm those limits ... She herself had only once responded with a natural ardour, but discovered on her husband's face an expression of having tasted something bitter, or of looking too deep. So, she replaced the mask which evidently she was supposed to wear, and because he was an honourable as well as a pitiable man, she would refrain in future from tearing it off. (p. 68)

This is a denial of 'self', of the sort that Peter Grimes refuses to accept, when, declining the mask of social respectability, he rejects Ellen Orford's assistance and assurance: 'Peter, we shall restore your name. / Warmed by the new esteem / That you will find.' (p. 92)

Mrs Roxburgh's suppressed emotions resurface during the visit to Van Dieman's Land. Faced with the overt sexuality of her brother-in-law, Garnet Roxburgh, she is alarmed to find herself responding. The hairs on his sturdy wrists – which remind her of her father – both attract and repulse:

> He had about him something which she, the farmer's daughter and spurious lady, recognised as coarse and sensual ... she noticed his thick wrists and the hairs visible on them in the space between glove and cuff. She turned away her head. She more than disliked, she was repelled, not only by the man, but by her own thoughts, which her husband and her late mother-in-law would not have suspected her of harbouring.
>
> To escape from her inner self she looked out across the country ... (p. 74)

By drawing parallels between the Cornish and Australian landscapes, White suggests that the savage world releases Ellen's innate desires. Entranced by her new environment she dozes in a small clearing:

> The delicious cool, the only half-repellent smell of rotting vegetation, perhaps some deeper prepossession of her own, all were combining to drug her, at first with mild insidiousness, then with overwhelming insistence. She could have been drifting at the bottom of the sea ... Then he was bending over her. (p. 82)

Garnet Roxburgh is an extension of the landscape to which Ellen feels increasingly drawn. He rides with her deep into the country and the consummation of their relationship upon a bed of rotting vegetation, a symbol of the sexual depravity she fears within her, anticipates her later experiences in the bush with the convict, Jack Masters:

> She was again this great green, only partially disabled, obscene bird, on whose breast he was feeding, gross hands parting the sweeping folds of her tormented and tormenting plumage; until in opening and closing, she might have been rather, the green, fathomless sea, tossing, threatening to swallow down the humanly manned ship which had ventured on her. (pp. 102–3)

Patrick White employs imagery relating to water and the sea to chart Ellen's spiritual and psychological progress. The young Ellen Gluyas immerses herself in the pitch-black depths of St Hya's well, hoping that this cold baptism will purify her and banish the 'presentiment of evil' which she senses:

> Presently, after getting up courage, she let herself down into the pool, clothes and all, hanging by a bough. When she had become totally immersed, and the breath frightened out of her by icy water, together with any thought beyond escaping back to earth, she managed, still clinging to the bough, to hoist herself upon the bank. (p. 98)

This 'cleansing' is a sublimation of her sensual desires, although the young Ellen does not fully comprehend this. White develops the association of immersion with sensual experience. At sea, revelling in her proximity to nature's elemental forces, Ellen records in her diary: 'Went on deck early and was intocksicated [*sic*] by a sense of freedom, of pure joy. Gulls approaching, then swooning off. At moments I felt dizzy with the air I swallowed, but sad to think I will never explore this vast land seen at a distance through spray and fog.' (p. 62) The libretto synopsis (Act I scene 8) reveals that White envisaged this scene as a musical climax:

> MRS ROXBURGH *appears calm, even exalted. It is like facing a new life with practically nothing of the old in her hands. As her bonnet ribbons are tortured in the gale, and her shawl and pelisse practically torn from her, she apostrophizes the country they see at moments.*

The spiritual potential of the sea, its power both to destroy and to restore, is voiced in White's libretto synopsis when Ellen sings an aria to her dead husband, confusing him in her '*fervish distress*' sometimes with Garnet Roxburgh and sometimes with the convict, Masters. '*She cannot be sure whether she has betrayed, or whom*':

MRS ROX: *... and time will not decide,*
neither light nor dark,
only water will wash,
if it does not drown.

In the bush, water's life-giving qualities are depicted in an 'Arcadian episode' where Ellen and the convict achieve a 'mystic union' while swimming in a lily pond. As Ellen dives to the bottom of the pond for a bulb, White's synopsis relates:

It was sad that they should destroy such a sheet of lilies, but so it must be
if they were to become reunited, and this after all was the purpose of the
lake: that they might grasp or reject each other at last.

The childhood games that they play beside the pool endow the eroticism of their actions with a kind of innocence, thus linking two 'redemptive' symbols, water and childhood.

Similarly, in *Peter Grimes* the sea acts as a metaphor for Grimes's subconscious: for example, in Act II the storm at sea parallels the storm within him. Grimes freely embraces the spirit of the sea; it is a symbol of his loneliness and alienation, but one which also contains intimations of rebirth and reconciliation:

What is home? Calm as deep water.
Where's my home? Deep as calm water,
Water will drink my sorrows dry
And the tide will turn. (p. 112)

At the end of the opera, Grimes is himself like a child, drifting between reality, fantasy and hallucination. He subconsciously yearns for a lost innocence, which he acknowledges has been destroyed by experience, and which can only be regained in the watery oblivion of the sea.

Ellen Roxburgh's journey and experience also compel her to confront the darkest depths of human experience. Inevitably, during this 'passage' her 'natural self', suppressed by the forces of convention, cannot be wholly denied. Despite the eradication of her Cornish accent and the imposition of an Italianate style of hand, she remains a 'farmer's daughter', unconsciously slipping back into her native dialect, particularly at moments of high emotion. At her new home in Cheltenham, she 'had printed on the glass TINTAGEL in bold, if irregular letters, and then was ashamed, or even afraid, for what she had done' (p. 68).[22]

In the same way, living in seclusion among the Aboriginals, whose spare, crude language has not been formulated out of social conventions but rather from a need to survive, the convict, Jack Masters, has become mute. Relying on '*congested gibberish*', he has forgotten the language of 'civilization'. White's libretto synopsis narrates: '*As language begins to seep back, MASTERS recalls the faces of human beings in a life lived before hell swallowed him up and the iron bit into him.*' He also instructs: '*Whenever aboriginals are used musically, they are voices without words – not an attempt to reproduce language, but a pure vocalisation.*'[23]

It is the unsophisticated language of children which is revealed to be the path to true communication. Ellen's relationships with the various children in the novel are complicated. We learn that during her marriage to Austin Roxburgh, Ellen Roxburgh has suffered a miscarriage, a still-birth and has borne a third child which died in infancy. She blames herself for these infant deaths, lamenting the insufficiency of her love for her children: 'Two years later Mrs Roxburgh again conceived, and this time bore a child, a perfect little boy, but who was with them so short a while, she did not even record his passing in her journal.' (p. 68) Later she struggles to find a capacity for love with Oswald Dignam, the young cabin boy who admires her. She approaches Oswald on the deck of the Bristol Maid, lapsing spontaneously into her own language, and begging, 'Cusn't I stay with 'ee?':

> It was too strange: a lady who could speak ordinary ... A certain innocence which life had not succeeded in exorcising from her nature made her long for him to accept her. As a little girl, which she had become again, only briefly no doubt, she might have bribed him with some valued possession. But here she had nothing to offer.[24] (p. 146)

Conscious of the guilt borne of her liaison with Garnet Roxburgh, Ellen later laments her loss of innocence: 'The afternoon dissolved into rain, which reduced every face, especially Mrs Roxburgh's, to the state of first innocence. What would she not have given for innocence enough to lean forward and stroke the round cheek of this boy who might otherwise remain closed to her.' (p. 175)

When the longboat finally lands on a sand bank, Oswald attempts to win her favour by hunting for shellfish for her to eat, but tragically he is swept from a rock ledge. Oswald merges with the sea, physically and symbolically: 'The wind behind him, Oswald quickly reached her, together with a lash of driven spray ... beads of salt encrusting his eyebrows were visibly translated into drops of water ... Alternatively sucked under and bobbing on the surface, he continued resisting his fate ... before the sea put a glassy stopper in his mouth.' (pp. 190–1) Emotionally and physically exhausted, Ellen falls into a troubled sleep, haunted by the 'ghosts of her lost children' (p. 192):

> The loss of this cabin-boy, which the colours of her dream had trans-
> formed into a major bereavement unloosed in her a need for affinity, a
> longing to be loved. (p. 194)

In the libretto scenario, she mourns the cabin boy as '*the one with whom she had been able to laugh and share little secrets'*.

Among the Aboriginals, reduced to material, linguistic and moral savagery, the 'wildness' of the young Ellen Gluyas resurfaces, and Ellen rediscovers her own childhood 'self'. Entrusted with the Headman's Wife's sick child to nurse, she initially finds it a '*poor, disgusting, infected little creature*': '*Poor thing, I should pity you, love you, but cannot*'. However, after her discovery of the half-eaten remains of a *Bristol Maid* crew member, Ellen turns to the children of the tribe to ease her horror and despair:

> They all lay about laughing a while. The young children might have been
> hers. She was so extraordinarily content she wished it could have lasted
> for ever, the two black little bodies united in the sun with her own
> blackened skin-and-bones. (p. 230)

Upon her return from the bush, it is the settlement children, not yet inhibited by 'civilized' society's restrictive codes, who offer Ellen a route out of the moral vacuum she inhabits. She hopes that the Lovell children, in whose house she is nursed back to health, 'might, by their innocence and candour, help her transcend her self-disgust' (p. 322), although she is troubled by the 'exquisite child's purity, rousing in her the sense guilt which was only too ready to plague her' (p. 343).[25] Witnessing the young Kate Lovell's cruel mutilation of an injured bird – 'The child was carrying the corpse of a fluffy chick, the head lolling at the end of a no longer effectual neck, the extinct eyes reduced to crimson cavaties' (p. 344) – she understands the child's mortification at being observed, sensing a parallel with her own former self. Comprehending that Kate is undergoing her own passage from innocence to experience, she does not judge. Child and adult are drawn closer by the understanding that both good and evil exist within us all: 'Kate slipped out of the school-room, and she and Mrs Roxburgh clung together for a short space.' (pp. 344–5) Ellen is thus able to reconcile past and present; she can accept that the ugly and the cruel can co-exist with the beautiful and good.

In contrast, despite Ellen Orford's hopes that caring for the apprentice boy could represent a 'new start', Peter Grimes fails to achieve such reconciliation. Ellen Orford tells the young boy, 'But when you came, I / Said, Now this is where we / Make a new start. Every day / I pray it may be so.' (p. 103); but although Grimes dreams, 'I've seen in stars the life that we might share: / Fruit in the garden, children by the shore, / A fair white doorstep, and a woman's care' (p. 108), ultimately he cannot exorcise the demons from his past. As his gaze falls upon the weeping boy, Peter Grimes is reminded of the former apprentices, and of his own violent childhood. Unable to connect with the child who might have 'saved' him, he sings with bitterness and fear:

> But dreaming builds what dream can disown.
> Dead fingers stretch themselves to tear it down.
> I hear those voices that will not be drowned. (p. 108)

Perhaps Ellen Roxburgh's relationships with children are complicated by memories of her own childhood, and in particular her relationship with her father. In a drunken state, alternatively violent and affectionate, her father had mistaken her for her dead mother: 'he stared at her, and asked in a distant, frightened voice, unlike his own, "Nelly" (he had never addressed her thus) "was it you knocked to the door? Or was it a token?" He might have been coming to her, but stumbled, and fell against the dresser, and was gone before she could take him in her arms.' (p. 58) Latent in her childhood memories are hints of her fears of sexual molestation by her father, and Ellen's recollections are thus coloured by reminiscences of her own sexual awakening:

> While she still was a little girl, he used to stroke her cheeks as though to learn the secrets of her skin. She would feel the horn-thing on his crushed thumb scraping her.
> On one occasion, unable to bear it any longer, she cried out, 'Cusn't tha see that I dun't want to be touched?' and threw him off.
> He brooded and sulked for a while, but it had been necessary, shame told her she was as much excited as disgusted. (p. 56)

It is worth remembering that Britten's working copy of Crabbe's *The Borough* contained many annotations and markings against references to Grimes's father, which may suggest that the father–son relationship was an important factor in Grimes's psychology in the early stages of development. The libretto drafts at the Britten–Pears Foundation reveal that Britten and Peter Pears originally intended to include scenes in which Grimes remembered episodes from his own childhood, clarifying the paternal-aggressive dichotomy which characterized his relationship with his 'surrogate' children, the apprentices. His father had shown him no love, only violence, and his treatment of the boys is shaped by this experience. Though touched by their vulnerability and innocence, Grimes is unable to articulate his empathy and, in his frustration, compassion turns rapidly to anger. A draft in Pears' hand records:

> [*Grimes*] *admits his youth hurts him, his innocence galls him, his useless-*
> *ness maddens him. He had no father to love him, why should he? His*
> *father only beat him, why should not he? 'prove yourself some use, not*
> *only pretty – work – not only be innocent – work do not stare; would*
> *you rather I loved you? You are sweet, young etc. – but you must love me,*
> *why do you not love me? Love me darn you.*[26]

Although a preface, in which Grimes's father appeared on his death-bed and solemnly cursed the young Grimes, was later excised, a strong association between Grimes's literal roots – his father – and his 'spiritual' roots – the sea – is apparent in the sketches:

> *I have a father in the sea*
> *Scolding from tides, and it was he*
> *Who made the laws that we shall disobey.*[27]

Living among the Aborigines, Ellen Roxburgh comes to terms with her 'primitive' self and liberates herself from the shackles of convention. In so doing, she learns that 'truth' is to be found within oneself. Paradoxically her moral epiphany occurs at the nadir of her circular passage to the depths of depravity and back to more 'civilized' worlds – with her act of cannibalism, a physical act from which she derives spiritual ecstasy:

> Just as she would never have admitted to others how she had immersed
> herself in the saint's pool, or that its black water had cleansed her of
> morbid thoughts and sensual longings, so she could not have explained
> how tasting flesh from the human thigh-bone in the stillness of a for-
> est morning had nourished not only her animal body but some darker
> need of the hungry spirit. (p. 248)

This ultimate transgression permits her a moment of stark, unalleviated self-awareness, which leads her to believe that she 'might have come to terms with darkness' (p. 249). Similarly, Grimes submits to the black void of the night, the fog, the ocean, for ultimately he has no human attachments, and is bonded only with the watery wastes which beckon him.

However, in contrast to Grimes, who remains true to his inner self, his visions, and welcomes the abyss even if the result is suffering or death, Ellen Roxburgh returns to take her place in civilized society. Her knowledge is a source of both joy and guilt; her descent to the lowest regions of humanity does not provide her with lasting fulfilment. Even though her experiences have enabled her to reconcile love, sensuality, self-knowledge and compassion, she persists in refusing to abandon her fringe of leaves in the bush, and clings to the wedding ring which is all that connects her to her former life. In the midst of her ordeal, faced with the choice between continuing the struggle or surrendering, Ellen chooses life:

> 'Kill me too, rather than hurt me,' but [she] knew at once that she did not want to die. … But she would not, must not die – why, she could not imagine, when she had been deprived of all that she most loved and valued. (pp. 224–6)

When she returns to society, Ellen suffers a mental crisis, descending, like Grimes, into delirium and madness, tortured by dreams and visions, daring not to sleep lest Jack Chance, the convict, appear in a dream and offer her his love. Yet, she reluctantly comes to accept that prison is both self and society; as there can be no escape from 'self', there is no escape from the society which oppresses individuals. Her understanding that no one is truly 'free' is empha-sized by the contrast with the views of others in the settlement community. In White's libretto drafts, Miss Scrimshaw, sensing Ellen's liberating transmuta-tion, declares:

> *A man is still a prisoner.*
> *I would have been an eagle!*
> *…*
> *Free, free, above a world spread out!*

Ultimately Ellen strikes a compromise between primitivism and civilization, between the dark and the light.

Some five weeks after his first letter to Britten, Nolan wrote again (12 September 1963), less optimistically, acknowledging that circumstances might make the project difficult but revealing his own penchant for the proposed opera:

> My dear Benjamin Britten,
>
> Thank you so much for your letter. I am driving up with Patrick White to the recital at Long Melford on Saturday ~~night~~ evening + then going on to spend the night at Aldeburgh at the Wentworth Hotel. We are coming back on Sunday afternoon for your concert returning after it to London.
>
> I mention all this because it seems the only chance now of meeting Patrick if you wanted to.
>
> We both feel that your time for the next two years seems fully booked and this makes another opera an unlikely prospect but I do not like to feel that I have not tried hard.

I have made further enquiries + it seems probable that the Sydney Opera House will not open until late 1967 or even early 1968 but this is only a private opinion although accurate enough I think.

Composer and academic, Edward Cowie – a friend of Nolan, who later collaborated with Nolan on an opera based on the Ned Kelly story – revealed that a meeting between Britten and White did in fact take place, with Nolan and Peter Pears also present.[28] Nolan had told Cowie that Britten and White took an almost instant dislike to each other; and that after a rather heated discussion the meeting ended acrimoniously, with Britten insisting that he had not read White's synopsis and had no interest in the project, and White protesting that he had been misled and his time wasted. There are many possible reasons why Britten was unwilling to commit himself to the project: for example, White had strong musical views of his own which he may have been unwilling to modify;[29] the opera had a female protagonist and there was no obvious part for Peter Pears; or perhaps he simply did not feel that White was someone he could work with.

White's anger about these events did not lessen over time: in a typically vitriolic letter (written to James Stern, 22 February 1970), he later described Britten as 'a nauseating county snob', adding for good measure that Pears had a 'nauseating voice'.[30] Yet, despite his reputation for ill-temper, stubbornness and a sometimes cruel candour, perhaps White's frustration is understandable. It seems unlikely that Britten would have refused to read a synopsis sent to him informally by a personal friend, or that he would then have agreed to meet White if he had no interest at all in the subject, whatever his initial misgivings.

When relations with Britten broke down, White attempted to find another composer for his project. Negotiations with Peter Sculthorpe began encouragingly, but later collapsed – largely as a result of White's loss of confidence in Sculthorpe's understanding of his protagonist. White wrote to Sculthorpe on 3 April 1964: 'I [should have] felt shattered in any circumstances to find you had gathered nothing about Mrs Roxburgh from the synopsis. You say you see the other characters, but all the others are there only for her sake. She is the only one who really interests me. ... You must have a mind the complete antithesis of mine – analytical, whereas I approach everything intuitively. Perhaps in the long run this may be a good thing – if it is not a complete disaster!'[31] And, he complained to Peggy Garland that 'the composer came to dinner last week and informed me that he didn't begin to understand my central character. I would have withdrawn there and then if it had concerned only myself, but Sid Nolan, from whose Mrs Fraser paintings I got the idea originally, is very keen on doing the opera … I am doing nothing for the moment except send the composer a biography of the character he doesn't understand.'[32]

Subsequent rumours that Stefan Haag had begun writing his own libretto on this subject for Sculthorpe, led White to set aside his text, but he did not abandon the idea. In January 1969 he wrote to Geoffrey Dutton that: 'Still, I sometimes take out the MS of *A Fringe of Leaves* and look at it. It still attracts me, and I may come back to her one day when she has recovered from the mauling she got from various little careerists when I was foolish enough to suggest the theme might be one for an opera.'[33] White finally returned to Mrs Fraser's story in 1974, following a trip to Tasmania during November 1973 to explore the landscape of *A Fringe of Leaves*. He wrote to Cynthia Nolan, 15 September 1975: 'The big relief was finishing *A Fringe of Leaves* yesterday morning … But is Sid still prepared to do it [the book jacket]? … He would have to read the book first to find out how different my Mrs Roxburgh is from his Mrs Fraser'.[34] Previously White had seen primarily horror and frustration in Mrs Roxburgh's ordeal, but now found reconciliation.

White had complained that Australian writing was stuck in the 19th century, determining (as his June 1958 letter to Nolan attests) never to concern himself with 'historical' subjects. When Sculthorpe had expressed his concern about composing an 'historical opera', White 'explained that my approach is not historical at all. That I deal with states of mind, and that the content is very contemporary although in a Victorian setting.'[35] Britten may have shared White's awareness that this was not simply a tale from history but one that had relevance for modern times and lives.

White later wrote:

> What may be our salvation is the discovery of the identity hidden deep in any one of us, and which may be found in even the most desperate individual, if he cares to search the spiritual womb which contains the embryo of what can be one's personal contribution to truth and life.[36]

Such an experience – 'salvation', achieved by even the most desperate individuals – is enacted by many of Britten's operatic protagonists: Peter Grimes, Vere, Owen Wingrave, Aschenbach. Moreover, White's opera scenario and subsequent novel explore themes and symbols which recur in Britten's operas: the 'outsider'; the 'visionary' artist's struggle in the face of social convention and hypocrisy; the cruelty of 'civilized' worlds and institutions; innocence and experience, and the purity, and vulnerability, of childhood; the physical and spiritual power of the sea. In particular, the parallels between *A Fringe of Leaves* and *Peter Grimes* seem striking: the critique of a narrow-minded and hypocritical community; the links between landscape and environment and psychology; the protagonist's visionary, creative sensibility, and descent into 'madness' and primitivism; the latent threat of sexual freedom and transgression. White portrays a society which lives by an elaborate set of conventions, espousing a morality of reason, duty and honour, but which is exposed as superficial, incongruous and artificial. He attacks the hypocrisy of upperclass, colonial notions of 'justice' and morality by revealing the cruel treatment of the convicts and the essential honesty of the Aborigines. In the same way, Britten exposes the hypocrisy of the Borough, which condemns Grimes but turns a blind eye to the inherent cruelties of its apprentice system and to its own misdemeanours. White does not always, as Britten does, so directly demonstrate how his characters and their behaviour are shaped by their environment. But the primary difference between White's Mrs Roxburgh and Britten's brutal, troubled fisherman is that Ellen is reintegrated into society – however ambiguous this reassimilation may be – whereas Grimes acknowledges that his visionary understanding ensures, even necessitates, his isolation and death. Ultimately, the epigraphs to White's novel, by Simone Weil and Louis Aragon respectively, could fittingly have graced Britten's operas:

'If there is some true good in a man, it can only be unknown to himself.'

'Love is your last chance. There is really nothing else on earth to keep you there.' (p. 6)

Notes

1 White's draft libretto and all correspondence cited are held at the BPF.

2 Barrie Reed, quoted in A. J. Hassall, 'The Making of a Colonial Myth: The Mrs Fraser Story in Patrick White's "A Fringe of Leaves" and André Brink's "An Instant Wind"' *Ariel* 18/3 (1971), p. 5.

3 *Patrick White: Letters*, ed. David Maw (London: Jonathan Cape, 1994), pp. 138–9.

4 *Ibid.*, p. 219.

5 Kenneth Clark, Thames & Hudson monograph, quoted in Brian Adams, *Sidney Nolan: Such is Life* (London: Century Hutchinson, 1987), pp. 154–5.

6 'A Letter to Humanity', in *Patrick White Speaks* (London: Jonathan Cape, 1969), pp. 105–10 at pp. 109–10.

7 'In The Making' (1969) in *ibid.*, pp. 19–23 at p. 23.

8 'A Noble Pair' (1978), in *ibid.*, pp. 69–71 at p. 69.

9 This conversation is reproduced in *MRLL*, vol. 1, pp. 404–7.

10 *MRLL*, vol. 1, p. 405.

11 *Ibid.*

12 *MRLL*, vol. 1, p. 406.

13 *MRLL*, vol. 1, pp. 406–7.

14 This incident is echoed by the protagonist's fate in *Owen Wingrave*. A full account of Britten's friendship with Dunkerley is given in *MRLL*, vol. 1, pp. 401–7.

15 Adams, *Sidney Nolan*, p. 204.

16 'I married her to a gentleman so that I could make her function at more than one level, and turn something which would otherwise have been a mere adventure story into a novel of psychological interest.' Letter to Allan Williams, 11 January 1976 in *Patrick White: Letters*, p. 467.

17 Patrick White, *A Fringe of Leaves* (Harmondsworth: Penguin, 1977), p. 17. Subsequent references to this edition are given in parentheses in the text. The sequence of events in both novel and opera scenario is largely identical. Text quoted from the typescript scenario (BPF) is italicized.

18 *Peter Grimes*, in *DHOB*, revised edition (1989), p. 99. Subsequent references to this edition are given in the text in parentheses.

19 *BBAA*, p. 21.

20 White, 'In the Making', p. 20.

21 Mr Roxburgh insists that the accusations against his brother were based on 'suspicion rather than evidence, and knowing my brother I am confident he was not guilty … He is not *bad*! It was never *proved*!' (p. 71) The 'unproven' charges against Garnet Roxburgh recall the cross-examination and condemnation of Peter Grimes; for despite Swallow's verdict that 'William Spode, your apprentice, died in accidental circumstances', 'that's the kind of thing people are apt to remember' and Grimes understands that: 'The case goes on in people's minds/ Then charges that no court has made/ Will be shouted at my head.' (p. 91)

22 Later she recalls how she had 'scratched the name upon an attic window, not out of affection she thought, rather from frustrated desire' (p. 248).

23 This 'vocalisation', had it found form in Britten's music, may have had much in common with the wordless and linguistically ambiguous melodies that communicate so powerfully in Britten's operas: the apprentice's shriek in *Peter Grimes*; the 'interview chords' in *Billy Budd*; Quint's unearthly beckoning; Miles' own 'Malo Song'; and Tadzio's entrance music in *Death in Venice*.

24 Following her escape from the bush, Ellen is introduced to the modest businessman Mr Jevons, her future husband. As they take tea together, he stumbles and spills a cup of tea into her lap. Ellen, concerned to lessen his embarrassment, reverts instinctively to her native Cornish dialect. The incident brings the couple closer together, and their honest communication contrasts greatly with the constricted, restrictive discourse that she shared with Austin Roxburgh. It might be suggested that, in the closing moments of *Peter Grimes*, Grimes' delirious utterances, similarly reveal a 'truth' which could not be expressed in the language of the Borough posse which pursues him.

25 Ellen's response to this innocence recalls the guilt experienced by some of Britten's protagonists, Grimes, Claggart, Vere, the Governess and Aschenbach.

26 *Peter Grimes*, libretto draft, held at the BPF.

27 *Ibid.*

28 In a private interview with the author, 21 March 1996.

29 White undoubtedly had a passion for, and strong views about, music. A letter to Mollie McKie, 12 October 1950, reveals: 'We listen to the wireless a lot now after being rigidly anti-wireless for so long, and I am drinking up music like a piece of blotting paper drinks ink.' (*Patrick White: Letters*, p. 83) And he explained to Ben Huebsch (8 February 1957): 'You talk about the "symphonic structure" of *Voss* – well, in the last ten years I think that music has taught me a lot about writing. That may sound pretentious, and I would not know how to go into it rationally, but I feel that listening constantly to music helps one to develop a book more logically.' (*Ibid.*, p. 110)

30 *Ibid.*, p. 358.

31 *Ibid.*, pp. 252–3.

32 *Ibid.*, p. 255.

33 *Ibid.*, p. 339.

34 *Ibid.*, p. 462.

35 Letter to Geoffrey Dutton, 5 December 1963, *ibid.*, p. 245.

36 'Australians in a Nuclear War', *Patrick White Speaks*, pp. 113–26 at p. 115.

11 Britten and France, or the Late Emergence of a Remarkable Lyric Universe*

Maéna Py

Since the 1990s the French public has become more and more absorbed by Benjamin Britten's operas. This was not always the case, however, and their acceptance as part of the French musical landscape did not come about without a certain number of upheavals, conflicts and negotiations. As early as the 1940s, Britten's instrumental pieces were frequently played in Paris,[1] and one could hear his orchestral music on the radio, in particular his *Simple Symphony*.[2] But in trying to win over the media and the Parisian music theatres, his operas were up against some hostile trends. The Parisian intelligentsia and the sectarian spirit of certain schools barred their acceptance. Judged too conservative, too far from the serial avant-garde which was in vogue at the time, Britten's lyric works also had to struggle against a general tendency of dismissing opera, an art form considered out of date and bourgeois. On the whole, Britten's music was only vaguely familiar, and damned with faint praise. 'It's well done, it's pleasant', as Mario Bois recalled in a news release for Boosey & Hawkes in June 1962 entitled 'Britten? … Connais pas!'[3] Nevertheless, he indicated that certain outstanding personalities of French artistic life were interested in Britten's latest scores:

> People like Charles Bruck, Frédéric Goldbeck, Jean Giraudeau, Manuel Rosenthal, Charles Panzera, and Pierre Pagliano, are watching for his latest score to appear and are ready to do their best work for it. As far as the dramatic works are concerned, in spite of the even sharper difficulties that lyric music is meeting in the provinces as opposed to Paris, admirable ventures have been carried to fruition, by men such as Roger Lalande, Jacques Pernoo, Pierre Deloger, Henri Bécourt, and others who, regrettably, cannot be mentioned here.[4]

Thus, far from Paris, informed and enthusiastic composers, orchestra leaders, singers, opera directors, and producers accomplished courageous and

---

* Author's note: 'Lyric' in this context refers to operatic, and 'lyric works' or 'lyric stage works' to operas.

pioneering work: the result was to establish Britten in France as a first-rate lyric composer. Let us then try to untangle and shed light on the personal, political and cultural networks which allowed Britten's operas to emerge in France.

Britten's operas in the musical, lyric and artistic context of Paris: 1945–65

Britten knew France well. He had made several visits there and had set to music texts by several French authors. The press and the Parisian public always noticed his presence in Paris, notably during his tours with the English Opera Group. As far back as 11 June 1948, *Peter Grimes* (1945) was presented at the Paris Opéra in Tyrone Guthrie's and Tanya Moisewitsch's production, directed by Karl Rankl, the same production which had been given at Covent Garden in 1947. Later on, *Billy Budd* (1951), *The Turn of the Screw* (1954), *Albert Herring* (1949) and *A Midsummer Night's Dream* (1960) were given respectively in May 1952, 1956, 1959, and 1967, in the context of international festivals organized by the municipality of Paris, such as the Théâtre des Nations. This particular festival aimed to establish Paris as the international capital of the scenic arts.[5] All nations were to be represented there, as well as all forms of theatre, dramatic or lyric. Thus, the dramatic cycle of the Théâtre Sarah Bernhardt was completed by a lyric cycle at the Théâtre des Champs-Elysées. The accent was placed on the notion of freedom for each work in the programme, in particular in 1952 during the 'Festival of 20th century work': 'free to experiment, free to express oneself, free to choose one's masters and one's arrangements, to choose irony or naïveté, to be esoteric or familiar.'[6]

Thus, one can understand the framework and context in which Britten's operas, given by the English Opera Group, were welcomed: as the emblem of lyric English productions in a space favourable to eclecticism, innovation and discovery. The articles appearing in the press praised Britten's work, but one can already see the beginning of a characteristic trait in the reception of his work in France during those years: an insistence on the novelty of Britain finally producing a national lyric composer. After having heard *Billy Budd* at the Champs-Elysées in 1952, one critic from *Le Figaro* wrote: 'A British musician who is quite simply founding English opera is entering into a career unencumbered by his elders; there is no example to respect, no prejudice to push aside.'[7] In short, an isolated case, an exotic species in the lyric landscape, far removed from the weight of musical history which was the object of musical quarrels in France at that time. This critic, emphasizing the good will of the Parisian public, concluded his article not on the opera itself but on Britten's anxiety when he had to conduct *la Marseillaise* and hesitated concerning the tempo: jokingly, the critic declared 'we mustn't hold it against him that, contrary to venerable British customs, he has failed up to now to spend his vacations on the Côte d'Azur, because he will participate in the festivals at Aix and Menton. All in all, Britten would be the very definition of the traditional Englishman if he had not chosen to make his living composing lyric works.'[8] It was the composer's Britishness which above all occupied the critics rather than his artistic merit. Similarly, in an article on 'L'école anglaise' in *La Revue musicale*, the same year: 'Since then Britten seems to have found his way and his true vocation – to become his country's great opera composer, by trying to find for the first time since Purcell, a kind of truly *national* opera inspired by purely native elements reflecting the character, traditions and ways of being of the British people.'[9] French critics were vying with one another to make this sort of criticism in the first years during which they discovered Britten's universe.

However, from 1952 certain critics, conscious of the crisis that French lyric music was going through, tried to place Britten's operas in a context beyond the merely anecdotal and to show the contributions they could make to the general landscape of lyric music. In particular, for Frédéric Goldbeck in relation to *Billy Budd*, the enterprise 'was successful in its adventure and its risk. A reasonable critic, if Britten had been so clumsy as to consult him ahead of time, would probably have found it necessary to warn him of the danger'.[10] For it was really a matter of taking a risk in the world of contemporary music in France, especially in Paris. In fact, the provincial critics seemed more shrewd, objective and dispassionate. A few months later, in July of 1952, during the fifth international music festival at Aix-en-Provence, Claude Rostand spoke about Britten's operas as a model to follow for getting out of the crisis of lyric music in France.[11] Audacious words at that time; but they came from the provinces, far from the musical wars in the capital.

In Paris, during those years, contemporary music was marked by the strong personality of Pierre Boulez, on a crusade against 'the stillborn music of our times',[12] who was attempting to enforce serialism as the only possible way for music to evolve. A remarkable organizer and manager, he could impose his ideas by creating, in 1953,[13] a tremendous venue on the Parisian scene for the dissemination of contemporary music.[14] But that could not happen without a strongly radical element, aimed at excluding and destroying everything that did not belong to the 'movement', to the 'generation'.[15] Of course, Britten, not being part of this movement, was far from the preoccupations of Darmstadt.[16] While he had in his youth participated in the festival of the International Society of Contemporary Music, the Parisian élite considered this society, which put on *Le Marteau sans maître* in June 1955, to be 'sly and reactionary'[17] and far from the avant-garde. Antoine Goléa's comments were absolute and sketched out the crusade which gradually took form during the 1950s to eliminate everything from the musical field that was not serialist: 'works by young people or semi-young people, young and semi-young born already old, who are nothing but pale imitators [of the] great ancestors.'[18] Thus, in Parisian circles, 'a certain music' made of 'impure sources', 'imitative disputes', 'old-fashioned, superseded pretensions',[19] 'threadbare emotive power' and which constituted a 'harmful'[20] activity was no longer tolerated. And when Boulez, in the context of his concerts of the 'Domaine Musical', programmed and directed the European première of Stravinsky's ballet *Agon*, at the Salle Pleyel during the 1957–8 season, Antoine Goléa mentioned a further victory over the enemy: 'It was the rout of all those who, for thirty years, have hoisted Strawinsky shoulder-high on their neo-classical faith, have made of him their beacon, their standard-bearer.'[21] Now these years corresponded precisely to Stravinsky's interest in serial technique and Britten's break with a composer whom he had so admired. Stravinsky joined the avant-garde clan, responding to Boulez's appeal in 1952, with the peremptory affirmation that 'after the discovery of the Viennese, any composer is *useless* outside of serial research.'[22] The same year, Britten seemed to oppose him in the press, declaring to a journalist from *Le Figaro* that 'to have the public understand, it is necessary to be simple, direct and human. Besides, how can one support a durable success on the ephemeral feelings which only exist while we are alive? The present always slips toward the past, and the most skilful construction would have every chance of collapsing.'[23] Clearly Britten and Boulez were not looking in the same direction. Britten conceived the musical heritage left behind by his musical predecessors as a formidable learning resource. In 1969 he suggested to a young composer wishing to undertake his first opera that he become interested in Mozart,[24] suggesting that an awareness of what others have done is 'useful'.[25] The two adjectives, 'useless' and 'useful' echo each other, separated by several years, marking off for each one an opposing musical territory.

The conductor Ernest Ansermet's discourse is even more radical than Britten's on serialism as a historic impasse and on enlarged tonality as the only viable evolution for music, and he developed the stature of the leader of those defending Britten abroad. Indeed, on 6 September 1965 he gave a speech in Geneva entitled 'La condition de l'œuvre d'art'. The historicist discourse is virulent and marked; one finds the same framework and the same debate, reversed, as in the avant-garde clan: 'It follows that music can be only tonal, even polytonal, but not atonal, for fear of losing its obvious meaning.'[26] Ansermet denounced Schoenberg, Messiaen, Schaeffer and Cage, and praised

Britten and Frank Martin. Works by the latter composers served as anchoring points for the opposition. The tone is polemic, the style caustic and the discourse extreme at times. Britten himself was much less aggressive than Ansermet and others. He did not stigmatize serial or dodecaphonic music, nor the composers who used those techniques: 'It has simply never attracted me as a method, although I respect many composers who have worked in it, and some of their works.'[27] Britten's pacifist tendency is easily recognized here, even concerning music. What is more, he appears reluctant to throw himself in the arena; yet, abroad, it was being done on his behalf.

As a countering gesture, a real cult dedicated to Boulez was then established in Paris,[28] a sectarian spirit hostile to any attempt to diverge from the movement and therefore hostile to Britten. In the Boulez clan the critics were not gentle towards composers coming to present their works in the context of the 'Festival of 20th century work' in 1952 in which Britten took part. Paule Thévenin noted that the public was 'not at all the brilliant Parisian public' and mentioned 'several spectacular and childish innovations (!)'.[29] Thus Britten's operas seem to have been more tolerated than accepted in Paris, insofar as they stayed confined to the restricted circle of the Théâtre des Nations. Unappreciated or deliberately neglected by the avant-garde, they fitted into the Parisian lyric landscape by their strange and exotic characteristics, rather than by their real musical or scenic innovations. The height of ostracism was marked when a German company gave *Albert Herring* in May of 1959 at the Théâtre des Nations; Emile Vuillermoz wrote in *Paris-Presse*: 'The perfection of the scene is stupefying. It must have taken an astronomical number of rehearsals. For the improvisers that we are, shows like these include rather cruel lessons and, alas, mix a little bitterness and envy with our sincere admiration.'[30] Yves Clarendon in *Le Figaro*, wrote 'The two shows given at the Théâtre des Nations by the Comic Opera of Berlin attest to the accuracy of André Malraux's severe judgement: we are certainly behind certain foreign countries in the area of lyric music, as for the production and the training of singers capable of playing comedy in the same way as tragic or comic actors.'[31] Nothing was said about Britten's work: only the qualities of the production and scenography of the German companies were praised! Unsurprisingly no Parisian opera house put Britten's operas on the programme at that time, and Paris had to wait until 1981 when the Paris Opéra produced *Peter Grimes*, and Charles Pitt put on a retrospective exhibition of Britten's work in Paris, accompanied by concerts and conferences. This may have appeared to be the first attempt at rehabilitating his reputation in France, but in fact such an interpretation neglects developments that had meanwhile been taking place in the provinces.

Lyric vitality in the provinces

Britten seems to have understood that his stage works (both operas and church parables) would not become well known in France by simply passing through Paris. In the mid-1960s he presented his church parables in the Touraine region during the Secondes Fêtes musicales, a festival founded by Sviatoslav Richter and which was directly inspired by the successful Aldeburgh Festival. *Curlew River* (1964) was presented on 1 and 2 July 1965, at the Grange de Meslay, in its original production and directed by Britten himself. The work would be given in two parts with *The Burning Fiery Furnace* (1966) at the Mai de Versailles in 1968. The third church parable, *The Prodigal Son* (1968), was presented in France by the English Opera Group at the Aix-en-Provence festival in 1970. Little by little, Britten's lyric works made a name for themselves in the provinces thanks to the tours of the English Opera Group.

Faced with this novelty, the opera houses became more and more interested. Colin Graham's production of *Gloriana* (1953) was presented at the 'Mai musical' in Bordeaux in 1967. But soon it was no longer the English troupes that were solicited to put on Britten's operas, but the opera houses of the provincial cities with French singers, sometimes singing translations, and the productions aroused a growing enthusiasm. A striking increase was noticeable during the 1960s: French companies produced *Albert Herring* and *The Beggar's Opera* (1947) at the Académie Internationale du Théâtre Lyrique in Vichy in 1964, *The Turn of the Screw* in Nevers in 1964, then in Marseille in 1965, and *A Midsummer Night's Dream* in Strasbourg also in 1965. However, this development did no more than build on the pioneering ventures of the lyric theatres in the east of France; towards the end of the 1940s, *The Rape of Lucretia* (1946) had been put on in Mulhouse (in April 1948, only two years after its British première) and *Peter Grimes* in Strasbourg (in March 1949).

These ventures were realized thanks to the vision of a small number of courageous, pioneering and artistic personalities. Louis Ducreux, renamed 'D'Artagnan-Ducreux'[32] for his innovative fighting for lyric music, regularly programmed Britten's operas[33] and in 1968 initiated a festival of contemporary opera in Marseille. Roger Lalande, successively opera director in Mulhouse, Strasbourg and Bordeaux, pursued the same direction, and proposed programming, directing and translations. Antoine Bourseiller became the director of the Nancy Opera in 1982. Concerned about his 'mission'[34] as dispenser of contemporary music, he was later behind the creation in France of two of Britten's operas: *Death in Venice* (1973) in May 1991 and *Billy Budd* in March 1993. Even during the 1990s the venture was daring. But, as Antoine Bourseiller insists, 'without taking any risks, there is no artistic creation.'[35] It is interesting to note that at that time the press continually underlined the courageous character of all these creations and productions in the provinces. For example, regarding the French production of *Billy Budd* we read: 'If the composer directed this work at the Théâtre des Champs-Elysées, in 1952, shortly after the Covent Garden production, it was necessary to wait forty years for a French theatre to dare to put it on';[36] and 'Courageously, Antoine Bourseiller is producing the work of a musician too long kept in the background for his French production.'[37] Those who admired Britten's work often came from the theatre world, such as Pierre Barrat, an actor and a director, and very interested in opera directing which he recognized as lagging well behind the spoken theatre. It was in discovering Britten's operas that he foresaw the possible renovation of the lyric theatre. In 1963 he assisted Louis Erlo in the production of *Albert Herring* at the Académie Lyrique in Vichy. He next produced *The Beggar's Opera* at the Maison de la Culture in Caen in 1965, *The Burning Fiery Furnace* at the Maison de la Culture in Angers in 1970 and finally initiated the French production of *Owen Wingrave* (1971) with the Atelier Lyrique in Colmar in 1996. In organizations such as the Maisons de la Culture or the schools of lyric art, like the Atelier Lyrique du Rhin, Pierre Barrat was very effective in promoting a growing awareness of Britten's work. In this he took as his model the English Opera Group for its group work and *esprit de corps*, far from the 'star system' of the great Parisian opera houses. But even there, his artistic entourage criticized him, as he reported: 'When I created *The Burning Fiery Furnace* in 1969, many critics or friends did not understand this choice, which they considered to be a regression in my contemporary adventure.'[38]

The provincial institutions, resisting this kind of criticism and profiting from increased prestige in the 1970s through the Landowski reform,[39] emphasized their divergence and advocated a new programming policy. Thus, during the 1961 revival of *Peter Grimes* in Strasbourg, the programme read: 'Not satisfied with having put it on the stage, Strasbourg revives it. ... our city is one of the first to admit *Peter Grimes* in our repertoire.'[40] Thus, the municipal theatre at Metz put on a French production of *Albert Herring* and warned the public in an open letter about the 'reason for being of a municipal theatre': 'its pedagogical ambitions demand ... that it save from oblivion works which are often masterpieces and that it enrich its domain with new pieces. ... These operas are performed almost everywhere, except in France.'[41] One sensed that people were beginning to talk in the provinces and Paris was being attacked for its sectarianism and its closed-mindedness. In 1962 Mario Bois, despite his reservations about Britten's music, declared himself amazed, and rightly so: 'Let us speak frankly, isn't it absurd that the Paris Opéra has not yet had its *Peter Grimes*, or the Opéra-Comique its *Albert Herring*? Why should the

French general public continue to ignore one of the two most often performed living composers in the world, whose main fault, to hear some critics, is to be pleasing?'[42]

Strategies and negotiations: the Parisian conquest

The artistic risk-taking was therefore taking place in the provinces. If successful, the production could envisage a revival in the capital, as was the case for Roger Lalande's company in creating *The Rape of Lucretia* in Mulhouse in 1948: they were invited to the Paris Opéra as a sign of recognition.[43] But the artistic links between Paris and the provinces remained strained and sabotage was not uncommon. Thus, during the first French production of *A Midsummer Night's Dream* in Strasbourg in 1965, the Paris Opéra, at the last moment, prevented one of its singers, Giovannetti, from creating the role of Bottom. This shows the contempt on the part of the great opera houses for what was being done elsewhere; but fortunately Derrick Olsen, called on in the emergency, saved the day.[44] The Paris Opéra was then experiencing a crisis. In 1965, André Malraux, the Minister of Culture, described opera as 'entertainment for concierges',[45] and in 1967, Pierre Boulez declared, 'We must blow up the opera houses!'[46] In the 1970s the Paris Opéra closed several times and was subjected to reforms and changes of management. Pierre Boulez and Jean Vilar worked on the problem and searched for solutions.[47] But the programmes still did not include works by Britten. In 1974 Adorno's biting text on 'the problems of the contemporary lyric theatre' was published:

> Henceforth, with Britten's style, we will no longer be able to brag among the specialists, nor win over an uninformed public with an art whose merits can be reduced to the fashionable quality of a cocktail, whereas concerning the musical composition we are simply faced with an insipid mixture of elements from a dead tradition and a few unimportant modern ingredients.[48]

When Rolf Liebermann became the head of the institution in 1973, it seemed possible to imagine that there was going to be a perceptible change. A great admirer of English music, he was also one of the pioneers in producing Britten's operas: 'I am proud of having put on the stage three of his works (*A Midsummer Night's Dream*, *Albert Herring* and *Billy Budd*) in Hamburg, in spite of the virulent attacks aimed at him during the 1960s because he still used the tonic and the dominant. Now that those battles are calmed and appear rather sterile, Britten recovers his true stature in the eyes of all.'[49] However, after he left his post as director in 1980, no Britten works were programmed. It was necessary to wait until 1981 to see *Peter Grimes* at the

Palais Garnier. The production was very successful, finally marking a turning point in Britten's reception in the capital. The Parisians discovered a forgotten masterpiece and the public was overwhelmed, applauding for a quarter of an hour and demanding 15 curtain calls.[50] A television retransmission was even considered to reach the public at large.[51] The supporters of modernity in contemporary French music began to re-evaluate their points of view, including Messiaen, who was struck by the dramatic power, the opulence of the orchestration, the melodic simplicity and the *tour de force* in composing within the diatonic scale.[52] Nevertheless, in the press one notes the familiar criticisms: Maurice Fleuret wrote 'more modernism than modern',[53] and Claude Rostand even wrote that the composer was 'more worried about the workmanship of his art than the art of his workmanship'.[54]

So it was not until the 1990s that Britten's work was truly accepted in Paris and the critics began instead to attack Parisian sectarianism and ostracism:

> We revere Strauss, Berg, Bartók; we almost never perform Britten's operas, some are never performed at all. Why this disrepute for one of the most gifted and productive creators of this century? To succeed in France ... one must be armed with a theory, belong to a school, an avant-garde movement; none of that for Britten, a musician by instinct, readily eclectic, a lover of beauty, an amateur of a pure kind, resistant to every system, a free solitary genius.[55]

The attacks were multiplied; pressure was put on the structures and institutions, as Jacques Doucelin suggested in *Le Figaro* about a production of *Billy Budd* put on in Nancy: 'Paris would be well inspired to invite it, for the capital has waited too long to discover Britten's music. But his hour is coming with the death of the serial dictatorship.'[56] In this more favourable artistic context, Britten's operas finally found a place in France which had previously been refused them. In 1996 *Owen Wingrave* was on the programme during the Festival of Contemporary Music in Strasbourg, *Musica*. For the first time in France, Britten was ranked with composers such as Dusapin, Aperghis, Dutilleux and Messiaen. A critic remarked in *Limelight*: 'There was a time when Benjamin Britten would have been out of place in a festival of contemporary music. But ... "Times change", and the English composer whose *Owen Wingrave* was programmed by Musica 96 truly deserves his place in the pantheon of composers.'[57]

Yet it still remained necessary to convince the Parisians. The archives of the Manufacture du Rhin, which have preserved Pierre Barrat's documents concerning this production, reveal a good deal. A co-production was the only way to put on the show at a lesser cost and to have it produced at a prestigious hall such as the Opéra-Comique. And so that hall was identified and an attractive date was suggested for the first Paris performance: 'What do you think about a Paris première on May, 16, 1996, on the occasion of the twenty-fifth anniversary of its world première, May, 16, 1971?'[58] A whole strategy of persuasion was put in place, a long-term venture which took more than two years; Pierre Barrat accepted the artists imposed by the Opéra-Comique, suggested financial arrangements, and assured the director of the support of sponsors such as France Télécom (which reserved many seats for public relations purposes), as well as representatives of the Britten–Pears Foundation.[59] Even today the only way for a production to gain national and international recognition is for it to be seen by many in Paris concert halls. Pierre Barrat considered this project to be indispensable in order to 'make progress in creating an important work of the twentieth century repertoire in France.'[60] Its success was so great that the Englishman Charles Pitt expressed the hope 'that England will have the good sense to welcome it.'[61] Thanks to Pierre Barrat's tremendous artistic and political energy, and talent in public relations, *Owen Wingrave*, a provincial creation, found a first-rate national and even international venue. And Britten found a credibility and a status in the contemporary world which had long been denied him.

Such has been the geographical, historical, political and artistic journey of Britten's lyric works in France. The composer, whose operas were performed very little in Paris and even deliberately excluded, was finally accepted in the great Parisian concert halls partly by means of provincial theatres which took more risks in their programming, dared to disagree with the artistic tendencies of the capital and suggested truly innovative approaches. His operas met with such success in the provinces and later in Paris that they served to establish Britten among the important contemporary composers in France. Roger Lalande, Louis Ducreux, Antoine Bourseiller and Pierre Barrat allowed him his revenge for the years that the Parisian intelligentsia and the Boulez circles kept him out of the mainstream. Supporters of Britten managed to attain their two goals without confronting the Parisian public head-on, by using a subtle conditioning strategy in the provinces. They made the public aware of contemporary music with works that are approachable without being simplistic, attractive without being vapid, and they gave a suitable place in the French lyric landscape to Britten's operas.

If the influence of these men of the theatre played a fundamental role in integrating Britten's work in France, one must not forget other factors which contributed to a more favourable context. Let us mention, in the 1990s, the end of the serial dictatorship, the acceptance of composers with a more personal and poetic language such as Dutilleux or Ligeti, the mellowing of Boulez's polemic, and a new craze for opera after the fashion for musical theatre had diminished. These changes in mentality, perceptible in the 1990s, may also have been eventually favourable to the understanding of Britten himself. In his operas the public found echoes of contemporary cultural issues (such as pacifism and homosexuality) but, even after the music was finally accepted, Britten's personality continued to arouse questions and some polemical responses. As Gilles Macassar noted, 'The situation of the composer remains paradoxical in France; his work, regularly performed, is always successful; but his personality remains disputed.'[62] Nonetheless, success had arrived and today's press is a witness to the fact that, notwithstanding these caveats, Britten's works are finally popular – and likely to remain so.

Notes

1 *MRLL,* vol. 2, p. 1243, n. 2. Britten and Peter Pears gave three concerts under the auspices of the British Council in February, 1945. On 8 March they recorded a programme from the Théâtre des Champs-Élysées for the French Broadcasting Company, conducted by Britten, which included *Les Illuminations, Soirées musicales* and *Matinées musicales.* On 10 and 11 March Britten and Charles Münch conducted the orchestra of the Société des Concerts du Conservatoire de Paris, at the Champs-Élysées, with Britten's *Serenade* and *Sinfonia da Requiem* on the programme. On 13 March Britten and Pears gave a recital including the French Folk-Song Arrangements in the concert hall of the Old Conservatory.

2 Archives of the French broadcasts held at the Institut National de l'Audiovisuel.

3 Mario Bois, 'Britten? … Connais pas!', *Boosey & Hawkes: société des grandes éditions musicales,* Bulletin d'information 16 (June 1962), pp. 1–4 at pp. 3–4. All translations from French to English are by Lisa Blauvelt-Weil.

4 *Ibid.,* p. 6. Charles Bruck and Jacques Pernoo were conductors who directed the Radio Symphony Orchestra of Strasbourg. Frédéric Goldbeck was a musicologist; Manuel Rosenthal and Pierre Pagliano were composers; and Charles Panzera and Henri Bécourt were lyric singers.

5 *Programme du Théâtre des Nations, IIIe Festival de Paris* (Paris, 1956), p. 10.

6 Nicolas Nabokov, 'L'Œuvre du XXe siècle, exposition internationale des Arts, sous les auspices du Congrès pour la liberté de la culture', *La Revue musicale* (Paris: Richard-Masse Editeurs, 1952), p. 8.

7 Claude Baignières, article from *Le Figaro* (May 1952) reprinted in the programme of the 1992–3 season of the Nancy and Lorraine Opera, pp. 5–7..

8 *Ibid.*

9 Rollo H. Myers, 'L'École anglaise', in 'L'Œuvre du XXe siècle', pp. 15–21 at p. 18.

10 Frédéric Goldbeck, 'A propos du nouvel opéra de Benjamin Britten', *La Revue musicale* (Paris: Richard-Masse Editeurs, 1952–3), pp. 200–2 at p. 200.

11 Claude Rostand, *Programme du Vᵉ festival international de musique d'Aix-en-Provence*, 11–13 July 1952, p. 37. For Rostand, Britten's operas allow one to 'seek a sort of lyric theatrical system which would correspond to the requirements of today's public and break with the clichés and routines presently making up the most solid and steadfast tradition of the opera genre, the one which is a main factor of what is commonly called the "crisis of the lyric theatre" '.

12 Antoine Goléa, *Rencontres avec Pierre Boulez* (Paris: René Julliard, 1958), dust-jacket notes.

13 1953 was the year of the 'Première Décade Internationale de Musique Expérimentale' organized in Paris by Pierre Schaeffer's team and in which Pierre Boulez participated.

14 Célestin Deliège, 'Pierre Boulez entrevu', Dossier Pierre Boulez, *L'Avant-scène opéra* 36 (Sep-Oct 1981), pp. 166–78 at pp. 174–5.

15 Pierre Boulez, 'Dix ans après', in 'La Musique et ses problèmes contemporains, 1953–1963', *Cahiers de la Compagnie Madeleine Renaud-Jean-Louis Barrault* 41 (December 1963), pp. 360–70 at p. 370. 'All that, when all is said and done, made up a *movement*'; 'I say us: this generation of composers who *recognized* each other, immediately after the war, by certain ways of behaving.'

16 Academy in Germany devoted to contemporary music. It brought fame to personalities such as Boulez, Nono and Stockhausen, who all began to teach at Darmstadt from 1956.

17 Goléa, *Rencontres avec Pierre Boulez*, p. 175.

18 *Ibid.*, p. 176.

19 *Ibid.*, p. 185.

20 *Ibid.*, dust-jacket notes.

21 *Ibid.*, p. 196.

22 Pierre Boulez, 'Schönberg est mort', in *The Score: Relevés d'apprentis*, ed. Paul Thévenin, collection Tel quel (Paris: Editions du Seuil, 1966), pp. 265–74 at p. 271.

23 Claude Baignières, article from *Le Figaro* (May 1952) reprinted in the programme of the 1992–3 season of the Nancy and Lorraine Opera, pp. 5–7.

24 Donald Mitchell, 'Mapreading', in *CPBC*, pp. 87–96 at p. 96. Transcription of Mitchell's interview with Britten for CBC, February 1969.

25 *Ibid.*, p. 96.

26 Ernest Ansermet, 'La condition de l'œuvre d'art', in *Le Robot, la bête et l'homme*, collection Histoire et Société d'Aujourd'hui (Neuchâtel: Editions de la Baconnière, 1966), pp. 117–41 at p. 124. Texts of the lectures and interviews edited by the Rencontres Internationales de Genève, with the cooperation of UNESCO, 1965.

27 Murray Schafer, *British Composers in Interview* (London: Faber, 1963), p. 120.

28 Pierre Souvtchinsky, in an article entitled 'Ceux du Domaine musical' in which he affirms that in France everything ends up by settling 'on a single personality, in order to transform the "*newcomer*" into "*chosen one*" ', of which the 'historic

utility' seems undeniable. In 'La Musique et ses problèmes contemporains, 1953–63', pp. 141–6 at p. 142.

29 Paule Thévenin, 'L'Univers en mouvement de Pierre Boulez', in 'La Musique et ses problèmes contemporains', pp. 355–9 at p. 355.

30 'Ce que dit la presse', concerning Benjamin Britten's *Albert Herring*, *Rendez-Vous des Théatres du Monde*, 30 année (May 15 1959), p. 8.

31 *Ibid.*

32 Emile Spiteri, *Marseille notre Opéra: petite histoire et grands événement* (Marseille: E. Spiteri, 1987), p. 96.

33 Marcel Schneider declared in *Combat* (21 January 1965) '*Wozzeck* dates from 1925, *L'Ange du feu* from 1930, *The Turn of the Screw* was put on in Venice in 1954: this time, thanks to M. Louis Ducreux and to the city of Marseille, we haven't waited too long.'

34 Antoine Bourseiller, *Opéra créateur* (Jarville-La Malgrange: Éditions de l'Est, 1992), p. 7.

35 Marion Thébaud, 'Antoine Bourseiller, la curiosité artistique', *Le Figaro* (6 October 2003).

36 Jacques Doucelin, 'Passions d'hommes dans un huis clos marin', *Le Figaro* (29 March 1993).

37 Dominique Fernandez, 'Un opéra sans femmes', *Le Monde* (25 March 1993). The expression 'courageous experiment' was also used by the director of the Maison de la Culture in Caen, in a letter to the personnel involved when Pierre Barrat put on Britten's *The Beggar's Opera* in a French version in October 1965 (Archives de la Manufacture). One could still find the same sentiment in *Le Monde* (25 February 1997) on the French production of *Owen Wingrave*: 'Thus we will be grateful to Pierre Barrat, the director of the Atelier du Rhin, for having dared to produce the French première and bringing about twenty or so representations in France, from Colmar to Massy. This is not the least daring effort of this exemplary organization, founded in 1974 and placed under the sign of creation.'

38 Reported by Marie-Noël Rio, 'Rencontre avec Pierre Barrat: metteur en scène et pédagogue', *L'Avant-Scène Opéra* 173 (1996), pp. 68–77 at p. 69.

39 Marcel Landowski, the first director of music, lyric art and dance in the Ministry for the Arts, approached the question of the decentralization of the lyric arts when he foresaw the regionalization of some lyric art institutions in the provinces, particularly in Strasbourg, Lyon, Toulouse and Bordeaux.

40 André Tubeuf, from the programme of *Peter Grimes*, Opéra, *Théatre municipal de Strasbourg*, 1961–2 season (January 1962), p. 203.

41 Abel Rilliard, artistic director, 'Lettre ouverte à Mme X...'. *TMMetz*, 1965–6 season, pp. 15–16.

42 Bois, 'Britten? ... Connais pas!', p. 6.

43 Roger Lalande, 'The Rape of Lucretia', *Opera* 2/6 (May 1961), p. 286.

44 André Tubeuf, 'Histoire du *Songe* à Strasbourg', *A Midsummer Night's Dream, programme Opéra national du Rhin,* 1997–8 season, pp. 42–3.

45 François Lafon, 'Théatre musical 20 ans après', *Le Monde de la Musique* 136 (September 1990), p. 97.

46 Pierre Boulez, 'Entretien', *Der Spiegel* (27 September 1967); quoted by Philippe Albèra, 'Avant-propos, Opéra', *Contrechamps* 4 *(*April 1985), p. 4.

47 See 'L'Opéra de Paris I: chronologie d'une crise (1967–1974)'. *Musique en jeu,* Spectacle-Musique I: Opéra/textes (Revue trimestrielle 14, May 1974), p. 108.

48 Theodor W. Adorno, 'Problèmes du théâtre lyrique contemporain' (1956), trans. H. Hildebrand, *Musique en jeu* (as note 47), pp. 65–72 at p. 69. This article had already appeared in the *Neuen Deutschen Heften*, 1956–7, and in the Programmheft *Tannhaüser,* Bayreuth Festspiele, 1966.

49 Rolf Liebermann, *Actes et entractes,* collection Musique (Paris: Éditions Stock, 1976), p. 114.

50 Serge de Beketch, *Minute* (February 1981).

51 *Humanité Dimanche* (1 February 1981).

52 Donald Mitchell, 'What do we know about Britten now?', *CPBC,* pp. 21–5 at pp. 24–5.

53 Maurice Fleuret, in *Le Nouvel Observateur* (9 February 1981).

54 Gilles Macassar, 'Un ange à la mer', *Télérama* (17 March 1993), pp. 66–7.

55 Fernandez, 'Un opéra sans femmes', p. 31.

56 Jacques Doucelin, 'Passions d'hommes dans un huis clos marin', *Le Figaro* (29 March 1993).

57 Alain Andlauer, *Limelight* (November 1996).

58 Archives of the Manufacture du Rhin. Letter from Lyse Richter, secretary-general of the Atelier du Rhin to Monsieur Pierre Médecin, Director of the Opéra-Comique, 21 June 1994.

59 Letter from Pierre Barrat to Pierre Médecin, from Colmar, 25 April 1996. 'Dear Pierre, I am taking the liberty of returning to battle to confirm that we will be presented at the Opéra-Comique next February 21 to 26. As you wished, we have retained David Heusel as conductor and for music preparation, Graham Lilly. We have tightened up expenses as much as possible as you can see in the budget that we sent you last February 23. I repeat our desire to present this creation in France at the Opéra-Comique. The Britten Pears Foundation is delighted with this collaboration and will be present at these performances. The France Télécom Foundation, which is supporting us throughout this operation, attaches particular importance to the Parisian performances.'

60 Letter from Pierre Barrat to Pierre Médecin, 28 June 1995.

61 Charles Pitt, *Opéra International* (November 1996), pp. 32–4.

62 Gilles Macassar, 'L'Homme orchestre', *Télérama* (18 December 1996).

12 Why did Benjamin Britten Return to Wartime England?

Brian McMahon

On 16 March 1942 Benjamin Britten boarded the MS *Axel Johnson* at New York to begin his long and dangerous journey home as part of an Atlantic convoy.[1] He had departed England three years previously ahead of the commencement of hostilities in Europe disheartened and feeling that the continent was doomed to fascism. With the subsequent widening of the international conflict his commitment to pacifism saw him at odds with prevailing world-wide political events. Now at the height of the Atlantic war he was departing North America to return home: but why? Britten's departure to the United States on the eve of the Second World War was regarded by many of his fellow countrymen as an act of betrayal and was possibly one of the most controversial decisions of his life. His stated reasons for leaving were based on the belief that there was no future for him in England and he needed to try his luck elsewhere. He was to spend almost three years in North America, during which time he achieved moderate success as a composer and performer, travelled widely and even contemplated making the US his permanent home. However, his somewhat sudden decision to return home at the height of the conflict has raised many questions. This essay will examine the context and some possible reasons for his decision to brave the wartime Atlantic in 1942.

There can be little doubt of Britten's deep sincerity when it came to his aversion to military conflict. But what informed this principled stance? Was it cowardice or conscience? A very personal fear of violence expressed as a heroic political gesture of pacifism or a sincere political belief that governments needed a better way to settle disputes rather than sending its young men to slaughter? Britten's pacifism, or at least his aversion to conflict, began early in his life. Humphrey Carpenter cites an interview with the composer in *The Guardian* in June 1971, where he attempted to explain the origins of his pacifism. He recalled his early schooldays and the shock at the administration of corporal punishment:

> I heard a boy being beaten, and I can remember my absolute astonishment that people didn't immediately rush to help him. And to find

it was sort of condoned and accepted was something that shocked me very much. Whether it [pacifism] all grew from that I don't know.[2]

He expressed his hostility to militarism early on as a schoolboy by refusing to join the Officer Training Corps unit at Gresham's Public School in Holt. According to the composer, this 'caused many hours and questioning of motives' before he was permitted to opt out.[3] Memories of the carnage of World War I were still fresh in the public mind, and these may have added to his aversion to military conflict. Britten's musical and intellectual mentor, Frank Bridge, also had a profound influence on his young pupil. In an interview in 1963 with the *Sunday Telegraph*, Britten stated 'A lot of my feeling about war came from Bridge.' Bridge also insisted that his pupil should argue and argue in order to clarify his position on a topic and then be true to his principles by sticking to them.[4]

In 1935 Britten joined Canon Dick Sheppard's Peace Pledge Union, the most prominent pacifist organization in the United Kingdom. This popular movement had been established the previous year following Sheppard's letter to the *Manchester Guardian* which called for opponents of war to send him the following message on a postcard: 'I renounce war and never again, directly or indirectly, will I sanction or support another.'[5] The huge response that followed saw the establishment of the mass movement with Britten distributing its leaflets door to door in his boyhood home, Lowestoft.[6] The following year Britten expressed his political views by composing the incidental music for the anti-war film *Peace of Britain* directed by Paul Rotha,[7] and in 1937 he set Ronald Duncan's *Pacifist March* to music. This became the anthem of the Peace Pledge Union, using an unlikely march tempo to promote pacifism:

> In our hearts we've no hate but complaint against the chainstore state;
> We will build peace for earth's plenty.
> March ... stride to resist strong with force not with fist.
> Against all war we shan't cease to construct force for peace,
> Now we're kept poor and merely exist to die, why?
> March ... stride to resist strong with force not with fist.
> March! March! March! March! March! March![8]

The collective memory of World War I in England certainly informed the pacifism of the 1930s. Idealistic anti-war attitudes and philosophies were commonplace in the aftermath of man's most destructive conflict to date. However, these opinions came under challenge in the face of militaristic fascist states who championed war and whose aggressive behaviour ensured that dialogue between reasonably minded opponents could never be relied on to settle international disputes. In 1939 Britten's utopian dream of a world without war was shattered. Many of his fellow pacifists from the 1930s enlisted, albeit with a heavy heart. Britten did not, but used another justification for his reluctance to participate in the conflict.

Could there be other motives behind Britten's declared hostility to military conflict? Martin Ceadel's work on pacifism, *Pacifism in Britain, 1914–1945: The Defining of a Faith* explores different justifications for the creed. However, he draws a clear distinction between the conscientious objector and the pacifist. The conscientious objector may refuse to fight for reasons other than those of pacifism. He may have political, social or personal objections to a particular conflict. One such personal motivation for refusal to enlist is discussed and dismissed as quasi-pacifism and this model holds some familiar resonances with the stance articulated by Britten during World War II. Ceadel describes the attributes of the objector thus:

> His reason which usually amounts to a claim for special treatment on account of particular characteristics of an individual. It is an elitist form based on the assumption that certain gifted individuals should, on account of their personal qualities, be excluded from having to fight.[9]

This description holds striking similarities with Britten's written submission in 1942 to the Tribunal for the Registration of Conscientious Objectors in London. Many of his compatriots who joined the conflict in the national interest were placed in occupations to which they were totally unsuited. However, Britten clung to the belief that he was special, and for this reason, should be excused military service. He described his position to the tribunal:

> The whole of my life has been devoted to acts of creation (being a professional composer) and I cannot take part in acts of destruction. Moreover, I feel that the fascists' attitude to life can only be overcome by passive resistance. If Hitler were in power here or this country had any similar form of government, I should feel it my duty to obstruct this regime in every non-violent way possible and by complete non cooperation. I believe sincerely that I can help my fellow human beings best, by continuing the work I am most qualified to do by the nature of my gifts and training i.e. the creation or propagation of music[10]

His petition suggests that his aversion was consistent, even if the motivation for his position was adjusted to suit the particular circumstances. But his expressed belief that passive resistance could possibly achieve success in the face of fascist oppression appears naive in the extreme, even in 1942.

The motives of an earlier celebrated British pacifist differed profoundly from those of Britten. The World War I poet Wilfred Owen became the inspiration for Britten's most celebrated artistic statement of pacifism, the *War Requiem*, composed in 1962. Appearing at the height of the Cold War, it resonated with a general anxiety of possible nuclear conflict and became a milestone in Britten's phenomenal musical career. However, the rationale behind Owen's pacifism stands in stark contrast to that of Britten. Owen's principles were of an active pacifism where the poet felt that he was in no position to criticize the folly of war unless he shared the burden with his fellow countrymen. He declared: 'I must get some reputation of gallantry before I could successfully and usefully declare my principles.'[11] Owen saw active service, suffered gas attack, shell shock, and sadly was killed in the last days of the war. However, unlike Britten he saw it as his duty, albeit under protest, to join in the conflict.

In analysing Britten's pacifism it is worth while examining the politics that informed his convictions. His association with the poet W. H. Auden and his circle had certainly increased his political awareness. He had witnessed, though not experienced personally, the depression of the 1930s with its hunger marches and means tests which challenged the capitalist system in providing for its population. Faced with the failure of capitalism and the looming spectre of fascism, Britten considered socialism to be the only acceptable political alternative.[12] The rise of fascism in Europe and its growth in popularity at home unsettled him. Here was a value system that threatened all of the virtues of democracy, would certainly not yield to reason and could only be stopped by force. As with so many like-minded socialists Britten now found himself in a dilemma: how to be both against war and yet also opposed to fascism. Britten recorded in his diary in March 1938:

> Hitler marches into Austria, rumour has it that Czecho.S. & Russia have all mobilised – so what! War within a month at least, I suppose & end to all this pleasure – end of Snape, end of concerto, friends, work, love – oh blast, blast, damn.[13]

His idealism of a world without war was unravelling and the harsh reality of the inevitability of military conflict dawned on him. Yet he was not prepared to become involved in defending the values that he held so dear.

Britten's decision to depart for America with his partner Peter Pears on 5 April 1939 was probably prompted by several factors. He was hugely influenced by Auden, who had already left for the United States with Christopher Isherwood. Britten's love life was in a mess and he needed to get away for a time.[14] However, the belief that war was inevitable was probably the principal factor that motivated the move. As a pacifist he had no desire to become involved in the coming armed conflict, and in the event of a Nazi victory, there would be little future in an England for a homosexual, pacifist, and composer of contemporary music. It seems reasonable to suggest therefore, that a fear of what was to happen to him personally informed his pacifism, and this is borne out by the diary entry quoted above. Indeed, looking back in 1960, Britten himself confirmed this analysis when he remarked: 'many of us young people at the time felt that Europe was more or less finished. There was a great Fascist cloud about to break at any moment and we felt that Europe didn't – nor did it have the will to – resist that.'[15]

Other musicians such as John Barbirolli, Thomas Beecham and Albert Coates also chose to stay abroad, and not without ignominy. Beecham flippantly made no secret of his cowardice: 'It was an emergency' he later remarked, 'so I emerged.'[16] Others such as Malcolm Sargent behaved more nobly. At the beginning of hostilities he was in Australia, having been offered a lucrative long-term contract to work there, but he refused to sign it, and out of a sense of honour returned home.[17]

Britten's years in North America were moderately successful from a professional standpoint, and the composer also made clear his political commitments on at least one occasion. During his stay he composed the *Sinfonia da Requiem*, a piece commissioned by the Japanese government to mark the 2,600th anniversary of the Mikado dynasty. It has been argued by Eric Walter White that Britten deliberately chose to use this work to protest at the Sino-Japanese War, with the 'Lacrimosa' and 'Dies Irae' movements expressing the terrors of the damned.[18] There could be little doubt that the composer was drawing parallels between the brutality of the Japanese onslaught and the torments of hell. In fact in a letter to his sister, Beth, he confirms that the work is 'combining my ideas on war and a memorial for Mum and Pop'.[19] The Japanese authorities eventually rejected the work, citing its Christian references as unsuitable. However, the composer had seized his opportunity to express his hostility to the militarism of Japan through the use of his art.

Initially, it appears that Britten and Pears intended to remain in the United States indefinitely. In a letter to his friend Wulff Scherchen in June 1939 Britten certainly shows no sign of wishing to return. 'I am thinking hard about the future', he wrote. 'This may be *the* country. There is so much unknown about it – and it is tremendously large and beautiful … and it is enterprising and vital.'[20] Two years later his enthusiasm for remaining showed little sign of waning, and he decided to alter his visa status. In spite of intrusive legislation which had been recently passed intending to root out communists and other political undesirables from the US, Britten and Pears chose to regularize their residency status there.

The 1940 Aliens Registration Act (Smith Act) required the registration and fingerprinting of all aliens in the United States over the age of 14. This law also required all alien residents to file a comprehensive statement of their personal and occupational status and a record of their political beliefs.[21] Having been subjected to this procedure, Britten's personal file would have been open to scrutiny by the authorities. Indeed, later events would show that Britten's presence in the United States was monitored by the FBI. Pears' association with communists was also noted by the Bureau. In a 1942 memo, unearthed by Donald Mitchell, the FBI informed the visa section of the State Department of this activity.[22] Interestingly, this note is signed by J. Edgar Hoover.[23] It is difficult to know whether the composer was aware that he had come to the notice of the FBI or if this had any bearing on his decision to return to England. However, in the post-war era and for the remainder of his life, the US State Department categorized Britten as a 'Prohibited Immigrant', which deprived him of automatic entry into the United States. Prior to each visit he faced an obligatory interview at the US Embassy in order to gain an entry visa.[24]

As a consequence of the Smith Act, Britten and Pears, like many aliens, applied for an adjustment to their visitor visa status. Once approved they were required to leave and re-enter the United States through an official port of entry where a record of admission for residency would be filed. In a letter to his sister Beth, in May 1941, Britten wrote:

> Peter and I have an invitation to go and spend some time in South California … and we want to go to Mexico so as to get on the labour quota (you have to go out of the country and then come back, so as to be able to work without hindrance) that all fits in well.[25]

By thus indicating his intention to apply for residency status Britten clearly demonstrated that he had no immediate intention of returning to England. But just four months later unease creeps into his correspondence. Writing from California to his other sister, Barbara, he noted:

> This place is a complete military hive now – crammed with soldiers, sailors and marines, with planes all over the sky, and lots of gun practice going on and rattling the windows. I suppose it's on account of the Japanese scare.[26]

In response to Japan's increasing aggression and specifically reacting to the advance of Japanese troops into southern Indochina in July 1941, President Roosevelt froze all Japanese assets in the United States. He also imposed an embargo on high-octane fuel which effectively terminated all trade between the two countries. This deprivation of fuel would prevent Japan resuming its

expansionist mechanized military campaign on the Asian mainland and therefore a conflict with the United States became a distinct possibility.[27] Just as in
pre-war England, Britten now seems to have been concerned for his future
and the possibility of a forthcoming conflict.

This anxiety may have been further exacerbated by events in Washington.
The United States, witnessing the fall of many European states to Nazi domination and the rise in militarism and threat from Japan, had determined to
increase its defence capability. The Selected Services Registration Act of 1940
was passed in October of that year, requiring all males (including aliens)
between 21 and 35 years of age to register for the draft.[28] While compulsory
induction into the military was on a lottery basis, there can be little doubt that
this would have unsettled the 26-year-old Britten; and the unease was heightened later when the selection process became more wide-ranging in the aftermath of the attack on Pearl Harbour.

So whereas in May 1941 Britten had every intention of remaining in the
United States, even planning to go to Mexico to change his visa status to that
of 'Resident Alien', it seems clear that by 18 October things had changed. He
wrote to Elizabeth Sprague Coolidge in New York: 'I have made up my mind
to return to England, at any rate for the duration of the war.'[29] Something
between May and October of 1941 prompted him to change his plans. The tim-
ing suggests that he once more decided on flight ahead of the coming conflict.
This, however, was never the explanation cited by the composer as his reason
for returning to England.

Britten later maintained that his decision to return during World War II
occurred in mid-1941 following his reading of E. M. Forster's article on the
18th-century East Anglian poet George Crabbe in *The Listener* magazine.
Crabbe's description of the East Anglian countryside, particularly his home
town of Aldeburgh struck a resonance with the composer. As he later recalled:

> it was in California in the unhappy summer of 1941, that, coming across
> a copy of the Poetical Works of George Crabbe ... I first read his poem,
> *Peter Grimes*; and, at this same time, reading a most perceptive and
> revealing article about it by E. M. Forster, I suddenly realised where I
> belonged and what I lacked. I had become without roots, and when I
> got back to England six months later I was ready to put them down.[30]

He would later base his most famous and successful opera on Crabbe's
writing. ('We've just re-discovered the poetry of George Crabbe (all about
Suffolk!) & are very excited – maybe an opera one day ...!!')[31] On the basis of
his subsequent testimony alone, then, it would appear, then, that a 'rootless'
Britten became homesick for Suffolk after a chance encounter with the poetry

of Crabbe.[32] It is, though, reasonable to suggest rather that the possibility of impending war in the US was the major factor in prompting Britten and Pears to decide to return. Certainly it would have been easier to gain the status of Registered Conscientious Objector in the UK, where he had some influential connections, rather than in a foreign land.

Eventually, after a wait of about six months, Britten and Pears crossed the hostile Atlantic as part of a convoy, arriving at Liverpool on 17 April 1942. Britten then appeared before the Tribunal for the Registration of Conscientious Objectors, armed with testimonials of the sincerity of his pacifism from many influential people, including the BBC management, Frank Bridge's widow and Britten's publisher, Ralph Hawkes. After appealing an initial unsatisfactory decision, he was granted the status of conscientious objector, an unusually rare decision where less than 5 per cent of applicants were successful.[33] Luckily, or by a strange coincidence, the chairman of the appeals tribunal, Sir Francis Floud was a father of a former school friend, Peter Floud. Mitchell records that in 1965, after Sir Francis' death, Britten, in a letter of sympathy to his daughter, wrote: 'He was good to me when I was in Gresham's [public school] once, and a wise and sympathetic judge at my tribunal in the war.'[34] Unlike his fellow composer Michael Tippett, who spent time in prison for his pacifism, Britten was exempted unconditionally from military service.[35]

His principal contribution to the war effort was to be his involvement with the Council for the Encouragement of Music and the Arts (CEMA). Together with Peter Pears he gave recitals in 'small towns all over the East of England … under the strangest conditions – playing on awful old pianos – singing easy, but always good programmes.'[36] Britten had informed the Tribunal for the Registration of Conscientious Objectors of his offer of service to CEMA and this probably was an additional factor in the composer's favour when their decision for exemption was made.[37]

With the end of the conflict Britten emerged to make his feelings known publicly. At a time when one could expect a conscientious objector to 'keep his head down' he expressed his protest, not only through his art, but in another of his few acts of overt political activism. After VE day, in July 1945, he called a press conference to discuss the Potsdam Conference. Britten's gathering took the form of a foodless lunch in protest at the danger of imminent starvation in the war-ravaged countries of Europe. Britten wanted to encourage and shame those who led public opinion about the urgency of the problem of hunger in Europe.

A report of the event was recorded in *Peace News* on 27 July 1945. Britten announced: 'Mr. Churchill's high living at Potsdam is an offence that stinks to high heaven. It is a political indecency – a moral crime.' He reminded his audience that Churchill had promised in 1940 that he would 'arrange for the speedy entry of food into any part of the enslaved area' but

> [n]ow it is in this wrecked, beaten, hungry country that the United Nations have met. And the first news we get is that they are gorging themselves on turkeys, hams, fresh eggs, juicy steaks, melons, straw-berries, wines and whiskeys. All round is the stricken enemy people, hungry and facing greater hunger; not far away are the people of France, Belgium, Holland and Norway. They have been hungry for years and are still hungry. ... Large numbers are getting half our food value ... Would we share what there was according to need? Or cling desperately to a privileged position – feed well at the expense of hungry friends? I'll take the risk of expressing England's answer – we're ready to share.[38]

The fact that someone who had avoided any part in the defeat of fascism should decide to expose himself to public attention and possible ridicule by commenting on the post-war political situation gives some indication of Britten's intellectual commitment. This activity and also his subsequent gruel-ling tour of relieved concentration camps in Germany with Yehudi Menuhin, demonstrate Britten's moral integrity, yet at the same time draws attention to the paradox of his personality. Here was someone with an acute sense of morality and justice, but who avoided the conflict and only engaged in the public debate when victory was assured. It could be suggested that his aver-sion to personal conflict also informed his reluctance to discuss his feelings publicly during the war.

When Britten was enjoying the success that his later compositions would bring, his distaste for dealing with conflict was ever-present and further served to demonstrate the less noble side of his nature. This habit was sometimes expressed at the expense of his colleagues. David Matthews refers to Britten's 'corpses', the list of people who were close to the composer, personally or pro-fessionally but then were informed at a later stage by a third party that their services were no longer required.[39] The composer seemed to find these face-to-face terminations difficult to deal with, and generally used others to per-form the unpleasant task. Basil Douglas, Manager of the English Opera Group that had been founded by Britten, was initially given the duty of informing artists that they were no longer needed; when his turn came, Britten's amanu-ensis, Imogen Holst, had the difficult job of disposing of him. Montagu Slater, the librettist of the opera *Peter Grimes*, was suddenly replaced by Eric Crozier. Stephen Reiss, the General Manager of the Aldeburgh Festival, who was forced to resign, noted Britten's dislike of confrontation: 'he didn't want the unpleasantness of calm confrontation – actually to go calmly to someone and say – "Please understand." '⁴⁰ Ronald Duncan, another 'victim' and a colleague of over 40 years, described the situation: 'The list of those who worked with Ben reads like a War Memorial of "Those who died" – in vain.' ⁴¹

The questions raised by the composer's decision to return to wartime England and his subsequent refusal to engage in the fight against fascism continue to puzzle. The critic Tom Sutcliffe discusses his confusion regarding Britten's timidity in this regard:

> The greatest mystery of all to my mind is how somebody with such clear political instincts and commitments could have been so resolutely uncommitted about opposing Hitler, whatever his feelings about violence. There is a strange lack of imagination and moral commitment about that crucial test, the Second World War – a deeply unattractive evasiveness amounting to a personality defect. Especially when writing from the US, Britten seemed to regard the war as a frightful inconvenience – something awfully tiresome for him personally to have to put up with in his life. And yet we know this was the genius who set a new agenda for opera, explored unprecedented themes and narratives, and provided a crucial repertoire of works in English with music of such convincing and fully realised evocativeness as to change his native country's entire outlook on the lyric stage.⁴²

To return to the question posed – why did Benjamin Britten return to wartime England? – it seems reasonable to conclude that the homesickness induced in Britten by the poetry of George Crabbe served as a romantic justification for what was, perhaps, a flight induced by human frailty and a strong desire to avoid personal disruption. The notion of a poetic siren-song of 'Our busy Streets and Sylvan-walks between, Fen, Marshes, Bog and Heath all intervene' ⁴³ calling Britten home is too simplistic and given the circumstances of the time, is not a particularly credible explanation. A more likely answer is that Britten chose to avoid conflict once again; but in doing so embedded further conflicts in his own personality that have remained, and will undoubtedly continue to remain, subjects for future discussion.

Notes

1 *MRLL*, vol. 2, p. 1026.

2 *HCBB*, p. 10.

3 John Bridcut, *Britten's Children* (London: Faber, 2006), p. 15.

4 Benjamin Britten, 'Britten Looking Back,' *Sunday Telegraph* (November 17 1963).

5 'A Brief History of the PPU', http://www.ppu.org.uk/learn/infodocs/st_ppu. html (accessed 12 December 2008).

6 *MCWR*, p. 11.

7 *HCBB*, p. 79.

8 Donald Mitchell, *Britten and Auden in the Thirties: The Year 1936* (London: Faber, 1981), p. 69.

9 Martin Ceadel, *Pacifism in Britain, 1914–1945: The Defining of a Faith* (Oxford: Oxford University Press, 1980), pp. 9–10.

10 Benjamin Britten to Local Tribunal for the Registration of Conscientious Objectors. Application to Local Tribunal by a Person Previously Registered in the Register of Conscientious Objectors, 4 May 1942. Held at the BPF.

11 *MCWR*, p. 7.

12 *HCBB*, p. 78.

13 Peter Stansky and William Abrahams, *London's Burning: Life and Art in the Second World War* (London: Constable, 1994), p. 137.

14 Michael Oliver, *Benjamin Britten* (London: Phaidon, 1996), p. 71.

15 Benjamin Britten, 'People Today: Transcript of BBC Discussion with the Earl of Harewood, 23rd June 1960', in *PKBM*, pp. 176–85 at p. 180.

16 Richard Aldous, *Tunes of Glory: The Life of Malcolm Sargent* (London: Pimlico, 2002), pp. 115–6.

17 *Ibid.*, p. 98.

18 Eric Walter White, *Benjamin Britten: His Life and Operas* (London: Faber, 1970), pp. 32–3.

19 *MRLL*, vol. 2, p. 803.

20 *MRLL*, vol. 2, p. 668.

21 Documents of American History, Aliens Registration Act 1940, found at http:// tucnak.fsv.cuni.cz/~calda/Documents/UnitList.html [1940s-Alien Registration Act] (accessed 23 October 2008).

22 See Donald Mitchell, 'Violent Climates', in *MCCC*, pp. 188–216 at p. 215.

23 *Ibid.*, p. 212.

24 *Ibid.*, p. 214.

25 *MRLL*, vol. 2, p. 920.

26 *MRLL*, vol. 2, pp. 972–3.

27 William Keylor, *The Twentieth Century World* (New York: Oxford University Press, 2001), p. 237.

28 US Department of Defence, Background of Selective Service, http://www.sss. gov/FSbackgr.htm (accessed 21 March 2007).

29 *MRLL*, vol. 2, p. 987.

30 *BBAA*, p. 21. Forster's article was revised and printed in *Peter Grimes*, ed. Eric Crozier, Sadler's Wells Opera Books no. 3 (London: Bodley Head, 1946), pp. 9–14.

31 Letter to Elizabeth Mayer, 29 July 1941, in *MRLL*, vol. 2, p. 961.

32 See also Murray Schafer, 'British Composers in Interview: Benjamin Britten', in *PKBM*, pp. 223–32 at p. 226: 'Perhaps it was partly a home-sick reaction – war and our eagerness to return home; one was aware of a sharp tug at one's heart right from the first.'

33 Stansky and Abrahams, *London's Burning,* p. 155.

34 *MRLL*, vol. 2, p. 1059.

35 *HCBB*, p. 152.

36 *MRLL*, vol. 2, p. 1089.

37 *HCBB*, p. 176.

38 Quoted in *PKBM,* p. 48.

39 David Matthews, *Britten* (London: Haus, 2003), p. 83.

40 *HCBB*, pp. 376–7 and p. 526.

41 Ronald Duncan, *Working With Britten* (Devon: Rebel Press, 1981), p. 144.

42 Tom Sutcliffe, 'Tell the Court the Story in Your Own Words', *Musical Times* 132 (October 1991), p. 515.

43 *George Crabbe: The Complete Works*, ed. Norma Dalrymple-Champneys and Arthur Pollard (Oxford: Clarendon Press, 1988), p. 364.

Index of Britten's Works

General Index